"*The Book of Old Ladies* is an inspiration for what life can be like in my future."

—SKY BERGMAN, award-winning filmmaker and professor of photography and video at Cal Poly State University

"In *The Book of Old Ladies*, Ruth Saxton offers readers, through curated conversation, the opportunity to defy the sweet-as-the-day-is-long stereotype and to examine the more fully developed and—thank goodness—realistic senior woman."

—JENNIFER KING, director of the Downtown Oakland Senior Center

"With an engaging, conversational style and feminist lens, Ruth Saxton guides us through an array of twentieth- and twenty-first-century novels and stories . . . An essential read."

—EILEEN BARRETT, editor of *American Women Writers: Diverse Voices in Prose* and professor of English at California State University

"Saxton's work will delight, inform, educate, and enlighten all who read her book."

—VIJI NAKKA-CAMMAUF, president of the Alumnae Association of Mills College

# The Book

of

# Old Ladies

## Celebrating Women
## of a Certain Age in Fiction

RUTH O. SAXTON

She Writes Press, a BookSparks imprint
A Division of SparkPointStudio, LLC.

Published 2020

Printed in the United States of America

ISBN: 978-1-63152-797-5
ISBN: 978-1-63152-798-2
Library of Congress Control Number: 2020902519

For information, address:
She Writes Press
1569 Solano Ave #546
Berkeley, CA 94707

She Writes Press is a division of SparkPoint Studio, LLC.

*To all the old ladies in my life
and in books who have inspired me
to see possibility, embrace change,
and find joy in becoming
a woman of a certain age.*

# Contents

# Introduction

I have always read fiction to find models for how to live, how to be. I am not alone; we search for ourselves in story, often seeing our own lives in fictional plots and imagining our potential futures through the lenses of fictional lives. Stories offer us ways to make sense of our pasts and to forge a way of being in our presents and futures. The stories we read, the plotlines we encounter, impact our sense of ourselves and what is possible.

From a childhood drenched in testimony and storytelling by old women, including my grandmother and her sisters, I learned a love of narrative, even as the plotlines offered to me as a girl were notably limited. I grew up feeling as if I personally knew the characters in my favorite girlhood novels. Louisa May Alcott's Jo March, Charlotte Brontë's Jane Eyre, Jane Austen's Lizzie Bennet, and Willa Cather's Antonia were my introduction to smart female characters who loved books and education, though their major life choice was only whom to marry. These books, and books like them, eventually led me to be the first in my family to go to college.

As a college student, I scoured my syllabi for books by any women at all, but the only fiction I was assigned to read was by men. As a young mother in the feminist movements of the 1970s, I returned to school for my master's degree and was introduced to American women such as Kate Chopin, Edith Wharton, Flannery O'Connor, Alice Walker, Toni Morrison, Tillie Olsen, Grace Paley, Zora Neale Hurston, and dozens of others, whose work I taught in my community college class-room and shared with friends. I read these books hungry for a story in which I could see myself, through which I might find plots that would aid me in my attempts to manage being a daughter, a wife, a mother, a feminist, and a teacher, but I often found myself torn between Virginia Woolf's Mrs. Ram-say and Lily Briscoe, never allowed both to rock the cradle and to write the book in the same (life) story.

When I was in a doctoral program in the early 1980s, sev-eral of my professors commented that there were simply not many women worth serious study; a graduate course on women writers, taught by a visiting professor, resulted in our discovery of original editions of eighteenth-century books with uncut pages shelved on the open stacks, unread. I continued to read the women writers I'd studied in my master's program, such as Woolf and Doris Lessing, whose female characters were not simply the foil for male characters' development.

Later as a professor, I taught, wrote, and edited books on Woolf and Lessing, as well as books about contemporary women's fiction, girlhood, mothers and daughters—always searching for female fictional limitations and possibilities. As I aged, my focus turned from the girl and the mother to the grandmother, or the woman my age, and I began to look for plots that might help me map a possible future beyond the familiar fairy tale where the old woman is stereotyped as either the wicked witch or the fairy godmother. In my forties, I had noticed that I was the age of all those dead mothers littering my favorite novels by women, the heroines always the adult daughter. In my sixties, I noticed once again the unseemly collusion of fictional portrayals with social stereotypes, the ways novels and short stories would caricature old women and confine them in plots like fictional shut-ins.

Those characters were not present, not still engaged with the messy currency of living. I kept running into the same old stories in which the older women are simply beside the point. From the formative nineteenth-century women's novels of my girlhood to contemporary fiction, older women are almost never the ones whose story matters; the older woman or grandmother is either absent or important only as she affects the (younger) heroine. Think, for example, of "Little Red Riding Hood," in which the granddaughter is the focus and the old woman is read as lacking desire and therefore vitality. Even in the various contemporary feminist revisions in which the wolf tells his version of the tale, the grandmother is still food for the wolf, and the fodder that generates the story. The story is never, really, about her.

And so, I began a serious search for fictional stories that have old lady protagonists who are not simply marginal. I found old women to be plentiful in detective fiction, and I enjoyed novels in which Miss Marple or Mrs. Pollifax is able to solve criminal mysteries precisely because her physical appearance as an old lady renders her invisible. But I wanted to read realistic fiction in which I could see through the eyes of an old woman, not simply appreciate her as an excellent plot device or character, just as I had so often viewed the world through the eyes of younger women. I searched for stories that get inside the heads of old women. I wanted to gather examples of good aging, of wise or surprising women over sixty and into their nineties, like beads on a string, a secular rosary to help fend off the fear of becoming elderly in a society whose mainstream vision of aging women is marked by fear, loathing, refusal, or reduction. I wanted to read the novels in which fictional older women prepare for the journey of aging, inhabit the territory, and become increasingly their truest selves.

As I read books touted to be focused on an older woman, however, I saw that she mostly remained a shallow cipher. And when she was central, the novel often fell into a category that I began to term "Deathbed Bookends"—opening and closing with her aged consciousness, the focus of the book being her memory of a youthful (usually romantic) past. In a cultural climate of advertising that urges us to postpone the inevitable by purchasing products or relying on plastic surgery to maintain the appearance of youthful bodies, perhaps it is natural that fictional old women are portrayed at the end of their lives remembering their youth rather than looking inward or outward at their present situations. Writers and readers may also have difficulty imagining new adventures for older women because youthful romance is such a familiar plot for women. However, I wanted to find stories about women's firsthand experience in the present time of life, not ones where they are stuck in the past.

Many novels explicitly about older protagonists disappointed me; the women not only bore little resemblance to me or my acquaintances in their sixties, but also were nothing like the many vibrant old women I have known throughout my life. My mother, aunties, and grandmothers enjoyed new experiences in spite of arthritic hands or swollen ankles. Grandma welcomed visitors until she died at 102. My mother stayed in touch through handwritten letters with family and friends all over the world. Elderly teachers took up painting or creative writing after retirement, and acquaintances in their eighties were raising great-grandchildren. I began to realize that by teaching novels in which the old women are trapped in memories of youthful romance, I was subtly colluding in a distortion of actual old women's possibilities. To discover whether the old women I have known were entirely unusual, I began research in nonfiction, including psychological and sociological texts, biographies, autobiographies, memoirs, and journals, all of which shored up my sense that *actual* old women have infinitely more plots than I had found in fiction. So, what was going wrong? Why were our stories not being written or published?

The lack of good fictional role models for aging women appears to be wrapped up in a larger problem of how we think about old age. In her short book of essays, *The Last Gift of Time*, scholar and mother Carolyn Heilbrun writes about the way that fictions about elderly protagonists end up devoting most of their pages to recounting or revisiting the women's pasts. She expresses her own surprise at discovering that she actually enjoyed her sixties. I wonder to what extent the difficulty for writers to imagine life in the present through the eyes of an old woman mirrors the same difficulty in modern life, where independence, speed, and productivity are highly valued and culture fails to imagine dependence, slowness, and wisdom as possible gifts.

In her famous essay on fiction and the role of the modern novel, "Mr. Bennett and Mrs. Brown," Virginia Woolf claims that the task of the novelist is to catch in words the old lady in the railway carriage. This book is the result of my searching contemporary fiction by women for glimpses of those elusive old ladies who, a century after Woolf's call for them, remain nearly invisible. Like Woolf's Mrs. Brown, an old woman may sit in the carriage. Or she may sit quietly on the bench of a London park, like the invisible women of Doris Lessing's novel *The Diary of a Good Neighbour*. She may sit quietly reading on an airplane, in a meeting, in the waiting rooms of public institutions. What does she notice? What does she make of the snippets of conversation she overhears? What is the interplay of present observations and memories in her mind? Does she enjoy the sun on her skin? Does she relish her flexibility after that recent hip replacement? Is she composing a melody or a poem as she pulls the needle through her embroidery? Woolf wrote that she never managed to tell the truth about the body, and I think most readers assume she meant the sexualized body. However, increasingly I think that fiction has often focused exclusively on the sexualized body rather than the embodied person as a whole. I looked and continue to look for stories of older women in which they notice not only their desire but also their strength, the beauty they apprehend through their sight and hearing, the life-giving breath that sustains them.

For this work, I have chosen fiction in which the protagonist reads as "old" and in which she is the main character even if the narrator may be younger. I include stories from the twentieth and twenty-first centuries that portray the complexity of older women's lives and the varieties of activism, creative pursuits, motherhood, friendship, labor, love, and sexual pleasure that they experience. *The Book of Old Ladies* seeks out the strong characters and vital plots that already exist, while critiquing the stereotypes and limitations that still abound.

As new stories have been published, my pile of eligible books has tripled; however, I have limited myself to a selection that gives readers a sense of the general outlines of the plots I have discovered and provides ways to think about these stories and others like them. Although there are many connecting threads among the stories I have chosen, I have arranged them into five chapters that frame the main fictional plots for old women: "Romancing the Past," "Sex after Sixty," "Altered Realities," "It's Never Too Late," and "Defying Expectations." In each chapter, I include six stories that I group into pairs to highlight the similar approaches and the range of possibilities within each plot.

In chapter 1, "Romancing the Past," I confront the romance plot as it takes shape in stories about old ladies. The older protagonists of the six stories in this chapter each reveal the continuation of the assumptions of the familiar marriage plot, with its celebration of the centrality of romance, its insistence that a woman must choose between marriage and artistic creativity, and its persistent notion that romance is limited to the young. As in all the chapters, I order these stories in pairs. On their deathbeds, Katherine Anne Porter's Granny of "The Jilting of Granny Weatherall" and Susan Minot's Ann Lord of *Evening* relive details of their unrequited youthful love in spite of everything else in their long lives, and readers may easily be drawn into nostalgic yearnings of our own before we recognize how much of life has been ignored. May Sarton's Hilary of *Mrs. Stevens Hears the Mermaids Singing* and Tillie Olsen's Eva of "Tell Me a Riddle" both have accepted the notion that love and marriage make impossible the nurturing of artistic potential, but they have made opposite choices. Doris Lessing's Sarah in *Love, Again* and Mary Wesley's Rose in *Not That Sort of Girl* both relive the past as they deal with current amorous possibilities, rejecting or accepting romance that extends into the present. Together, these stories demonstrate how dwelling on passionate youth limits women's possibilities in life and in fiction.

The protagonists in chapter 2, "Sex after Sixty," all reveal the continued sexual desire of older people that is rare in fiction, from yearnings for intimacy in old age homes to the reignition of forgotten passion in long-dead marriages. In the first pairing, Bernice Rubens's *The Waiting Game* and Elizabeth Taylor's *Mrs. Palfrey at the Claremont*, residents of homes for healthy seniors pursue erotic and tender connections in the midst of their narrowing lives. The next pairing, Toni Cade Bambara's "My Man Bovanne" and Jeanne Ray's *Julie and Romeo*, consists of two light-hearted tales in which adult children's embarrassment at their mothers' obvious sexuality does not deter their mothers' sensual behavior. In the final pairing, "The Liar's Wife" by Mary Gordon and "Dolly" by Alice Munro, women who have settled into passionless partnerships find their feelings reawakened by unexpected visits from former lovers. This chapter shows a range of passionate emotions and actions for characters at ages where women are often thought to be beyond desire.

The novels in chapter 3, "Altered Realities," portray old women as old and aware of their current situations without undue attention to their pasts as they face altered realities and their mortality. In the first pair of novels, Muriel Spark's *Memento Mori* and Helen Yglesias's *The Girls*, the authors blend comedy and poignancy in depicting older women who confront their impending deaths. In the second set of novels, Michelle Herman's *Missing* and May Sarton's *As We Are Now*, the protagonists are losing their grasp on their memories, and each of the narratives deals frankly with the loneliness that accompanies such loss. My final pair for this chapter comprises two of my favorite books to loan to friends and assign to students: Leonora Carrington's *The Hearing Trumpet* and Debra Dean's *The Madonnas of Leningrad*. Each of these two novels moves beyond the realistic into a surreal or magical realm in which we encounter laughter and beauty from the perspective of an old woman who has gained in imagery and beauty more than she has lost in rationality. These six books allow us to explore the end of life and reconsider the assumptions we make about it.

Chapter 4, "It's Never Too Late," introduces six novels that take up the ways in which the inevitable terrible losses and difficult changes to the daily fabric of life for the aging person may result in profoundly meaningful growth. Elizabeth Strout's *Olive Kitteridge* and Margaret Drabble's *Seven Sisters* explore the loss of a long-term partner and the process of rebuilding a life in that new world. Penelope Lively's *Spiderweb* and Anita Brookner's *Visitors* portray the impact of the fundamental changes that follow retirement or an altered living situation. I end this chapter with Stephanie Kallos's *Broken for You* and Linda Olsson's *Astrid and Veronika*, in which a solitary woman is forced to examine her familiar sense of self, to reprise her opinions of others, and to take unexpected risks. Each protagonist in this chapter is believable, and their stories help to deflate a common narrative that the final decades of life are only a downward spiral to death.

Chapter 5, "Defying Expectations," builds on the hopeful vision of change offered in "It's Never Too Late." The six stories in this chapter are among the most satisfying of my accumulation of old lady books. Each introduces a protagonist who not only defies common notions about older women but also manages to surprise and delight the reader as she chooses options beyond the limits of familiar plots of marriage, motherhood, and artistic practice. Cathleen Schine's recent *They May Not Mean To, But They Do* and Vita Sackville-West's 1931 *All Passion Spent* delight us with witty and bracingly bold stories of old women who shock their adult children by their insistence on joyful companionship that is not centered on their children. In *The Fountain of St. James Court* by Sena Jeter Naslund and *The Love Ceiling* by Jean Davies Okimoto, the novels' old women combine successful mothering and artistic practice in defiance of the still depressingly topical presumption that women cannot mother and be successful or ambitious artists. I end this chapter with two novels whose unfamiliar plots and memorable characters defy expectations both of aging women and of stories about them: Catharina Ingelman-Sundberg's *The Little Old Lady Who Broke All the Rules* and Emma Hooper's *Etta and Otto and Russell and James*. Both use form in surprising ways to rescript the stereotypes of fictional and personal possibility. The stories in this chapter show us what it looks like to make room in fiction for a richer array of personalities and plots for older women.

I end the book with a short reading of Margaret Drabble's recent novel *The Dark Flood Rises*. This is self-consciously a novel about the ways we tell the stories of aging: how those stories are shaped in and by minds and bodies, while those minds and bodies are simultaneously shaped by and within larger forces of humanity, nations, and nature. Despite that lofty description, it is also a terrific tale about a distinctly likable heroine—Fran, newly single in her seventies, who "dresses with bravado" and spends her time driving across England evaluating nursing homes and retirement villages, places in which she is determined not to have to live or, more precisely, to die. The novel reflects our own present reality, the way we deal with aging bodies and an ailing world and yet continue to find hope and connection. I follow this final fictional story with a postscript on my own journey into old age. A car accident propelled me into a new way of experiencing the world and myself, one that was initially circumscribed by loss but has become defined by adaptability and insight.

This is a book that champions older women's stories. It is a curated conversation that challenges the limiting outcomes we seem to hold for aging women. Our society is unkind to aging people across the board. However, we allow for the possibility that old men may have richly complex interior lives, imagine them able to create art and have erotic potential, political capacity, business acumen; we do not see their sexuality as a punch line or imagine their personhood to be only in service of others. In this book, I have gathered novels and short stories that represent possibilities and realities for aging women that move beyond stereotypes, showing a range of options for their elderly female characters. I look forward to a future in which we can read about more older women protagonists from an expanded selection of writers with different cultural identities and life experiences. I hope *The Book of Old Ladies* inspires new fiction and leads to discovery of the novels I have not yet read, and I hope my discussion of the stories in this book will make you want to pick them up and begin your own search for models of aging that defy the restrictive plots that do not represent women's true possibilities.

Chapter 1

# Romancing the Past

"The Jilting of Granny Weatherall" (1930)
   by Katherine Anne Porter

*Evening* (1998) by Susan Minot

*Mrs. Stevens Hears the Mermaids Singing* (1965)
   by May Sarton

"Tell Me a Riddle" (1961) by Tillie Olsen

*Love, Again* (1996) by Doris Lessing

*Not That Sort of Girl* (1987) by Mary Wesley

When I saw the book jacket description of Susan Minot's *Evening*, about a woman in her mid-sixties, I was delighted. The venerable *New York Times Book Review* declared, "Susan Minot has set forth a real life, in all its particularity and splendor and pain." The *Boston Globe* told me that Minot "gives us a novel of spellbinding power on the nature of memory and love." But as I delved into the beautifully written novel, I consigned it with considerable disappointment to what I had then begun to call my "Deathbed Bookends" pile, a phrase I had attached to Katherine Anne Porter's short story "The Jilting of Granny Weatherall," in which, on her deathbed, Granny remembers the long-suppressed experience of being abandoned on her wedding day. By "Deathbed Bookends," I mean fiction in which a major portion of the story is the aged protagonist's deathbed memories. Her present situation serves primarily as a container for the central narrative of her past. "Bookend" is my term for the structure of an aging present that is primarily a support within which the youthful heart of the story exists. In such texts, the woman's impending death prompts a revisiting of a romance from her youth, often passing over the years of life experience in between and circumventing any evidence that she has matured rather than simply aged since her girlhood.

In this chapter, I consider the seductive power of the bookend structure to engage even the most critical reader in a story in which an old woman's present life is conveyed in relatively few words in comparison to the richly rendered romance plot of her youth. Just as the Deathbed Bookends plot promises us that romance remains vital, it also comforts us with a soft-focus vision of death. The reader is assured that youth is perpetual and love cannot die. Are we unable to imagine passion in the present tense for women of a certain age? Are memories of youthful passion so strong—for the character, the author, and the reader—that they overwhelm any other plot interest?

Of course, romance excites us, and even after a century of women broadening their spheres, the romance plot remains the most common one for female characters. But in a story of a female protagonist who has reached the end of a long life, the omission of a lifetime of experiences beyond young love is glaring, particularly in contemporary fiction. Nineteenth-century plots about women often center on their need to make a successful marriage, and readers become vicariously engaged in the pursuit, the chase, and the dangers of wrongful entanglement. In a historical moment when marriage was the main source of (and threat to) economic and personal security for certain classes of women, this emphasis makes sense. The plot focuses an often-critical lens on women's limited options. However, the continuation of this limited plot in stories of older women in late twentieth-century and twenty-first-century fiction runs counter to the lived experience of many women readers. What plotlines compete with the romance plot, at any age? Where are the plots of second chances?

I will be exploring the ways in which the romance plot precludes a nuanced portrayal of an older woman's life in her present. Whether the stories dwell on unrequited romance, serial romantic muses, or outgrown romance, the focus on romance implies that between the romance plot and the burial plot, not much else matters. The six works I chose for this chapter fall into a series of three pairs that illustrate different versions of the romance plot. The first pair, "The Jilting of Granny Weatherall" and *Evening*, are clearly the Deathbed

Bookends, in which an early romantic relationship has defined the protagonist. In the second pair, May Sarton's *Mrs. Stevens Hears the Mermaids Singing* and Tillie Olsen's "Tell Me a Riddle" have in common a structure in which the present experience is a bookend frame within which the author gives us a reflection on the woman's life, with its chosen and rejected paths of creativity and domesticity. While these stories are descriptive rather than prescriptive, they still prioritize the romance plot. In the third pair, Doris Lessing's *Love, Again* examines varieties of love and friendship throughout life and ends with a renunciation of passion by its widowed protagonist, whereas Mary Wesley's *Not That Sort of Girl* uses its bookend structure to point to a future of passion for its widowed protagonist.

In all six of the narratives I've chosen for this chapter, the stories are infused with a romance plot so familiar that perhaps only by imagining it functioning for an aging male protagonist do its limitations become visible. In a novel by Philip Roth or John Updike, the aged protagonist does not pine over lost loves; rather, he lusts after young women. He may rue his difficulties with prostate functioning, but he does not ever need to choose between love and art, as do Hilary in Sarton's *Mrs. Stevens Hears the Mermaids Singing* and Eva in Olsen's "Tell Me a Riddle," nor has his artistic life been ignored because of marriages and children. In three of the stories in this chapter, the female protagonist, like a character in Virginia Woolf's *To the Lighthouse*, must choose between romantic and artistic fulfillment. The perpetuation of this dichotomy is troubling at a time when women continue to outlive men and our fictional plots are so meager in contrast to the rich plotting of our actual lives. I continue to search for fictional plots that portray the complexity of women's full lives and are not limited to their past loves.

~∾~

# "THE JILTING
# OF GRANNY WEATHERALL"

## by Katherine Anne Porter

"The Jilting of Granny Weatherall" is the first of the two clearest "Deathbed Bookends" I include in this chapter, and I chose it because it shows how an otherwise complex character can become lost in the romance plot's obsession with youthful love. Even the title of Katherine Anne Porter's 1930 short story suggests that Granny Weatherall's jilting is the most important aspect of the story. Associated with youth and romance, the "jilting" of a granny feels oxymoronic, the two words seeming to cancel out one another. As a reader, I anticipate the old woman has reconciled herself to whatever jilting occurred in her past, and in some ways she has. In the story, Granny reviews her life as she is dying, and she becomes overwhelmed by the memories of being left at the altar that she has struggled to suppress for years. On the one hand, Porter's story offers us a refreshingly sane alternative to Victorian notions of pining heroines, refusing a Miss Havisham ending in which an abandoned bride wears her wedding dress for the rest of her life. On the other hand, despite her defiant desire not to succumb to it, the jilting has been at the core of the protagonist's life; she has been defined by it.

Even on her deathbed, Granny comes across as a strong, feisty old woman. The story opens with a quick, defiant flick of her wrist as she pulls her sheet up to her chin and orders Doctor Harry to "get along now," viewing him as a "brat . . . in knee britches" and insisting "there's nothing wrong with me." In response to his paternal instructions to "be a good girl," she insists he not address "a woman nearly eighty years old" without due respect. Granny is an engaged, authoritative subject who refuses deference to anyone.

Granny is tenacious and irascible, and it is only as we read further that we begin to see any weakness in her. With Granny, we overhear the whispered conversation between her daughter, Cornelia, and the doctor. We are privy to her disgust at Cornelia for always being tactful, kind, and dutiful. Granny's spunky outburst and her insistence that she took to her bed only to escape her daughter's hovering show that Granny takes pride in her independence, and yet the narrator tells us "it was too much trouble" to wave goodbye and that her vision is wavering. We see her emotional strength in the face of physical decline and her impatience with stereotypical feminine submissiveness in the face of male authority.

Granny's abrupt responses to the doctor and Cornelia reveal a lifetime of giving commands to others and a sense of accomplishment in completing the hard tasks of life competently—from keeping an orderly house to raising her children and grandchildren. She is irritated at Cornelia, who speaks in whispers and acts as if somehow because of her age Granny is "deaf, dumb, and blind." She rehearses in her mind the evidence of her continuing worth at the age of eighty as a confidant and a source of advice. She recalls that her son still drops in and asks her opinion because of her "good business head" in contrast to Cornelia, who "couldn't change the furniture around without asking." She recalls "fencing a hundred acres once, digging the post holes herself" and imagines telling her dead husband, John, about how she "was sitting up nights with sick horses and sick negroes and sick children and hardly ever losing one," and remembers that he "could understand" and she "wouldn't have to explain anything!" Her internal conversations with John indicate the strong, intimate connection between them, which makes her dying focus on her former lover George even more disturbing.

The reader is as startled as Granny when the memory of that long-ago jilting that she worked so hard to suppress returns. As she nods off for a nap, unaware that she is dying, she begins to battle with the forbidden memory, projecting that memory onto the pillow that she senses is rising up to "smother her" in a battle she uncharacteristically loses. The intense effort to subdue the recollection is revealed in the words that describe her encounter with the pillow, which "pressed against her heart" and "squeezed" the memory from it. The day of her ill-fated wedding returns to her mind, first as "such a fresh breeze blowing and such a green day with no threats in it." Then she reflects, "But he had not come, just the same. What does a woman do when she had put on the white veil and set out the white cake for a man and he doesn't come?" The images that follow are confused in a "whirl of dark smoke" that covered the day, and she describes the experience as "hell."

We sense that her entire life has been a battle to "get the upper hand" on her feelings about having been jilted. She has prayed for sixty years not to remember George, "and against losing her soul in the deep pit of hell," but now losing him and losing her soul are "mingled in one, and the thought of him was a smoky cloud from hell that moved and crept into her head." Past and present merge for Granny, and the jilting of so many years ago is fresh in her mind, along with the remembrance of being told not to let "wounded vanity" overcome her and to "stand up to it." In sifting her memories, she realizes she wants to confront George with the information that she "had my husband just the same and my children and my house like any other woman," and she is defiant in wanting him to know she "was given back everything he took away and more."

The ending of the story reveals that the jilting has shaped Granny's entire existence in spite of her ability to take charge of her life and look out for others. Death catches her by surprise—no more subject to control than the long-submerged anger and shame. As she curls within herself, there is "again no bridegroom and the priest in the house." And she "could not remember any other sorrow because this grief wiped them all away." Her last thought is that she will "never forgive it," suggesting that the failure to forgive may damn her to hell even after an entire lifetime of trying to bury the memory. Her last action, blowing out the candle by her bed, may be seen as a firm refusal of death, or it could be read as her loss of the battle to move beyond her youthful failed romance. Granny's spunk and strength and pride are complicated by the enormity of her submerged grief, even though she meets it with her customary audacity.

While I admire Granny's resilience and her defiance, her strong independence and capable achievements, I am distressed that the core of her being, the motivation for her life, is that early jilting. Does this memory erase her whole life's control and orderliness? Has she tried to suppress the memory of abandonment because she has never forgiven it, a sin that she assumes in spite of her prayers will damn her to hell? Does the story inscribe romantic abandonment as the central definer of her being, something from which she can never recover— not even in the afterlife in which she believes? What is Porter saying about the centrality of first romance and about the permanence of that early romantic rejection? Granny dies—in spite of her Catholic belief in absolution and redemption— adamantly refusing to forgive the young man and actively denying his effect on her. Her character is strong and resilient, but in terms of plot, this early romance remains the most important story of her adult life.

Maybe blowing out the candle is a defiance of forgiveness—an action at the end of her life that echoes the defiant actions she took as a young woman in creating a life with John and drawing on her own physical and emotional strength over the decades, even as a widow. Throughout sixty years she has repressed the shameful jilting, pouring her energies into creating a future rather than succumbing to hurtful memories. Only on her deathbed, when her defense mechanisms are no longer necessary, are the memories released.

Perhaps it is only when she lets down her guard at the end of her life that she can safely reveal to herself and to the reader the cost of such vigilance against the obverse power of the jilting and the extent to which she has hardened her heart against forgiveness, even to the possibility of facing an eternal hell. Nevertheless, I continue to be angry that the story paints that failed romance not as a bullet dodged but as a stain that colors the fabric of her life in its entirety.

# EVENING

## by Susan Minot

While in Porter's story, Granny offers up her life in memory to prove to the no-show groom of her youth that she has managed to create a full life in spite of that abandonment, in Susan Minot's *Evening* (1998), the old woman equates her most vital self with the self she experienced in the grip of passion during one weekend in Maine when she was twenty-five. Rather than seeing her life after that encounter as full and complete, she disregards it as superficial. She dies only after reliving the weekend in memory and imagining a reunion, a Catherine and Heathcliff moment in the world of spirit that eclipses all the real, experiential texture of the story of her life. I chose to include this novel because it helps us see how an old-fashioned romance can disguise itself as a story about an old woman, even though her present life is beside the point.

The heart of the novel, not only in number of pages but also in intensity and vivid description, is the romance plot. The old woman exists primarily as the source of the evocative romance story. In the novel, Ann Lord is on her deathbed from cancer, and under the influence of morphine to deaden the pain, she drifts into memories of her former lover Harris Arden and even imagines a reunion with him. The reader, along with Ann, is made to feel a quiet sense of relief as this version of Harris admits that she has always mattered to him more than she thought.

In both past and present, Ann is defined by Harris. Through her brief affair with him, she discovers what she valorizes as her most essential self. On the day she meets him, she feels "both a stranger to herself and more herself than she's ever been." Later that weekend, after they make love, when he tells her he has a fiancée, she still feels as if he revealed the world to her: "This is . . . life. This was the point." All her precious defenses disappear, and now everything "is in focus" and "she was solid, whole." When he touches the small of her back, "his hand on her back seemed to say, this is you. This is who you are under my hand."

The day after her night with him, in spite of her knowledge that he is engaged, "her instinct told her that this was what one based one's life on." She feels an immense emotion that she believes him to share, based on nothing more than his "sighing into her neck." She is sure that his feelings for her are stronger that his feelings for his fiancée, and because of Harris she has a new sense that "she would accomplish something in her life." Even in the moment, though, she realizes that having his arms around her is "part of it, but not all," and she wonders if she could have experienced the same powerful emotions and sense of purpose if she had never met him. The novel never follows through on this gesture that there is more to her or to her life than her status as a youthful, responsive lover. Forty years later, she remembers "how sweet it had been with Harris Arden" and recalls everything he had opened in her, "the jolt she got each time he made her feel a new thing." Her memories of him are the most vivid of her life.

In contrast, the rest of her memories are oblique. Lying in her sickbed years later, she watches her thoughts, and in response to a remembered question from Harris regarding where she worked, she cannot recall. Minot provides a list of jobs and apartments that "all floated by, random and nearly transparent. They were the props of her life but she had no more sense of them than one does for the stage scenery of a play one saw ages ago then forgot." Memories of her husbands and children, and even the death of her son, pass through her mind in vague flashes that contain none of the vibrant detail and narrative thrust of her memories of Harris Arden.

The crescendo of the entire novel is in the sensual, vivid account of Ann and Harris's passionate lovemaking. That erotic account is their *Midsummer Night's Dream* in the forest of Arden, outside all time and reason, magical and impermanent. Immediately after recounting the scene, the narrator tells us of her loss of singing, music, and stars, explicitly presenting her youthful romance as the only portal to her own creativity and vision. Ann has a vague sense throughout her life "that she's lost something: and that to remember that night might be unbearable." As she is dying, she is conscious that after having kept the story secret, "pushed down by reason and habit" and years of working "to rub it out," the ending of the story means more to her than the ending of her life. She tries, too late, to tell the story, repeating his name, and in a direct echo of Catherine's famous claim, "I am Heathcliff," she declares, "Harris was me." Throughout the novel, we receive hints that Harris was not as profoundly affected by Ann as she was by him, and that perhaps she was merely one of several women he cheated with. This characterization of him is worse than if he were presented as an ideal lover. Ann remains seduced by him throughout her life, and the novel's honoring of her distortion reduces her value.

I admit that I enjoyed reading *Evening* and that I was most engaged when the passages returned to the past. I am also aware of colluding in a myth I find troubling in its implications about women, our psyches, our multiplicities, our layered lives, which may well include enormous passion and abandonment but which are more spacious and complex than the portrait Minot has fashioned. Minot's novel reinscribes romance as the central truth of a woman's life and creates an older woman whose entire life in retrospect appears to be superficial in comparison to the emotional and physical intimacy of one weekend with a stranger—that enchanted evening that so disregards everything except young lust masquerading as love. It is not the fact of the weekend that troubles me; it is that Minot makes it the centerpiece of an old woman's life, using the deathbed reality as a mere container for the old familiar story and somehow blurring its familiarity by the new setting, so that what otherwise might seem overdone is somehow made to seem new and enticing.

Like "Jilting," *Evening* is a story of repression in which a young woman is told by others to overcome or deny her emotions. Ann was taught by her mother to tamp down her feelings, so the value Ann places on the weekend with Harris could be more about letting herself go than about Harris himself. From her mother, Ann "had learned to rein in the expression of feelings and eventually the feelings themselves, treating them as if they were unruly children who ought to be tamed instead of allowing them free expression as a sort of fuel drawing her into life." Only the feeling with Harris "was too great to check and she did not check it." But even if *Evening*

were a story portraying the effects of repression, Minot doesn't
do anything to explode the myth that romance is the gateway
to women discovering themselves and becoming fully alive.

What is so disappointing in *Evening* is that Ann Lord
dies with the illusion that the tragedy of her life was losing
Harris Arden, but if we step back from the romance plot, we
see that tragedy as a lifetime separation from herself and her
life. *Evening* reminds me that love and lust may be indistin-
guishable in memory, that one's first complete giving over to
passion may become magical in memory. If memories of that
magical weekend are allowed to surface under the painkilling
drugs and make dying easier for Ann, a reader can appreciate
the escape it offers. However, if in contrast to such memories
of that weekend, she has never been truly alive to the rest of
her experience, if she never really knows or is known by her
adult children, if none of her three husbands ever matters to
her, I find the novel tragic. Due to the many pages devoted
to memories of that weekend obsession with Harris, *Evening*
suggests that to Ann, even losing her child was somehow easier after having lost Harris because she had hardened herself
against feeling. We get the sense that Ann has not been fully
present in her own life for forty years and that everything has
paled after her romantic moment. Critics have lauded *Evening*
for telling the truth about an old woman, and about memory
and love. If their praise is at all correct, we are in a sad state
of affairs.

What dismays me about responses to *Evening* more than
their tendency to equate the lust of that fling with true love is
their general acceptance of the idea that Minot's portrayal of a
dying woman's last days is somehow illuminating of the lives of
old women. In my personal quest to find novels to accompany

me as I grow old, I see *Evening* as a cautionary tale. Beware of repressing your feelings. Do not equate your self-worth with another person. Learn from life's losses. Become acquainted with your children, let them know you, be present to them. Make memories throughout your life. Don't shut down after abandonment or any other major loss.

## MRS. STEVENS HEARS
## THE MERMAIDS SINGING

### by May Sarton

Unlike the protagonists of "The Jilting of Granny Weatherall" and *Evening*, Mrs. Stevens is not on her deathbed. However, the Bookends plot is also the backbone of May Sarton's *Mrs. Stevens Hears the Mermaids Singing* (1965), as a comparatively brief introduction and conclusion in the present tense of the elderly poet serve as brackets for an overview of her life, a life marked by a series of romantic passions for persons that only from the perspective of long experience and age can she name "muses." Rather than dwelling on what might have been, Hilary Stevens channels her long-ago romantic passions into her art, but her attempts to reconcile the larger-than-life passions of her past with her current aging self suggest a woman's whole life is primarily entangled in the romance plot. This is the first of two stories in this chapter that imply that even in a capacious lifetime, a woman has room for only one of two choices: personal expression or devotion to others. I include it both because it explores more about passion and sensation than many novels about older women and because it shows what still remains to be explored.

Sarton divides her novel into two major parts—"Hilary" and "The Interview"—separated by an interlude and closing with a brief epilogue. The second section, in which the two interviewers spend several hours asking about the past and the previous books of the newly famous Hilary Stevens, is more than twice the length of the first, which follows Hilary in her present. Though we receive a much fuller portrait of an old woman here than in *Evening*, this portrait is still undermined by a focus on youthful passions.

The portrayal of Hilary in her present reveals the effects of age along with her continuing battles between self-doubt and determination. We learn that she depends on lists and that her handwriting is becoming illegible. She battles the inner demons that continue to doubt the value of the accolades her most recent book of poems has received, wondering if outliving her contemporaries rather than achievement is the cause of critical interest. However, she remains vital and intense. Like Porter's depiction of Granny, Sarton shows Hilary's physical strength and endurance as well as a sense of reduced energy and frailty. In the garden, she hauls rocks with her whole strength, experiences a bit of vertigo, and addresses herself as a "fool," yet she is active, and is thinking of writing "that not impossible poem, the thing that would justify it all, and stop forever the whirling of the past with all its images, make the whole world stand still!" Like Granny Weatherall, Hilary is, in this bookend introduction, a fiercely alive and engaged elderly woman with opinions and attachments, fully grounded in the present and seemingly able to "weather-all" with defiant insistence on her own critical awareness in the face of the inevitable vagaries of age.

Hilary still delights in sensation, aesthetic appreciation, the admiration of others, and the fire, however banked, she feels in her encounters with Mar, the young man who helps her in the garden and wants to be a poet. She seems surprised that he can restore to her some of what her past lovers—"the muses"—have given her, and we notice that she comes most alive when she can balance such encounters with solitary time at her desk. She complains about the myriad mundane tasks and the attention she must give others, but she loves being wanted, needed, and sought after. With Mar, she has bitter fights and "rage that shot adrenaline through her," giving "her the strength to begin a poem again," though "she had not imagined that she would be so fertilized by a human being again." She discovers that age does not diminish her power to attract and to be attracted to someone—"old, young, male, female"— and that her capacity to "be touched, to be involved, to care was . . . still that of a young girl." I appreciate this portrayal of Hilary in her present as vital, passionate, and creative, and yet there is a huge assumption here about who is capable of feeling—that it is unusual or unnatural for an old woman to feel strongly. Hilary's character, the capacity of her desires, is presented as the exception rather than the rule.

Sarton portrays Hilary Stevens in her seventies as deeply conflicted about aging, and about her sensitivity. Dazzled by the beauty of a long, slanting slab of sunlight on her kitchen wall, she considers sitting down to spend a while simply appreciating it but decides not to. She admits that she "had always imagined that one of the blessings of old age would be that one might live by and for these essentials . . . the lights on a wall" but that "instead one dragged around this great complex hive of sensation and feeling." To distract herself from feeling part of the older generation, Hilary turns to the obituaries in the *Times* and tackles her pile of letters. But the letters are filled with requests from the young, and Hilary feels her fame at this age has resulted in nothing but "a vast debt to be paid to the world" after years of escaping it.

Hilary gives priority to her reasonable and artistic self and views sensation and emotion as parts of a carapace that still detracts from what she sees as her essential identity. The narrator characterizes the warring twin entities of her younger and older selves as "a hortatory and impatient person" and "a doddering servant who was getting old." This internal split, not limited to the aged, may resonate for any reader who has longed to luxuriate peacefully in bed and yet faces an appointment. However, Hilary delineates the tension entirely in terms of age. She stands "rather shakily" addressing herself in the mirror as an "old crone, with hardly a wisp of hair left, and those dewlaps, and those wrinkles," while also enjoying the experience of regarding herself. She looks with compassion at that self, "her life companion, for better or worse," and rejoices that "I am still myself. They haven't got me yet," even though she is not sure who "they" are. Though she recognizes her familiar self in her aging body and in her strong reactions, she views both as troublesome baggage that her "real" self carries, as if she is forever babysitting an annoying, childish version of herself. Her true self, she feels, is the one who governs her passions and sensations and turns them into art.

Sarton devotes the bulk of the novel to the interview, which focuses on Hilary's past loves, as the interviewers' questions about Hilary's work provide scaffolding for her memories. When the interviewers ask Hilary about each book in chronological order, after beginning to reply, she then disappears into her private memories of the person who fertilized her imagination in ways that led to that book's poems. Consideration of each book brings to the surface unarticulated thoughts through which Sarton reveals to the reader Hilary's past lovers, who are mostly female. When Hilary returns from her unspoken memories to the questions she has been asked, she shares little of her recollections; nevertheless for the reader, her memories of youthful loves propel the narrative.

The plot of the book and the protagonist herself offer a formula in which unrequited love can be channeled into art, repurposing the romance plot. Hilary's garden helper Mar, a tormented young writer reeling with the discomfort of his unrequited passion for a male teacher, serves as a pupil for Hilary, a sounding board for her philosophy on the ways in which art can channel the passions. When Hilary is interviewed, the novel presents the relationship between love and art as one that requires more sacrifices from women. Through the conversations of the interviewers with each other and with Hilary, the notion of two opposing plots for women emerges: a woman can be either an artist or a caregiver, but never both. The brief section on the interviewers sketches them as masculine and feminine symbols of this tension: he is the male professional interviewer, she the female who claims to want to write and also to be a "regular woman" with a husband and children, evoking the barely masked condescension of Hilary, who seems to believe that marriage and children cancel out art for women, an assumption not countered by the narrator.

Hilary's responses to the questions of the young interviewers draw on what she considers her own "masculine" and "feminine" selves. Her answers include assertions about women, about art, about the classic split between masculine and feminine, between mind and feeling. Though she claims to speak only about finding her own way, she insists that art emerges from violent conflict and is somehow the result of unrequited rather than requited love and passion. In spite of her publishing success over forty-five years, Hilary continues to feel aberrant both as a woman and as a poet, and in her telling, the reader finds writ large the age-old dichotomy: the hand that rocks the cradle is not able to produce art.

In spite of critical praise of the novel by feminist writers, I am troubled by the distinction Hilary and the novel draw between feminine bearing of children and masculine creation of art. I wonder to what extent the aging poet has assuaged her romantic disappointment or rationalized her own narcissism with assurances that her art has required a series of intense romantic passions that ultimately had to die if the poems were to exist. In her 1974 introduction to the 1965 novel, Carolyn Heilbrun agrees with Hilary's insistence that young women like the female interviewer are mistaken if they assume they "can have the whole bag—marriage, children, and art." Heilbrun praises *Mrs. Stevens* because "its homosexuality is not seen in its social or shocking aspects at all" but rather "is used, thematically, to discover the source of poetry for the woman artist." Nevertheless, Heilbrun herself combined marriage, children, and an outstanding professional career as a professor and writer during the years Sarton was writing, and I hope that fifty years after the publication of *Mrs. Stevens*, the sharp distinctions between mother-woman and artist are permeable rather than fixed.

# "TELL ME A RIDDLE"

## by Tillie Olsen

Tillie Olsen's 1961 "Tell Me a Riddle," like Sarton's *Mrs. Stevens*, implies that traditional women's roles are not compatible with personal and artistic fulfillment: Mrs. Stevens is an artist who does not mother, and Eva of "Riddle" is a mother who does not write. Like all the stories in this chapter, it uses an old woman's present to reflect on her youthful possibilities. However, rather than romanticizing a dying woman's youth, the story centers on the old woman's present life, offering a glimpse of the end of a life that is being lived, not just remembered.

After a long marriage, Eva and David live intertwined lives, not caught in a youthful fantasy of "happily ever after." Olsen's story includes memories of hard times, and poverty is the backdrop of their lives, but the plot does not sentimentalize that poverty any more than it romanticizes youthful passion. In "Riddle," the old spouses, married for forty-seven years, bicker over how to live the latter years of their lives. Their bickering is animated, and each is equal to the other in bitterness, name-calling, and insult. The roots of their quarrel, we are told, reach back to the early days of their marriage, but the story does not dwell on their early courtship or the loss of another, more idealized romantic entanglement. While its anti-romantic gist deflates the romance plot, the story is also haunted by the past, portraying the ways women suffer not only the brunt of poverty but also the cost of being "forced to move to the rhythms of others."

The couple's seven adult children pity their parents, feeling that "at least in old age they should be happy." However, instead of happily ever after, Eva and David argue constantly now that "the needs of others no longer shackled them together." The reasoning of their quarrel and their bitterness erupts on every page. David yearns for life in a retirement home where he will have company and diversions, whereas Eva wants to enjoy the solitude she feels she has earned in years of tending to the needs of her family. He wants for once in his life to "be carefree" and no longer have the responsibility of worries about money, owning a home, fixing a broken vacuum cleaner, changing the storm windows, or running errands on the streetcar. And she, after tending to housekeeping and meal preparation for decades, wants now to be able to "cook and eat how I want." He tries to ply her with promises of a reading circle, whereas she is filled with resentment that he never relieved her of childcare years ago when she would have loved to go out on her own. Her memories are not of abandonment by a passionate lover but of irritation at a young husband who returned from late meetings, stimulated and ardent, and tried to pry her away from the only time there was to read after nursing the current baby. She mourns the writing that domestic life made impossible for her.

Unlike Ann Lord, Eva is not aware that she is dying of cancer and her memories are not drug induced. After a misdiagnosis of her fatigue and being blamed for her lack of energy, Eva is examined by another doctor and immediately rushed into surgery. Doctors discover that her cancer has metastasized and predict just a few more months of living—basically pain free. Her family agrees not to tell her the prognosis or to upset her by selling the house, but instead to borrow money for travel to visit each of the children. No explanation is given to Eva for why they must visit all the children in their homes rather than be allowed to settle into her dream of solitude.

Not understanding the cost to Eva of motherhood, her daughter wants her to hold the newest baby, assuming she will derive comfort, but Eva is disturbed by "what the feel of a baby evokes." "It was not that she had not loved her babies, her children. The love—the passion of tending—had risen with the need like a torrent; and like a torrent drowned and immo-lated all else. But when the need was done—oh the power that was lost in the painful damming back and drying up of what still surged, but had nowhere to go." In the presence of the new baby, her memories torment her. While they think she is napping, she hides in a closet and attempts to shield herself from invasions of her past.

Maybe the romance plot is extraneous to this story, yet the children and the reader yearn for the reconciliation and peace somehow promised or implied as the outcome to a long marriage. Olsen reveals the cost of that plot, the absence of alternative ways to see the mother when she is old, to even imagine her as continuing to grow and change or to have ever suppressed her self in raising children. In this way, the plot may be more like the others in this chapter than it at first appears, in that what has been repressed comes pouring out when Eva is dying, and that outpouring is—like in the other plots—the outpouring of her girlish self that had so long been submerged in the day-to-day outcome of the romance plot lived out by the working poor. While Olsen's story refuses the idealized romance plot and calls needed attention to the grinding requirements of domestic life without extensive resources, it does not allow for a more appealing alternative to the romantic fantasy.

After visiting all of the children and grandchildren, Eva finally learns she is dying. On her deathbed, she is cared for by Jeannie, who resigns her nursing job to care for her grandmother. Eva does not return in memory to a distant youthful romantic script of unrequited love or abandonment. She insists, "Let me feel what I feel," and declines her pills. She chants and vomits. She refuses to go the hospital. She rants at her husband for leaving her and always running, and he sobs to Jeannie, who tells him, "She needs you, Granddaddy . . . Isn't that what they call love?" Olsen portrays the complexities of a mature love that somehow has existed and changed over decades of hardship and poverty.

While Eva does not revisit past romance, she does release the songs and poetry that persist from her youth of impassioned activism, and in this way, she resembles the protagonists of the other stories. From her mouth pours what David imagines must be everything she ever read or heard. She tells Jeannie bits and pieces of her history, growing up in Olshana, being taught to read by Lisa, a highborn lady but a Tolstoyan she was forbidden to visit, repeating half-memorized phrases from books, in and out of delirium, talking of death and the pole star. She becomes light like a bird, and like a bird, "sound bubbled in her throat while the body fluttered in agony." She voices the world of their youth, their beautiful beliefs, that "joyous certainty, that sense of mattering . . . of being one and indivisible with the great of the past, with all that freed, ennobled."

"Riddle" ends with the italicized words of Olsen's dedication "for two of that generation": "Death deepens the wonder." The reader has known the plot would end in death but perhaps has not anticipated the sense of wonder. Olsen does not explain what she means by these final words, and the reader is left to unravel them.

Eva makes me sad as I see the hardness of her life, the withering of talent unused, the identification of herself with the physical tasks of a lifetime at such cost to her poetic potential. In three of the plots explored thus far, the underlying assumption is that romance and maternity cancel out art and all creative endeavors, although romance is fickle. In *Evening*, Ann loses her music after Harris; in *Mrs. Stevens*, Hilary resists attachment to protect her poetry; in "Riddle," Eva has no time to read and write. These three plots, despite their differences, agree that a woman cannot have a loving partner, children, and artistic fulfillment.

## *LOVE, AGAIN*

### by Doris Lessing

The final pair of stories in this chapter focuses not only on the romance and creativity of youth but also on the passions of the present. Doris Lessing's *Love, Again* (1996) has much in common with her other fiction, and this is what I find both gratifying and frustrating about the novel.

Doris Lessing's work was a major motivation for my return to graduate school, where I determined to develop the habits of mind necessary to explain to faculty colleagues why I considered Lessing's work important. (Some male colleagues considered all of her books after her first novel, *The Grass Is Singing*, as second-rate fiction because of her focus on women's issues.) Lessing has a way of writing "to the bone" that I love. Her portrayals of women are psychologically complex, the women often combining satisfying work with motherhood, intellectual achievement with steamy sexual encounters. Having read all of her fiction, in which female characters often delight in their sexuality, I was excited by the promise of the book jacket blurb for *Love, Again*: "An exhilarating and disquieting meditation on old age and romantic love." The plot summary intrigued me: "Widowed for many years, with grown children, sixty-five-year-old Sarah Durham is a writer who works in the theater in London. When she falls in love with a seductive young actor, the beautiful and androgynous twenty-eight-year-old Bill, and then with the more mature thirty-five-year-old director Henry, Sarah finds herself in a state of longing and desire she thought the province of younger women."

I read *Love, Again* for the first time in my fifties. On that reading I anticipated that by sixty-five years old, Sarah Durham would have come to terms with her physical self. I held out hope that unlike her predecessors throughout Lessing's fiction, she had outgrown the internalized judgmental male gaze when facing her mirror and maintained her capacity for desire. I really wanted Lessing to present a mature woman who was not so hard on herself. What I discovered about Sarah's attitude toward her body and her romantic feelings was mostly discouraging.

Sarah is not obsessed by reliving her youthful passions; rather, she is quite surprised to experience all the emotional and bodily responses of passion she thought she had outgrown. She feels invaded by sensations and emotions she has not experienced in twenty years, and she fights the invasion with her mature, reasonable self as if it were a disease to be avoided at all costs. Although several younger male members of the summer theater project claim to be in love with her, she resists their declarations. Her claims that they are too young, married, gay, unsuitable, looking for a mother figure, and so on make sense to her, and as a reader, I was not disappointed that she maintained her boundaries. However, I was upset when she stood naked in front of her bedroom mirror and critically judged her body parts, echoing mirror encounters in *The Summer Before the Dark* and in *The Diaries of Jane Somers*. I have written elsewhere about such a confrontation with the mirror, in which sexualized parts—neck, shoulders, breasts, hips—are examined and critiqued, the mirror framing the visual image. Just as Jane in Lessing's *Diaries* refuses an assignation with the man she loves for fear he will find her aging body distasteful, so Sarah compares her present body to her remembered youthful body, and fears exposure.

I was furious. How dare Lessing so limit Sarah? Yet several of my middle-aged female students and friends did not share my anger, telling me that Lessing was revealing what many women experience: distaste for their aging bodies and refusal of sexual pleasure, fearing that revealing their soft peach skin and changed bodies to a new partner would result in disgust. Even so, I wanted Sarah to be able to enjoy her changing body and not judge it negatively against youth—her own or anyone else's.

Now in my seventies, having reread the book, I see a daring in Lessing's portrayal of the allure Sarah has for Bill, Henry, Andrew, and Benjamin—all of whom are *much* younger than she is and yet fall in love (or in lust) with her. In my initial disappointment that Sarah accepts the double standards of her society even in the context of summer theater, I did not immediately recognize how rare it was for an author to portray a female character of Sarah's age experiencing passionate desire. Who else was writing in the mid-nineties about older women's desire with its bodily wetness, throbbing heart, sweaty palms? Lessing had gone beyond many other writers in allowing Sarah to experience desire in her sixties, the present tense, even though Sarah is dismissive of such feelings and considers falling in love a kind of madness.

Lessing both reiterates and undermines the social expectations of women of a certain age. Sarah muses that perhaps "one falls in love with one's own young self" even as she is raging with desire and a restored erotic identity. She notes that women of a certain age have to dress carefully so they will not "be accused of mutton dressed as lamb." Sarah determines to grow old gracefully and repeats many of the clichés about aging, such as "the flesh withers around an unchanged core" and "mature ladies are expected to put their troubles under their belts and get on with it" and notes that old women have to monitor their speech and censor it in front of the younger generations.

By the end of the novel, Sarah's anguish lessens. She experiences "moments of quiet enjoyment, drawing vitality as she had all her life from small physical pleasures, like the feel of a naked sole on wood, the warmth of sunlight on bare skin, the smell of coffee or of earth, the faint scent of frost on a stone." This peaceful description, for me, is undercut by the following sentence. Lessing writes, "She had returned to being a woman who never wept," and I cringe at Sarah's stoic refusal to experience a range of emotion. Once she has killed all desire, she again looks in her mirror. This time she realizes she has aged by ten years, her hair is turning gray, and she has "acquired the slow cautious look of the elderly." The cost of aging gracefully seems to be not only a rationalization of the quenching of her erotic self but also a reduced range of feelings and a resignation to becoming old.

This quiet substitution of safe sensory pleasures does not satisfy me as a reader. Why is the suppression of feelings, the stoic refusal to cry, presented as an accomplishment? The caution I take from this novel is that if you suppress or ignore one feeling, you risk flattening and deadening all feeling and becoming prematurely elderly, constricted inside the life of your own creation, a life that still breathes with potential, including a wide range of sensual and sexual experiences.

## NOT THAT SORT OF GIRL

### by Mary Wesley

Mary Wesley's six novels are all set against the backdrop of World War II. The war changes social relations, loosens sexual rules, and creates a "seize the day" atmosphere. Bombs falling on cities and rural areas heighten awareness of the fragility of life and simultaneously strengthen and weaken the rituals and practices of daily life. Sex is lively, casual, and seemingly guilt free, regardless of outcomes. In *Not That Sort of Girl* (1987), Wesley presents Rose's life through her memories following the death of her husband. The structure is similar to that of *Evening*, in that the backstory is revealed chronologically through Rose's memories, but the ending differs dramatically. Married at nineteen, forty-eight years later, at the age of sixty-seven, Rose is truly alone for the first time in her life. In the privacy of a small hotel room, she looks back on her life, her safe marriage to Ned and the secret love affair with Mylo, and the promises she made and kept to both men through nearly five decades. Unlike Ann Lord, Rose is not dying but planning her future; she remembers what she has kept secret from others, not what she has suppressed, and she will reunite with the love of her life in reality, not in fantasy. The novel moves beyond the deathbed endings of "Granny," *Evening*, and "Riddle," as well as beyond the comfortable familiarity of *Mrs.*

*Stevens* and *Love, Again,* by extending an older woman's life and her romance into the future.

The novel opens with a conversation between two of Ned's old friends, who have just read his obituary in the *Times* and are speculating about how the "old girl" will be devastated. When Nicholas and Emily drop by with Beaujolais and pâté, Rose is packing a small bag to go away, place unknown, for a few days of solitude after his death, cremation, and funeral ten days earlier. After she leaves, they speculate about whether "at her age" she may have an assignation, wonder if there may be more to her than meets the eye, but generally agree that she is "not that sort of girl."

Settled in her room at a small hotel where she is unknown, Rose is amused that she has managed to keep her secret. During her brief stay at the hotel, Rose reminisces about her life, and the plot moves chronologically over the decades as she tries to untangle her feelings and admits to herself that she chose safety over love in marrying Ned. Wesley allows Rose to keep her promises to Ned during his lifetime and to look forward to enjoying her old age with Mylo, the love of her life. Her conventional marriage and her passionate love coexist.

We see the past primarily through Rose's eyes throughout the novel, and although Wesley frequently calls into question the validity of memory and includes omniscient narrative interludes, the reader's focus is disproportionately on Rose's times with Mylo, and the reader shares her preference for him. Wesley interweaves brief glimpses of sixty-seven-year-old Rose, who wonders if she has grown too old for joy and hope with her leg "seized with cramp in her old age." She questions the reliability of her memory, and throughout the novel, readers notice that she and Ned seldom shared similar memories or tastes. For example, he claims to have fallen in love with her at the winter tennis party, but that is when she fell in love with Mylo and went unnoticed by Ned until nearly nine months later, months in which she and Mylo met frequently and were deeply in love. She thinks of how young and innocent she and Mylo were at age eighteen and nineteen respectively, how eager her mother was to get Rose married, and she wishes they could have waited. Yet she also admits that she eventually grew fond of Ned, and she "wept for Ned for the first time since he had died."

Plot high points for Rose, and thus for the reader, are memories of Mylo's calls, his visits, the drama of his participation in the French resistance. Her intimacy, romance, and passionate sex with Mylo sustain her throughout her life, but so does the role she inhabits as Ned's wife, and her development as Christopher's mother. From a tentative young girl and the only child of ill-matched and ineffectual parents, Rose matures into a capable and wise woman, sure of herself as she learns to garden, to care for the farm animals, and to avoid repeating the sense of entrapment and anger of her mother. Her secret life with Mylo, a man who risks his life for others during the war, not only causes yearning and despair, it nourishes her.

She feels sick with desire just thinking of Mylo, "at my age," and wonders if she is confusing hungers since she had no breakfast, echoing her first conversation with Mylo, when she questioned whether his lovesickness was caused by hunger. She recalls how over the years they met at intervals, no more than twice a year, often less, rationing their joy. They discussed books, plays, and films, talked about their children, his work. They hurt one another. They made a trip to Venice in their fifties. She and Mylo sustained conversations about literature, music, and current events after they discontinued their passionate sexual trysts because of the emotional pain such meetings increasingly caused. Rose recognizes that she has been shaped as much by her marriage with Ned as she has by her love of Mylo. She has not been impoverished, nor has she needed to support herself at any time in her life. Unlike the other protagonists in this chapter, Rose looks back on a full life while still looking forward to continuing passion in old age.

# CONCLUSION

Though romance enthralls us in fairy tales and romantic fictions, it troubles me when authors make it uncomplicated and claim that it represents entire lives. While the traditional heroine's plot—marriage or death—has been well mined for its limitations by feminist critics, I believe it is even more dangerous when such a plot erases all nuance in narratives about the end of an elderly protagonist's life. While we may shake our heads at the neat package of romantic fiction, we may also speculate that even Elizabeth Bennet and Jane Eyre may have had complex lives within their marriages if their stories were to continue into their old age. But in many of the twentieth-century texts I examine in this chapter, we face the burial plot with the knowledge that nothing at all ever gets better or matters more than the passion of youth. The deathbed plots with which I began this chapter disturb me in their insistence on making a fetish of youthful romance as the only plot for a woman. Nostalgia and fixation on unrequited love may be staples of fiction, but they are problematic for women in general. They shrink the possibilities of a full life for a woman in ways that foreclose her development as a complete human being throughout a long life of experience and growth.

In the first pair of stories in this chapter, "The Jilting of Granny Weatherall" and *Evening*, Granny and Ann's dying moments become an opportunity for them to revisit their early romances, which seem to have dictated the course of their whole existences. Porter and Minot make me wary, as they help feed the idea that the romance plot is the defining plot for women's lives. In the second pair, *Mrs. Stevens Hears the Mermaids*

*Singing* and "Tell Me a Riddle," the authors show us more of the old women's present lives, but their youthful choices still define the stories. Sarton equates the feminine with child-rearing, and insists that Hilary has avoided marriage and children as the price of her masculine art. In Olsen's story it is clear that young marriage and raising children have been the heart of Eva's life, but it is not clear what the cost of this has been until the end. I question the way these stories continue to portray the choice between maternal and artistic life as a necessary one for women. In the third pair, the narrative structure echoes that of the other four stories in that the present situation gives the protagonists a point to reflect on their pasts, but it's not the end of their lives. For Lessing, it is the end of passion, and for Wesley, it's the beginning. I am drawn to stories in which life after sixty is the next chapter of life.

Though each of these stories centers on youth, they still improve upon the bulk of stories that make old women into minor characters with no complexity at all. In contrast to plots in which an old woman is iconically wise or foolish or evil, four (Granny, Ann, Hilary, and Eva) of the six old women portrayed thus far retain in their aged bodies a girlish self. She is not wise or emotionally "grown-up." She is never really understood by her parents or her children. She does not experience "true love" as it is celebrated in fairy tales and imagined by the young. Her body in age no longer meets her expectations of strength, whether she is ill or in health. Almost unnoticed is that each protagonist avoids hospitalization or nursing home care at the end of her life. She remains in contact with family or youthful friends and retains a sense of self, no small feats. Both Lessing and Wesley, writing in their own seventies, portray vital women in their sixties who are not on their deathbeds.

They allow their protagonists contentment—whether Sarah's quiet satisfaction in avoiding drama and accepting the pleasures of her single life or Rose's promise of deferred passionate pleasure. Although I have been harsh on stories of unrequited youthful romance as the most crucial story of an old woman's life, I do like the possibility of romance that is sustained beyond youthful choices in a story that imagines a future for its elderly protagonist.

While it's satisfying to have found these texts, it's clear that we as a culture have not gone far enough and that there's still more work to do. I want readers to be aware of the stereotypes that limit portrayals of old women, not just of young women. I want them to anticipate pleasure throughout their lives and to see that women of a certain age are still capable of wonderment and surprise.

Chapter 2

# Sex after Sixty

*The Waiting Game* (1998) by Bernice Rubens

*Mrs. Palfrey at the Claremont* (1971)
by Elizabeth Taylor

"My Man Bovanne" (1971) by Toni Cade Bambara

*Julie and Romeo* (2000) by Jeanne Ray

"The Liar's Wife" (2014) by Mary Gordon

"Dolly" (2012) by Alice Munro

n this chapter I have gathered six stories that portray varieties of sexual expression in female characters of a certain age. From plots about intimate encounters in homes for the elderly, to ones in which adult children are embarrassed by the sexuality of their mothers, to ones that reveal the results of allowing desire to deaden over decades of marriage, these stories remind us of the importance of passion, desire, and intimacy far beyond sixty.

The first two stories in this chapter focus on residents in old age homes who crave affection. In *The Waiting Game*, a British comic novel, Bernice Rubens entertains readers with the antics of elderly people whose desire for intimacy may shock readers into laughter, but her mockery extends beyond the old folks' home to the society that creates such places for people to await their deaths. The novel also evokes tenderness for the inhabitants of The Hollyhocks Home for the Aged, as its bold portrayal of varieties of sexual behavior and continued desire for intimacy among the elderly makes the characters more than stereotypes. In *Mrs. Palfrey at the Claremont*, Elizabeth Taylor tempers the humorous portrayals of residents in an upscale home for the elderly by creating a compelling character in Mrs. Palfrey. Like Rubens, Taylor makes fun of several stereotypical behaviors of the elderly. Yet the story reminds us that there is no reason to assume that by growing old one gives up a need for attachment. Mrs. Palfrey, like her fellow residents, wants to matter to someone. Her surprising friendship with a young, nearly penniless writer provides her with a delicious secret and allows the reader a satisfying ending.

While adult children are conspicuously absent in these first two novels, they are actively present in the two stories that follow, where they loudly proclaim their disapproval of their parents' sexual behavior. In Toni Cade Bambara's short story "My Man Bovanne," Miss Hazel dances sensually with the neighborhood blind man she thinks her children have treated rudely. Her children are furious, and their response to her dancing results in her leaving the neighborhood event early with the blind man. However one interprets the ending of the story, Miss Hazel is determined to be her own person. Like "My Man Bovanne," Jeanne Ray's *Julie and Romeo* features an older woman who refuses to be shamed by her children. Ray builds a funny tale upon the scaffolding of Shakespeare's original play, the tragic tale of young lovers separated by family. Ray recasts the romance plot with grandparents who must escape the interference of their adult children. Unlike its sixteenth-century counterpart, Ray's tale is a comedy that allows happiness to flourish for its star-crossed lovers and depicts desire beyond youth.

By the early twenty-first century, the notion of women in their seventies rediscovering a zest for life and rekindling possibilities of passion is no longer dependent on comedy. Both Alice Munro and Mary Gordon portray their women of a certain age with empathy and nuance as they face surprise visitors from the distant past. In Gordon's novella "The Liar's Wife" and Munro's short story "Dolly," a woman who has lived a full life experiences an important internal shift and a heightened appreciation of living when a visit from a former lover prompts a renewed sense of vitality in the former and a relaxing of rigidity in the latter. I end the chapter with these two stories because I enjoyed reading them and because they remind me that even after years of increasing routine and familiarity, one is capable of pleasure and that the opening of old memories can sometimes allow an unexpected release. Unlike the "Deathbed Bookends" stories of the previous chapter, these plots explore passion in the present.

# THE WAITING GAME

## by Bernice Rubens

Bernice Rubens's 1998 Booker Prize–winning British novel, *The Waiting Game*, is described by readers as a hilarious, unsentimental portrayal of old age—honest and humane, and taboo-breakingly funny. I agree with these descriptions and also appreciate that much of the generous good humor and taboo breaking relates to the novel's bracingly frank descriptions of its aging characters' sexuality. I chose the novel for this chapter primarily because of Rubens's portrayal of the continuing sexual desire of the characters in an old age home: Mrs. Pringle at age eighty-six secretly masturbates to chat lines in her room; Mrs. Thackeray, a nearly eighty-year-old widow, suffers a horrific honeymoon complete with whips and ropes in a last-minute marriage to the home's newest resident, unaware of his proclivity for bondage; the war criminal Mrs. Green engages in an exaggerated flirtation with Mr. Rufus, not knowing he is an undercover inspector; and the retired military officer, The Major, and Mrs. Feinberg, the home's "token Jew" admitted only after rumors of racial bias at The Hollyhocks Home for the Aged, develop an increasingly intimate friendship.

Today, there are many more studies than ever before about how elderly adults remain sexual beings, and Rubens captures this through her depictions of characters' range of sexual responses. It's interesting to note how the family and staff respond with shock and struggle with the residents' sexuality, and when I initially read the book I identified with this perspective. However, in rereading *The Waiting Game*, and perhaps due to my age, I admire Rubens for taking on the topic and showing the residents' yearnings for sexual satisfaction as well as connection. I imagine that even including this in her fiction in 1998 would have been groundbreaking. I wish that she had been able to get below the surface and explain what was going on for the residents, in their minds, and yet even to include as much as she did was—and is—brave and unusual.

Though the novel is amusing, I find myself conflicted about its humor. Rubens's attention to the varied sexual appetites of these elderly characters can be entertaining and readers can be amused when imagining their elders as still capable of sexual activity only because her novel mirrors the bias of a youth-obsessed society. The laughter the novel invites is built on the premise that sexual longing is somehow outrageous for old people. BDSM, masturbation, bawdy jokes, and escaping into drunkenness would not seem as funny if the protagonists were younger. However, this kind of levity could be what allows a book about the harsh realities of the end of life to be appealing to many readers. It may be that one endures the indignities of failing minds and bodies by making sick jokes.

I read this short novel as a cautionary tale about lacking meaning in old age. Rubens delves into the lives of fifteen characters—between the ages of seventy-four and ninety-five—who are still ambulatory and not frail. Outward appearances hide closely held secrets of previous and current indiscretions, unmet needs, and acute loneliness. Rubens entertains her readers by revealing the web of gossip, lies, and pretense of the residents, and hinting at a mystery throughout the novel. The narrator's glee in unmasking the most dishonest characters may provoke a reader's laugh. Yet when we look beyond the residents' attempts to deceive one another by altering their autobiographies to enhance their personal histories, we discover a glaring lack of personal meaning and a spiritual vacuum. The residents' lack of meaningful engagement with others heightens their susceptibility to secondary interests—whether dependence on horoscopes or more sinister occupations. Even a funeral is an event that enlivens the deadliness of ordinary daily life. Their days are filled with an awareness of approaching death, yet without any religious or philosophical beliefs, they give little thought to questions of life's meaning; rather they wonder how they will die, hope it will be during their sleep, and until then each is "playing the waiting game." Lacking depth and self-awareness, the characters sometimes seem caricatured, making them more amusing than if Rubens had developed their inner lives and allowed them to be reflective. She touches upon their loneliness and desires, and she may have felt that in order to do so she needed to make light of them.

The third-person narrator opens the novel with an assertion that The Hollyhocks' location, near Devon in the UK—"on the road to Paris"—provides a "touch of class," which is what "The Hollyhocks was all about." We quickly learn that the woman known as Matron, the resident director of The Hollyhocks Home for the Aged, admits only those who are at least gentry. Rubens's tone and point of view invite amusement as we read that Matron had no pedigree of her own but "could smell it in others." The Hollyhocks appeals to a snobbish class of wealthy and healthy people. Matron selects residents of a certain class who are ambulatory and in good physical and mental health. Therefore, the home has none of the apparatus of assisted living residences or nursing homes, such as wheelchairs, walkers, or canes. In fact, even incontinence is to be feared and hidden from Matron, as it could result not only in a rubber sheet on the bed but also in expulsion from the home, and signs of mental instability lead to the final residence on the way to the grave—whether in the hospital or a nursing home.

Rubens's characters may lack depth, but they also do not fit stereotypical portrayals of sweet old ladies or dirty old men. Each character is distinctly himself or herself, with strengths and flaws, many of which are now useless in the shrunken scope of their world. Matron balances compassion for her residents with concern about the bottom line. Her attention to appearances contributes to the atmosphere of gossip, lies, and secrets and makes her susceptible to a blackmail scheme perpetrated by Lady Celia, who claims to have descended from a seventeenth-century poet and treats blackmail as a sport. We quickly learn that most of the residents hate Lady Celia, fearing she will outlive them, and that Jeremy Cross, whose single goal is to win the waiting game by outliving all the residents, hates her the most because she probably will win. The residents of The Hollyhocks continue to want to matter just as they did in their youth. They continue to seek approval, they want to be proven "right," and they are subject to embarrassment and humiliation if seen as mistaken or "wrong." They distort and inflate their personal histories to impress one another even as they assume only the partial truthfulness of one another's anecdotes. They jockey for invisible position and seek to enlarge their sense of self-importance. Rubens treats them with a mix of amusement and tenderness.

As in Muriel Spark's *Memento Mori,* which I discuss in the next chapter, one by one the elderly characters die—from various causes, both natural and unnatural. Rubens's omniscient narration, like Spark's, holds the characters at arm's length, and we see them from the outside. That distancing allows us to feel curious or outraged, to sympathize or blame, without penetrating their deepest emotions. We read about them with mild interest, as if skimming the obituaries in the daily newspaper. We care about but we do not mourn their deaths, in part because we do not really know them and in part because most of them are narrow-minded and bigoted. Though we learn that there is more to them than we originally thought, we never get inside their heads. We do not know how much to believe the stories they tell one another, having been warned that they tamper with the truth.

The tone of the initial pages suggests a lightweight tale, one in which we, like the Matron, may enjoy the company of the titled and smile in slight condescension at their bigotry, bias, and petty foibles. However, eventually we begin to see through Lady Celia's pretense, understanding her gleeful entanglement in blackmail as somehow getting even with her adulterous dead husband, and we may even feel sorry for Jeremy Cross's single-minded focus on outliving his fellow residents, which reveals his lack of friends and suggests his lifelong fear of intimacy. Each time he celebrates his comparative longevity by adding a name to the list of deceased residents he keeps on his wardrobe door, we wince at his petty triumph.

Rubens portrays the humanity of her elderly characters, describing their pride even as they continue to lose their influence in a diminishing world of physical and mental loss. The Major still relies on his firm, booming Mess Hall voice, projecting a former confidence and safety that appeals to Mrs. Feinberg, the token Jew among the residents, whom we eventually learn has lost her entire family in a concentration camp and has tattoos on the arm she never bares. We come to understand the fictions Mrs. Thackeray concocts about her so-called happy marriage when we learn of her abusive husband and her endurance of decades of uncomplaining but unwanted degradation from his whips, stains, and smiles. The surface comedy of characters' actions—whether overt flirtation or waiting to leave the lounge until everyone else has left—becomes increasingly complicated as we learn of the underlying causes. Small victories have significance beyond our initial observations, and even the most placid exteriors hide secrets and mysteries that range from the merely amusing to serious blackmail, suicide, and Holocaust war crimes. History and the legacy of war permeate the background and add to the novel's tension.

While these characters are limited in many ways, they are still very much alive. The residents struggle with whether to suppress or release their passions, but they are most certainly not beyond erotic desire. The most demure-appearing characters, such as Miss Bellamy, Mrs. Primple, and Mrs. Hughes, shake the home with their occasional outbursts of profanity and sexual truth. Even Matron celebrates and respects the newfound strength of Mrs. Thackeray after her disastrous honeymoon, when she finally speaks up for herself for the first time in her life and insists that her cruel new husband be evicted. In such instances Matron, their feared and yet appreciated authority at The Hollyhocks, is revealed to be more complex and layered than she initially seemed—not only to the inhabitants of the home but also to the reader.

Desire in this novel includes but goes beyond sexual desire. Nearly every character is lonely and wants some excitement to counter daily boredom. Most have outlived their families and friends, and they envy Mrs. Hughes and Mrs. Feinberg, who have invitations for the Christmas holiday. As a reader, I pity Mrs. Hughes, the sweet, doting great-grandmother whose boastings about the childish sayings of little Minnie bore her fellow inhabitants. When Mrs. Hughes becomes incontinent, leading to the dreaded rubber sheet on the bed, she recognizes her growing loss of independence. After this, coupled with an extended period of no family visits, she is overcome with sadness that she will not live long enough to watch little Minnie grow up. Mrs. Hughes begins drinking the cherry cordial gifts from her family that have accumulated untouched for years in her room, drowning her profound sadness in drunkenness. Her resulting inebriation and rudeness shock her family, the residents, and the reader, whether viewed as humorous or as a sign she has given up on life.

Rubens, known for her exploration of the pathetic secrets of damaged souls and celebrated for her combination of mordant humor and acute psychological insights, was quoted in interviews during her lifetime as saying she really wrote about only one thing: human relationships. She published *The Waiting Game* when she was sixty-nine, just seven years before her death at the age of seventy-six. Going beyond her many fictional accounts of relationships within families, in *The Waiting Game* Rubens portrays the endurance of intense emotions and loneliness, combativeness and grievances, and desire and sexuality into old age. As readers follow the twists and mysteries of the plot, we gradually develop some insight into each character's longings and fears. An unexplained desire to marry, for example, is revealed as the result of one character's perversion and another's attempt at satisfaction after her long abusive marriage. One character's need for safety meshes with the longing of another to provide protection. Meek, quiet women eventually gain strength to speak their rage and take pleasure in their newly discovered strength.

Rubens treats death lightly, as the obvious conclusion to all individual plots. Her characters want to prolong their lives, and they hope for painless, quick deaths, but they do not contemplate questions of the meaning of their lives. Most religious traditions and many psychological theories portray the end of life as providing an opportunity in which to review one's life, to make amends, to accept the person one has grown to be. Erik Erikson sees old age as the seventh stage of human development, in which an individual has the time and inclination to review and come to terms with earlier stages of development. Rubens's characters are instead trying to escape their pasts, to protect their reputations, and to outwit one another.

While the book jacket of my copy of *The Waiting Game* includes the words *hilarious, intelligent,* and *funny,* describes Rubens as gleefully extracting comedy from the most unlikely sources, and calls the novel "wickedly wonderful," I feel a pervasive sadness after reading this short novel. That I feel sadness rather than glee may be due in part to my distance from British humor, with its pleasure in revealing the pettiness of the privileged, its emphasis on the importance of a stiff upper lip and proper behavior. Rather than simply laugh at the comedy, I also feel the underlying pain at the heart of it. I am the same age as the youngest of The Hollyhocks' residents, and my life observations and experience make my personal response to the loneliness of Rubens's fictional characters one primarily of compassion and sorrow. The Hollyhocks is not a nursing home, and its residents are well treated and are not being driven mad by cruel caregivers, but nobody wants to end up in even the best old people's home, bereft of family and friends, and Rubens's comedy is at odds with my wish to avoid such a lonely ending to my life.

In imagining her characters' empty interior lives, even in such a lovely setting, Rubens manages to write wittily about topics we often avoid thinking about: the sexual longing of very old people or the loneliness that persists apart from family and friends in even the best old people's homes. It may be easier to imagine that old people are without sexual desire than to contemplate the sadness of their lives when desire and a need for connection linger, not only unsatiated but unacknowledged. If, like Miss Hazel's grown children in Toni Cade Bambara's short story "My Man Bovanne," readers may be embarrassed or uncomfortable in the presence of flirtation and sexual desire in parents or elderly people in general, then *The Waiting Game* is a poignant and amusing reminder that desire has no age limit.

# MRS. PALFREY AT THE CLAREMONT

## by Elizabeth Taylor

Though Elizabeth Taylor, like Rubens, finds humor in a story set in an old age home, she allows the reader to see through her main character's eyes, showing more of the subtleties of loneliness and desire. *Mrs. Palfrey at the Claremont*, first published in 1971 and reissued in 1982, is set in the 1960s and reflects postwar English life in shabby, genteel Kensington. It is an account of life in a hotel for the elderly—the dreariness and deprivation, but also the unexpected friendship between Laura Palfrey and the penniless young writer Ludo Myers. The two meet after her fall on the sidewalk outside his basement flat, and as a result of that initial meeting, she begins to enjoy the final months of her life, and he completes his novel. During her nine months at the hotel, Mrs. Palfrey and Ludo's relationship develops through the unlikely fiction that he is her grandson; he treats her with tenderness and respect, and she gradually begins to appreciate that she is still alive. I include this book because it shows the intricacies of building a tender relationship later in life—something rarely explored in fiction. The novel portrays the subtle mutual gifts of an unusual friendship between two strangers—a lonely old woman and a lonely young man. Taylor's account of their actions and their kindness to one another is not sugarcoated. It is nuanced, gently comical, and refreshing.

Like Elizabeth Strout's character Olive Kitteridge or Anita Brookner's Dorothea May (both discussed in chapter 4), Mrs. Palfrey is not someone I would want for a mother, a sister, or even a close friend. She is too stuck in an outdated role—wife of an English foreign service officer between the two world wars, confident of an innate entitlement that allows her to look down on colonized people as mere "natives" to whom one can lie without any sense of guilt, and who need governing by the British. She is preoccupied with external impressions. Her actions stem from an ingrained sense of duty and an adherence to unquestioned rules. Or, as one character notes, she must have had a very good nanny. Mrs. Palfrey is not curious about her fellow residents in the Claremont Hotel, managing to avoid offending others because of her own sense of dignity rather than any generous regard for their feelings. She has no close friends, no passionate interests or hobbies, no larger social or religious community. She has few self-indulgences beyond her favorite biscuits from the Food Hall at Harrods and her enjoyment of poetry, and even the poetry seems to be more a habitual self-discipline than a comfort. Yet I admire her self-discipline, her refusal to complain to the other residents, her attempt to make the best of her situation as a recently widowed woman after a lifetime of trying to please her husband. As I read about her dreary days, her lack of internal motivation beyond self-discipline, I sympathize with her. Loneliness is inevitable to someone who has not been a mother or grandmother who fostered affection, or allowed friends to get beyond her well-practiced reserve.

Mrs. Palfrey's introduction to the hotel is bleak. Through her eyes, we notice the winter rain, the taxi sloshing, the almost deserted road, and we absorb her shock when she discovers the driver has not ever heard of the hotel. We see her try "to banish terror from her heart" and note her "alarm at the threat of her own depression" as they arrive at the hotel that she selected from an advertisement. She has traveled alone by train from Scotland after the death of her husband and a short visit with her daughter, Elizabeth, who is too preoccupied with her own interests to care about her newly widowed mother. Mrs. Palfrey would not make herself vulnerable to her daughter; she is a woman who has relied on social rules to define her life. Yet we glimpse Mrs. Palfrey's real despair at her husband's death, hinted at in her comment that he died "in the face of all her prayers." We note Mrs. Palfrey's relief at the hotel's respectable appearance and her assurance that "she had always known how to behave—even as a young bride in Burma, when she had an image of herself to present to her husband, to herself, and to the natives—where she always reminded herself, 'I am an English woman.'" We can both appreciate how she once gained power from the role of "Englishwoman" and also see the ways her reliance on social rules has precluded self-knowledge and intimate relationships.

The narration is very close to her point of view, and we experience her utter misery of her first days at the hotel as well as her attempts to manage it with a stiff upper lip. The other residents criticize one another silently in their thoughts and in mean gestures behind one another's backs, trying to bolster their own fragile sense of importance. They gloat over every visit from a friend or relative and harass one another when expected visits do not take place. Mrs. Palfrey eventually realizes the extent to which the residents exaggerate their connections to family and friends and compete with one another to appear less lonely than they are. She soon wishes she had never mentioned the existence of her daughter, Elizabeth, and Desmond, her only grandson and heir, who works at the British Museum. They never visit, and their absence becomes a source of cruel comments. The dreariness of her life is painfully obvious when we learn that she feels "quite elated" to be asked by arthritic, nosy Mrs. Arbuthnot to exchange her book at the library because Mrs. Post is too ill to run this regular errand.

It is on this errand that Mrs. Palfrey meets Ludo, a caring young man who literally rescues her. Returning from the library at dusk, delighted at having had a reason to get out of the hotel, she suddenly slips in the drizzle, turns her ankle, and falls. More than the pain of her bleeding knee, she feels shame, and she struggles to recover her dignity on the empty street where she is sprawled, shaken and afraid. She drags herself up by the railings and leans there, trying to quiet herself, afraid she will never get home. She holds back her tears. A door opens, light streams across wet stones, and we hear the steps of a young man hurrying up the stairs from his basement room. Taylor writes, "He took her in his arms and held her to him, like a lover and without a word, and a wonderful acceptance began to spread across her pain, and she put herself in his hands with ungrudging gratitude." He helps her slowly down the steps to his flat, and we notice that once again she is concerned with appearances, having not wanted to be "looked at lumped against the railings, disorganized, disorderly." Once inside, she immediately apologizes, but he tells her not to talk yet, bringing her a cup of water and her handbag. She is temporarily shocked by the dirty towel with which he bathes her bleeding leg, yet she appreciates his tenderness as he bandages the wound with a handkerchief and offers her tea in his chilly flat. They introduce themselves, and she learns that he is writing a novel in the Banking Hall of Harrods, where it is nice and warm and he can save money on heating. She takes in his poor surroundings, and although she thinks he is hard up and hungry, she also thinks of the word *glee* as she looks at his face. He seems to be rather enjoying this adventure. After he "whistles up a cab," she invites him to come as her dinner guest on Saturday as a way of repaying his kindness. After an initial expression of astonishment, he is pleased and accepts her offer.

At the hotel, after announcing that she will have a guest for Saturday's dinner, Mrs. Palfrey allows her fellow residents to assume that the guest is her grandson. We learn that she has never before lied except on her husband's behalf, and she is immediately anxious about being found out. She bravely visits Ludo at Harrods and tells him of the "misunderstanding" she had not bothered to correct, as well as her fear of being taunted by Mrs. Arbuthnot. Much to her relief, he assures her he will enjoy going along with the deception and is happy to protect her from her fellow residents' taunts.

We recall that Ludo gave up acting to write a novel, and he plays his part well on his first visit. She introduces him as Desmond, and they both enjoy the pretense. She appreciates his company, and he appreciates the decent meal. He takes mental notes on everything about the elderly residents for use in his novel. Ludo is handsome and far more caring than Desmond, and Mrs. Palfrey is charmed by his behavior and by their shared secret. Although his visits are few, she enjoys his attention as well as the emotional protection his visits provide among the gossipy residents. It seems also that each of them gains real pleasure in each other's company, despite their obvious social differences. This crossing of boundaries is new for Mrs. Palfrey, and the novel suggests that only through her forced vulnerability—through her move into the Claremont and then her literal fall on the sidewalk—has she become open to the possibility of genuine friendship, one that is not derived from external roles or limited by her internal dictates.

Mrs. Palfrey's feelings for Ludo are complex, and she is surprised to recognize they resemble the early feelings she once had for Arthur when they were courting. She genuinely cares about him, and when he does not return to see her at the hotel, she misses his visits. Ludo is preoccupied with his pursuit of a young woman, Rosie, and unaware of how much Mrs. Palfrey misses him during the long periods between his visits to her hotel; Mrs. Palfrey does not escape her reliance on appearances and is distraught when she eventually loans him money against her own principle of never lending money to family or friends. Despite these problems, they give each other intangible gifts of corporeal mercy that allow the reader a quiet sense of joy. As the book jacket claims, "even the old can fall in love." Mrs. Palfrey tends to Ludo, giving him a sweater she had knitted for her neglectful grandson, Desmond, and Ludo brings her violets and lovingly calls her Grandmama in front of the other residents. She visits him with a warm steak and kidney pie and a smart Harrods carrier bag, insisting it will make him look more authentic as a shopper when he goes to the Banking Hall to work on his novel. When he tells her she thinks of everything, she silently thinks, "*I do where you are concerned, my dear Desmond. I try to go one step ahead of you, to discover what you want.*" And she suddenly feels tired "from love."

What a contrast between that evening as she takes a taxi from the Claremont to Ludo's flat for supper and the morning of the taxi ride when she first arrived there. The spring evening is "beautiful," the lilacs are budding, a man is wheeling a barrow of daffodils and irises, and Mrs. Palfrey is "full of happiness." These are among the happiest scenes in the novel. During supper Ludo realizes that there has never been anyone like Mrs. Palfrey in his life—"no spoiling aunt, or comfortable Nannie, no doting elder sisters—just he and his mother living in too close quarters, and quarrelling." No one before in his life had "stood in awe of writers." They both know they have a "strange friendship." The supper is a success, and their conversation includes his asking her a set of questions from a quiz to determine a person's level of friendliness. She answers each one truthfully, and when he tallies her score, he announces, "You have an average capacity for friendship." She is somewhat surprised, and tells him that it was easier to make friends as Arthur's wife than as a widow and that as one gets older, "people die, or drop out of one's life for other reasons. One is left with very little." As he helps her into her coat and walks her home, she tells him this is the "nicest evening . . . since Arthur died." She makes a splendid entrance at the hotel, he blows her a kiss, she goes to bed in bliss, and he hurries back home to write up his notes on everything he had noticed about her for his book on aging.

On the day Mrs. Arbuthnot leaves the Claremont for a nursing home because of her incontinence, all the residents feel down. Mrs. Palfrey strolls by Ludo's flat, just to catch a glimpse of him, waves when she sees the sweater she gave him, and then is jealous when she realizes a girl is wearing it. When Rosie describes "some old girl there waving," Ludo reminds her that he has told her of Mrs. Palfrey, but she has no interest in old people or his writing. Although he likes Rosie, she soon enough has a new boyfriend, and Ludo later reflects on the "appalling inequalities" of love. "There is always the one who offers the cheek and the one who kisses it. There was Mrs. Palfrey doting on him, and Rosie being doted on by him, to his exasperated sense of loss."

Before Ludo visits Mrs. Palfrey again, Desmond shows up unannounced on a rainy summer night when the residents uncharacteristically are all seated together in the lounge after dinner. Not wanting the residents to see the real Desmond, Mrs. Palfrey rushes to the entry hall and hisses at Desmond that he is not welcome. She rushes him out in the rain for a walk around the square and concocts all sorts of lies about not wanting him to meet the crazy residents with whom she lives. His reply that he came only because "Mother said I had to" lends some humor to the account of their dismal walk. She enjoys his discomfort much more than she deplores her own, and as readers we agree with her preference for Ludo and her silent solace that she "could find no patience for this pompous grandson; her love lay elsewhere."

Although she seldom sees Ludo, she continues to bask in their friendship and becomes somewhat less harsh in her judgments of the other residents. She feels sorry for Mrs. Arbuthnot and Mrs. Post, and even slightly less critical of Mr. Osmond, who, in spite of his dirty jokes and excessive pride whenever he gets a letter published in the *Times*, is obviously lonely. Although Mr. Osmond has never had rapport with anyone at the Claremont, he begins to develop a certain respect for Mrs. Palfrey because "she looked so wonderfully like a man," behaves like one, and scorns trivia. On a whim, he invites her to be his guest at the annual Masonic Ladies' Night, and she accepts, aware of the stir it would cause and the opportunity it would provide to dress up.

Later that evening, Mrs. Palfrey's conversation with the other residents is interrupted by the surprise entrance of Ludo. It had been so long since she last saw him that she felt almost panicked: "She had been trying hard lately to forget him, like a young girl with an unresponsive, but beloved boy." Claiming they have family business—the same excuse she used previously for hustling Desmond out the door—Mrs. Palfrey can scarcely get out of the room quickly enough. When Mrs. Palfrey realizes Ludo wants financial help because his mother has been evicted after discovering her lover is a con man, she suddenly feels overwhelmed and hails a taxi, too weak to walk the short distance back to the Claremont. Nevertheless, as Ludo helps her into the taxi, she tells him she will send him fifty pounds in tomorrow's post. Ludo feels his mother has humiliated both of them and determines to repay the loan with interest when his book is published, but Mrs. Palfrey does not know that. She is worried about taking money "from capital . . . the thing she must never do: for some unknown woman of loose morals and, worse than that, untidy thinking."

Like Mrs. Palfrey, Ludo is honorable, and he feels dreadful about borrowing the money. But instead of telling her, he stops visiting and writing and takes a job as a waiter to earn the money to help support his mother and to repay her. "Ludo had disappeared from Mrs. Palfrey's life," and she feels as if in giving him the money she had "rid herself of perhaps the only person she now loved."

A second and much more serious fall lands Mrs. Palfrey in the hospital with no knowledge of why Ludo has stopped visiting. Desmond comes to the hospital briefly because he found out from his mother that Mr. Osmond has proposed, and is worried about losing his inheritance. Later, Ludo shows up at the hotel because he's finally saved the fifty pounds to pay Mrs. Palfrey back. But upon learning she's in the hospital, he rushes to her bedside. When Mrs. Palfrey sees Ludo standing there, she tries to gesture a welcome with her hand. He sits beside the bed and softly tells her "whatever came into his head, invents messages from the home, and reassures her that she will live." He asks if her daughter is coming, learns she is not, and then arranges for her to have a private room. When he discovers she wants her own nightgown and her beloved book of poetry, he fetches both from the hotel. These practical acts of mercy comfort her, and he never mentions the loan, simply slipping an envelope with the money beneath her pillow. No longer alone and frightened, she asks Ludo if he remembers a poem about daffodils. He recalls it from his school days and recites what he can before she slips into her final sleep.

The day after Mrs. Palfrey's passing, instead of doing his writing at Harrods as usual, Ludo writes in his basement room, where he finishes his manuscript about life in a home for the aged and titles it *They Weren't Allowed to Die There*. We understand that their love has altered him, just as it altered her. In this novel we see the small pivots that change a life, the sea changes that are entirely internal, and whose effects transform one's experience from dreading each day to waking with a sense of renewal and hope.

# "MY MAN BOVANNE"

## by Toni Cade Bambara

The first two stories in this chapter deal with loneliness and longing in old age homes. Adult children and grandchildren are largely absent, wrapped up in their own lives. In the next two stories, children are very much present, and their concern about their elderly parents' sex lives creates drama. The first of these, Toni Cade Bambara's short story "My Man Bovanne," initially appeared in *Black World* in October 1971 under the misleading (or suggestive) title "Mama Hazel Takes to Her Bed." The story is narrated by Miss Hazel, a widowed matriarch in her sixties and mother of three adult children who are embarrassed by her sensual behavior with an elderly man at a fundraising event. I include this story in this chapter because of Bambara's portrayal of the contrast between the way the adult children see their mother and the way she sees herself. They see her as Mom and Bovanne as the old blind man who used to repair their broken toys. They are appalled at the mere suggestion of sexiness, especially from their mother. Although the setting is the 1970s, the failure of children to see their parents as sexual could occur in any community in any era.

Neither Miss Hazel nor the reader has any idea why the young people have invited their elders to the event. Nor do Miss Hazel and her friends know, until after the scolding by her children, that there is an unspoken agenda that requires the appearance of a unified community. She learns that she and several other elders in the neighborhood, including Bovanne, the nice old blind man who repairs broken things such as toasters and skates, have been invited "all on account of we grass roots." At the gathering, Miss Hazel notices that the young people ignore their elders except to greet them hurriedly. They rush by the blind man, saying, "My Man Bovanne," without stopping to get him a drink or a sandwich, or even to explain what is going on. She feels sorry for him and pulls him up to dance, and they weave their way among the tables set up throughout the room. Miss Hazel reaches for Bovanne because she empathizes with him and dislikes how the younger folks are marginalizing him by falsely calling him "My Man" without even stopping to chat with him. We don't know whether or not the dancing would have been the extent of Miss Hazel's involvement with Bovanne if her children had not pulled her away from him.

The young people had been hoping that Miss Hazel would behave in a certain way that would advance their agenda, which is ultimately to raise money for a free breakfast program for neighborhood children and to gain donated space in the local church. The young people see their elders primarily as resources, and certainly not as adults with complex needs and emotions, so it shocks them to see their mother not only as a separate adult but also as an adult with sexual desires. The newly politicized "children" are sentimental on the one hand about grassroots, tradition, and the elders, but at the same time are also deeply ashamed of Miss Hazel's appearance in her wigs and her head rag. They want her to look respectable, to wear her hair in a natural fashion, and to avoid standing out in the crowd. Disgusted by her skimpy low-necked dress, they unwittingly fall into ageist stereotypes that make them embarrassed by their mother's presentation of herself as seductive.

Bambara portrays both generations with humor and affection, not blaming Miss Hazel's children—Elo, Task, and Joe Lee—for their embarrassment, while also revealing Miss Hazel's sensitivity—her hurt feelings, her sadness, and her defiance in disregarding their attempts to use her as a pawn in their political strategy rather than see her as herself. Miss Hazel's close dancing scandalizes her adult children, who "haul" her into the kitchen, where they scold and humiliate her "like I got hoof and mouf disease." Elo talks about her own mother as if she were not there, saying "she had too much to drink" and describing her as "like a bitch in heat." Task complains that she was "makin a spectacle" of herself, "like one of them sex-starved ladies getting on in years and not too discriminating." He says her dress is too short, too low cut for a woman her age, with her "boobs out" and her "hem up to [her] ass." Joe Lee tells her, "You embarrass yourself and us too dancing like that." They make fun of Bovanne as a "tom," with no appreciation for the years he mended their broken toys, and they criticize how he looks without dark glasses to cover his blind eyes. The story includes hints that Miss Hazel is continuing her sexual behavior, not that it is something new, and as a reader I wonder how her children have managed not to take into consideration her seductive behavior when they assumed she would be useful to them in their attempts to influence the minister at the fundraiser. They have been so caught up in their strategies for a worthy cause that they have lost sight of individual people, whether Bovanne or their mother.

When I assigned this story in my graduate course "Coming to Age," my students assumed that Miss Hazel planned to have the blind man, Bovanne, spend the night in her bed, focusing on the intimate bodily "hummin" that Miss Hazel uses to describe their close dancing. Because Bovanne cannot see her, she relies on touch, and that touch is powerful. Although my students were sympathetic toward Miss Hazel, they admitted their discomfort in thinking of their own parents as sexual, even as they felt awkward in acknowledging their own failure to see older people as still capable of sex.

Miss Hazel appears to brush off her children's criticisms, though she yields to them to some extent. Instead of staying to listen to her niece give a prepared speech about the breakfast program or to speak a few words of support as a token grassroots elder, Miss Hazel pulls Bovanne out of there and tells him her plans to take him to buy dark sunglasses to camouflage his eyes. Then they go to the supermarket to shop for the next day's family dinner. These two errands reveal her response to the children's comments even as she rejects their disapproval of her appearance and sexuality. She takes seriously her children's remark about Bovanne's need for sunglasses and knows she will cook the family dinner the following day, as expected, while also defying her children's expectations by continuing to act seductively. She tells Bovanne she will take him to her house, draw a nice warm bath with healing herbs, provide a rubdown, and talk, brew tea, and massage his face. We smile when she insists she means to do her part for the old folks, and we recognize not only her practical action in buying Bovanne the sunglasses but also her sense of humor and desire in suggesting that old folks need sensual touch, not just camouflaging glasses. She responds teasingly to Bovanne's compliment, "I imagine you are a very pretty woman, Miss Hazel," with "I surely am, just like the hussy my daughter always say I was."

Is Miss Hazel really desirous of Bovanne, or is she, like her children, using Bovanne to make a point to her children, or to herself? Her behavior mirrors that of her children to the extent that she, too, has an unspoken agenda. She wants to get even with her children by doing just what she pleases, regardless of their opinions. Her sense of responsibility does not make her deny her own desire—whether to defy her children or to enjoy being a "hussy." In both situations, their goals seem to overlook the means, and to be complex and layered. The children's goals for community progress blind them to their treatment of their mother, and Miss Hazel's kind invitation to Bovanne to dance evolves into a reaction to her children's harsh comments.

On the other hand, in agreeing to host the family dinner and in taking seriously her children's comments on Bovanne's appearance, Miss Hazel recognizes the need for the community to work together. She tells Bovanne that you "gots to take care of the older folks. And let them know they still needed to run the mimeo machine and keep the spark plugs clean and fix the mailboxes for folks who might help us get the breakfast program going, and the school for the little kids and the campaign and all. Cause old folks is the nation." Regardless of her tone, which reads as a bit sarcastic, Miss Hazel understands the importance of engaging with her adult children and building up the larger community, but not denying her own vitality. She demands to be her entire self—and she expects her children to respect the fact that not only are old folks "grass roots," the "old folks is the nation." Sight and blindness thread through the story. Although the surface focus is on treatment of the blind man, the adult children themselves are blind to the complexity of older people, whom they see only in one-sided, limited roles.

Read through the prism of age, Bambara's story interests me because of its awareness of how profoundly adult children can refuse to see their parents as still capable of sexual desire. They are conditioned, as everyone is, to believe that old people are "beyond" sex.

## JULIE AND ROMEO

### by Jeanne Ray

Like "My Man Bovanne," Jeanne Ray's *Julie and Romeo* (2000) portrays the horror of adult children when they begin to see their mother as a sexual adult and not exclusively as Mom. And as with Bambara's story, we get to witness the unapologetic desire of an older female character. Variously described as a comic gem of a love story, charming, and a little jewel of a book by newspaper reviewers, this novel celebrates second chances, romance, and sexual passion beyond sixty. Using the feuding families of Shakespeare's classic play as scaffolding for the plot, Ray's novel is a satisfying comedy in which the generational conflict ends not in tragedy but in happy unions.

It is the terms of the happy ending and the romantic focus on a couple of "a certain age" that make this novel particularly rich for my project. The symbolic power of Shakespeare's iconic lovers is inextricable from their youth; their innocence, idealism, and romantic fervor are shaped in direct and painful contrast to their jaded, callow, and prosaic elders. In Ray's revision, the lovers are in their sixties; in contrast to their hot-blooded, adult children, their experiences, losses, and financial concerns have, at least until their love emerges, long deadened romantic passion.

The novel's feud between two families began with Romeo's mother, Mrs. Cacciamani, and Julie's father, Mr. Roseman. Though their families do not discover the cause of the feud until the end of the novel, Mrs. Cacciamani and Mr. Roseman's hatred and virulent competition was imbibed without question by their children (Romeo and Julie's generation) and grandchildren, impeding the youthful romance of Julie and Romeo's children and threatening the late-in-life romance of Julie and Romeo. The plot consists of the latter's burgeoning romance amid the past and present damage of the feud.

Despite the source material, Ray's novel is not tragic, and it depicts Julie's romantic awakening as a happy event. The lightness of Julie's narration and the fairy-tale quality of this witty reversal of Shakespeare's tragedy make Julie's discovery of her dormant sexual desire a purely positive development rather than a cause for psychological analysis, as in Lessing's *Love, Again*, or even a source of embarrassment or humor, as in "My Man Bovanne" or *The Waiting Game*. The comedy occurs not at the expense of the aging but rather in the twists of plot in which the widowed Romeo and the divorced Julie discover one another as attractive adults in a business conference setting, away from the context of the mysterious family feud. Whatever the magical elements of the story, the portrayal of internal conflicts between Julie and Romeo's personal desires and their deep love for their adult children is entirely plausible, and their conflicts do not detract from their enjoyment of each other. I chose *Julie and Romeo* for this chapter because of Ray's charming portrayal of Julie's recognition of her own sexual desire at age sixty. She is so happy, so alive, so surprised after decades of a waning marriage to someone her parents chose for her, the letdown of being abandoned by her husband for a much younger woman, and her tendency always to put her grown daughters and grandchildren first.

Ray relies extensively on dialogue, making it easy to forget that Julie is the narrator and that her point of view saturates the text. She confides the story to us, and it is easy to believe her account and to relish the details of her falling in love with the attractive man she had always perceived as the enemy. Ray uses the romantic trope of tension to good effect in her delineation of the lovers' relationship (think Benedick and Beatrice in *Much Ado About Nothing* as well as Mr. Darcy and Elizabeth Bennet in *Pride and Prejudice*, and countless films and novels). The age of these lovers makes this a new and valuable take on a well-loved story.

The novel is set against the backdrop of competing florist shops, not only providing real-world financial heft to the feud that endangers the livelihood of both families but also offering a symbolically loaded environment in which romance can bloom. The novel opens with Julie's vivid childhood memory of her father spitting on the concrete floor of his florist shop when she was five years old and calling the Cacciamanis pigs. Half a century later, she realizes she has no idea what caused the feud between the Cacciamanis and the Rosemans, the only two florists in the small town. She remembers only the deeply held mutual prejudice, in which the Jewish Rosemans considered themselves normal in contrast to the "idol-worshiping" Catholic Cacciamanis and "that continued through three generations and was never explained." Julie inherited the prejudice but was not personally affected by it until her teenage daughter Sandy and Tony Cacciamani wanted to get married. Both families—including Romeo and Julie—sat down together in a room and forbade the marriage, claiming the couple was too young, although the real reason was the virulent hatred of the feud.

Fifteen years later, Julie and Romeo meet again at a seminar called "Making Your Small Business Work." Julie walks into a nice-looking Italian man wearing the name tag *Romeo Cacciamani* and is surprised that she has no remaining twinge of the inherited hatred. Instead she feels sorry for him, realizing that his shop must also "be going bust." Julie relays how Mort Roth was chosen for her by her parents and how he had full control of the family florist shop after their deaths until he left her, five years before. Although she loves being back among the flowers, she has been unsuccessful running the family business. After a lifetime of pleasing her parents and then her husband, she has little experience of herself as a whole and separate being.

The narration that follows Julie and Romeo's meeting is remarkable for its domestic, suburban setting and its gratifying portrayal of their developing sexual relationship. The couple's courtship unfolds in the banal surrounds of the Sheraton Hotel and a local Starbucks. Their feelings are thoughtful, empathetic, and grounded in shared histories and family details rather than in the heightened euphoria that characterizes many romantic tales. We get to see Julie and Romeo luxuriating in their discovery of each other's bodies without self-consciousness or any negative comparison with their younger selves. I love Ray's portrayal of two mature adults who are living in the present and enjoying themselves and one another. They are not "settling" for second best nor substituting a gentle, cerebral affection for passionate sex.

When Romeo shows up unannounced at her flower shop early the morning after the seminar and invites her to dinner that night, they have trouble figuring out how to meet without being seen by their families. They finally decide to go to the local CVS at 7:00 p.m. and to create cover stories. They are afraid of being discovered by their children, and the novel is filled with a sense of excitement as they try to outwit them. Part of our enjoyment of Julie's account is that the adults are put in the position of teenagers. Their thwarted love and sense of risk add to their anticipation and revive a pleasure usually not associated with mature adults, who are often portrayed as overly cautious.

While waiting in the CVS, Julie walks up and down the aisles, where she feels assaulted by foundation that claims to make your skin young and dewy, nail polish called "Fetish," lipstick called "French Kiss," magazines whose covers blatantly promise to provide information on multiple orgasms and great sex at twenty, thirty, and forty. There is no promise of great sex at fifty or sixty or after, and Julie wonders, "*Were we finished? Unentitled? Too thrilled to be taking our grandchildren to swim practice to even think about sex?*" The pharmacy displays lubrication creams next to adult undergarments, and then a wall of condoms, which is where Romeo finds her, and asks, "Shopping?"

To her response of "This may be the single worst instant of my life," he says, "Good. Then things can only go up from here." He takes her to a sushi restaurant for raw fish, which she considers reckless food. He holds her hand. Later in the evening, he tells her he had sought her out at the seminar after glimpsing "this beautiful woman" he felt he knew. Before they separate for the evening, he kisses her, and she feels "washed back by the sea of tender kissing" and "lighter," her best self. She feels unusually sure of herself.

At home, she compares her current self to her youthful self and appreciates that her body can still respond to kisses even though she is "older, more sensible." Nevertheless, she feels "eaten up by desire. Sex." Later that night, Romeo returns, throwing pebbles at her window, and they sneak away to the spare room at his shop. The comedy occurs when they find Romeo's son sleeping in the spare room and have to encounter his outrage at Romeo's bringing a Roseman into "Mama's shop" to "fuck."

Any discovery of a secret sexual rendezvous is embarrassing, but Ray's account is funny rather than humiliating. The outrage is not directed at Romeo's sexual interest in another woman but rather is due to their unexamined feudal wounds. The familial disapproval not only frustrates but also inflames adult desire. But unlike the disapproving parents of a young couple, Romeo and Julie realize that they've been complicit in never questioning the family hatred; they are responsible for their children's bias.

Ray retains the plot device of the feud but relocates the judgmental pressure in the children rather than the lovers' parents. The story quickly moves into dramatic accounts of furious behavior of the adult children in both families when they realize their parents are not only talking to the enemy but also lying about their dates and having sex with each other. Julie, as a caring mother and grandmother, does not lose those ties in her new relationship with Romeo, but her enjoyment of her erotic self does impinge on the practical relationships in her life, a particular instance being when Julie's date with Romeo causes her to forget her regular commitment to babysit Sandy's children. When Julie arrives home late, both Sandy and her older sister, Nora, are initially worried. But when they learn that she was having dinner with a Cacciamani, they become livid. They have so internalized the learned hatred and bias that the fissures in the feud undermine their unexamined prejudices and complicate their sense of who they are. Despite their disappointment and anger, though, we get no sense that either daughter disapproves objectively of their mother's sexuality.

When Julie and Romeo finally make love, Ray portrays a tender reawakening of the sexual passion that has been dormant for so long. Afterward, Julie romantically recalls her sense that Romeo was the one she had always been waiting for. She describes their lovemaking and says, "Sex stays with you, even in the years you never call it into service . . . full of memory and response." She remembers making love so deeply that she felt the very shape of her body changing. They tell each other of their love. While such language may seem predictable or even cliché if they were young, this level of erotic specificity and gentle sensuality is unexpected in stories about old people.

The story's happy ending is predictable yet satisfying. All the loose ends get tied up, the younger generation finds love, and the origins of the feud are finally revealed. Julie and Romeo merge their businesses, keep a secret third-floor walk-up for lovemaking, and are in no rush to marry. On the final page, Julie tells us, "To anyone who ever thought that love and passion were for the young, I say, think again. I am speaking from personal experience here." At the age of sixty, she is more surprised by passion and love than any classic young heroine, and the struggle for autonomy from family constrictions adds spice to the tale of forbidden love.

# "THE LIAR'S WIFE"

## by Mary Gordon

In the final pair of stories in this chapter, women whose lives have become comfortably predictable or even stagnant gain perspective and renewed passion as the result of unexpected visitors from the past. At the heart of the first of these stories, Mary Gordon's novella "The Liar's Wife" (2014), is a surprise reunion between Jocelyn Bernstein and Johnny O'Shaughnessy fifty years after she abandoned him in Dublin and ended their short marriage, fleeing to her childhood home in New Canaan, Connecticut. This story shows us how life can be shaken up in simple but delightful ways, even late in life.

Gordon's omniscient narrator tells the story from the point of view of its seventy-two-year-old protagonist, who is startled by the appearance of a yellow Frito-Lay truck parked outside the home she inherited after her parents' death, where she returns periodically while her husband, Richard, vacations at the home he inherited on Nantucket. Before seeing the unwelcome truck, Jocelyn had been savoring the early evening outdoors surrounded by the comforting trees and familiar late-summer scents of childhood. She is frightened by the unfamiliar sight, fearing burglary, kidnapping, or terrorism, and is even more frightened when a stranger rings the doorbell and calls her name.

As the story unfolds, we learn that Jocelyn has always feared life, whereas Johnny, who shows up in the yellow truck with his common-law wife and fellow troubadour, Linnet, has always embraced it. During the few hours of their unexpected visit, Jocelyn's memories provide the background narrative of her protected upbringing as the only daughter of conventional and caring parents, her ardent seduction by Johnny, their seventeen months of marriage in Dublin, and her inability to adjust to Irish customs and to Johnny's stories, which she experienced as lies.

Although the story takes place in fewer than twenty-four hours, the memories span Jocelyn's entire life. We learn she had completely amputated all memories of her time with Johnny. As readers, we feel present to her suddenly remembered scenes of passionate lovemaking, her bewilderment as a young bride, her misreading of Irish culture and the Catholic religion. She had never conceived of a spectrum of truth-telling in which stories both entertain and soften the brutality of hard facts. Her New England directness equated the subtle nuance of Johnny and his friends' stories with outright lying.

She remembers her bewilderment over Johnny's wild stories and his omissions of painful personal information. After Johnny told an elderly aristocrat that Jocelyn was probably a direct descendent of Rogier van der Weyden because she resembled a woman in a van der Weyden portrait, she didn't know how to say "that's not true." When he refused to take her to a family funeral and she mentioned her disappointment to her friends, she learned it was the funeral of his father, a man Johnny had claimed died a decade earlier. Her friends explained to her that Johnny might have made up such stories "probably because he wanted them to be true, and he thought

89

you'd like to hear them." After confronting him, she fled, leaving him a note that read, "I had to go home." She recalls "navigating the choppy seas of what they would call stories and what she could only call lies. Not knowing what was firm, dependable ground, the ground of fact, the ground on which words and facts met—it had made her woozy . . . It was why she'd needed to leave him; she needed to be on firm ground again. And she had been living her life, one foot before the other on the sweet firm earth."

Until Johnny's reappearance in her life, Jocelyn had attributed her increasing sense of general loss primarily to aging. She appreciated her marriage, her family, and her financial security. She had accepted that her sexual passions had tapered to quiet contentment, that the once immensity of maternal love had settled into mixed feelings toward her adult daughter and son, and that she had tamped down her expressive emotion toward growing grandsons who were beyond nuzzling and snuggling. She and Richard vacationed separately since her several bouts of skin cancer had made her afraid of being out in the sun at their seashore home. While still deeply responsive to nature, to the scent of flowers and the dazzle of the night stars, she nevertheless felt that the best of life was behind her.

The surprise visit brings up feelings that Jocelyn thought she had left behind. From the time she cautiously answers the front door through the awkward conversation with Johnny and Linnet in her living room, she is acutely uncomfortable. She asks what they want to drink and then admits there is no beer in the house but that she has liquor and wine. She pours them the pinot grigio she had been drinking, and they exchange brief facts about their lives. We learn that Johnny has been married twice and that he was recently friended on Facebook by his adult daughter. They ask to spend the night at her house rather than sleep in the truck before continuing their last cross-country delivery prior to leaving the US for Dublin. She agrees to let them treat her to an Italian dinner in exchange for her hospitality.

Throughout dinner at the Tower of Pizza, where the pair gives a singing performance in exchange for their meal, Jocelyn is again uncomfortable. She criticizes herself silently for her snobbishness, her inhospitality, her initial judgments of their poorly dyed hair, their ill-fitting dentures, their grammar, but mostly for her continuing discomfort with Johnny's "lies"—both past and present. At the restaurant, Tony, the owner, tells her to say hi to Mick next time she sees him, and she discovers Johnny has told him that she left him to go off with Mick Jagger. Later, the waitress says she understands that "Ruby Tuesday" was written for Jocelyn. Not only is she embarrassed, she is trembling, engulfed in all the anger of her youth. She tries, however, to enjoy the evening, telling herself to *"get out of your rut. God knows, Johnny was never in a rut."* When Linnet corrects Johnny for one of his Irish expressions such as "having a gas" or "great crack," Jocelyn actually laughs out loud, "a laugh she thought would have embarrassed almost everyone she knew. It would definitely have embarrassed Richard."

Feeling pleasantly light-headed from the Chianti, Jocelyn asks why they are going back to Dublin. Johnny at first tries not to tell their "woes," but Linnet confides, "It's the Big C," and explains that because they do not have insurance, they are returning to Ireland where "the state'll take care of him." When Tony hands Johnny his guitar and introduces them as Dixie and Dub, "two singers on their way to Ireland from sunny California," they break into song: "We got married in a fever / hotter than a pepper sprout . . . " and Jocelyn realizes she doesn't care if the song begins with a lie. Knowing that Johnny has cancer, Jocelyn understands that he has come to say a final goodbye, and she begins to temper her initially harsh judgments. And then, when Johnny and Linnet sing to his guitar, she along with many diners in the restaurant begins to cry. As readers, we sense that her familiar assumptions suddenly strike her as unkind, and yet she has not known how to think or behave differently.

She notices more about Linnet too. She is not only a bleached blond with a boob job but has a pure, natural voice that lifts everyone into her song, "I am a maid of constant sorrow. I've seen trouble all my days." Johnny's introduction of a song "for a very special lady, and some very special memories" touches a responsive chord throughout the room, and he invites them to sing along, "Oh, the summertime is coming / and the trees are sweetly blooming." He ends with the speech from *The Tempest*, and his own rendition, "Have ye no homes of your own to go to." Nobody wants them to stop.

Jocelyn softens her harsh viewpoints as she is caught up in their songs and the awakening of shared feelings in a room of strangers. She realizes she enjoys the Chianti and the delicious Italian foods in the pizza joint on the wrong side of town just as much as the fine wines and expensive meals she and Richard are accustomed to in restaurants on the other side of town. And she "felt suddenly smaller than the two of them with her safe life, her safe home, her safe marriage . . . disliking everything about herself." As the singing ends, and everyone in the restaurant is clearly moved, Jocelyn questions why, yet she knows the reason—"they had made something happen in this ugly room . . . had given people something. Hope? Belief? A sense that we are not alone, that we will not be left, finally, unaccompanied."

The narrative is bittersweet. Johnny's goodbye visit reminds Jocelyn of events in her life that she had completely erased, including her youthful, passionate self. His disregard for financial success contrasts with Richard's wealthy life as a lawyer with his specialty in intellectual property, and Jocelyn recognizes she does, in fact, appreciate the life she has chosen. Yet she also sees how much Johnny has always loved life in stark contrast to her own fears. She is surprised and touched that "they had been young lovers" and "They are grandparents." The author repeats these two lines, emphasizing their importance to Jocelyn.

After their return from the restaurant, Linnet tactfully withdraws to prepare for bed. Johnny and Jocelyn connect as friends—long-ago lovers, now grandparents—and Jocelyn invites Johnny outside, where she suddenly has the urge to dance under the stars. He tells her she was always a "Great girl" and "No regrets," and she agrees, knowing she speaks truthfully. "She would have been less had she never known him, without the glimpse of something offered, something she knew she couldn't hold on to. Didn't want. Without Johnny she wouldn't have known, really, who she was. Because he had taught her who she was not."

As she wakens early the next morning to the sound of the yellow truck pulling out of the driveway, she knows they will never again see each other, that she can never tell anyone about what happened the previous night, that people might say she dreamed it. No one would even think she had it in her to make it up. By coming back, Johnny "changed some-thing. Moved some rock that had sealed something over. The sealed-up understanding that she'd had, as if she knew what life was and would always be." She is pleasantly dizzy, thrilled by the word *unsealed*. We glimpse the effect of that unsealing. Her immediate sense is that she can never return to the Tower of Pizza, but she counters with the thought that "maybe she would, with Richard, and if anyone said anything about Mick, she'd just put her finger to her lips and then wink."

Through Jocelyn, we, too, catch something of Johnny's zest for life, his contagious sense that not understanding every-thing about life is "great" because "anything can happen, you never know what it's going to mean."

# "DOLLY"

## by Alice Munro

Like "The Liar's Wife," Alice Munro's 2012 short story, "Dolly," tells a tale of a visit that stirs up old emotions. Set in Canada, "Dolly" is an interior monologue narrated by an elderly woman whose name we never learn. The narrator recollects a visit from a saleswoman who turns out to be her partner's long-ago lover, a woman he memorialized decades earlier in a published poem whose raw power has always disturbed her. The narrator also recounts the details of the thoughts and experiences that bracket her life before and after the visit. Munro's story explores the ways in which life-changing epiphanies are possible, even when one is old and mired in seemingly unchangeable habits and behaviors. Her quiet but powerful narrative demonstrates how a life is made up of the stories we tell ourselves and how small shifts in perspective may open new chapters and revelatory capacities to choose new narratives, even—and perhaps most importantly—within our existing stories, our current lives. Dolly's visit changes the way the narrator "reads" her common-law marriage and revitalizes her and her partner's experience of one another and their options.

Munro does not introduce the Dolly of the title until nearly halfway through the narrative. The story opens with the narrator's account of an even more distant time in the past, prior to the upsetting visit, when she was seventy-one and her partner, Franklin, was eighty-three, and they were contemplating mutual suicide because they both assumed that their predictable lives were unlikely to contain anything of future importance. On a perfect autumn day, they went searching for just the right location for their deaths, wanting privacy yet also wanting fairly quick discovery. However, after locating the ideal spot, in the woods near a country road, they disagreed about whether or not to leave a note explaining their actions. This disagreement led Franklin to pronounce his wife too young to make the decision, declaring that they would revisit the discussion when she reached seventy-five. When she told him that she was actually bothered by his assumption that nothing more of any importance was going to happen in their lives, he pointed out that their argument about leaving a suicide note was an event, and one sufficient for him to decide the entire subject needed to be postponed.

In this interaction, Franklin evinced little passion—they usually avoided all arguments and assumed that whatever was right for him was right for her. We get a glimpse into the dullness into which their lives had settled, a dullness both undercut and oddly reaffirmed by their planned mutual suicide, itself rendered a task whose details became minor irritations, annoying enough to him to insist on sidestepping the conversation.

Recalling the argument about the propriety of, or need for, a suicide note, the narrator ruminates on other ways she and Franklin differ. He is a retired horse trainer and a poet, though he downplays his occupation as a poet, seeming to be embarrassed by the apparent idleness of writing poetry in contrast to the obvious busyness of training horses. She describes him as a reticent man except for his best-known poem, a blatantly explicit account of a two-week sexual adventure with a woman named Dolly, a poem that the local folks, and he himself, still call "pretty raw." She describes herself as a retired high school mathematics teacher who tried staying home with Franklin after retirement, grew bored, and began writing "tidy" yet entertaining biographies of little-known Canadian women novelists "who have been undeservedly forgotten or have never received proper attention." Although she duly credits Franklin's reputation as a poet for helping her get acceptance as a writer, she admits to having more sympathy for novelists than poets. She is generally satisfied with her solitary days at home and usually enjoys the control and quiet of writing on her own after years in classrooms.

About halfway through the story, we get the impression that age seventy-five has come and gone prior to her next rumination with no further talk of suicide. The narrator recalls an afternoon when she yearned for some company and so, uncharacteristically, invited a door-to-door cosmetic sales-woman into her home, a saleswoman who (unbeknownst to them both) turns out to be the Dolly (real name Gwendo-lyn) of her husband's poem. The narrator compulsively relives every detail of that initial encounter with Gwen/Dolly as if it were happening in present time.

The scene is one of mutual discomfort and awkward con-versation across class lines. Gwen has brassy, thin hair, is ill at ease, requests an ashtray, and then apologizes for interrupting the narrator's letter writing. However, when she learns that the narrator is writing the biography of a neglected woman writer, not a letter, Gwen gushes, "You must be one smart per-son. Wait till I get to tell them at home that I saw a book that was just getting written." We learn that Gwen's common-law husband has died, and the narrator surprises us, telling Gwen that she, too, is unmarried. We sense she is trying to find a way to connect with her less-sophisticated acquaintance.

Although she does not use cosmetics, the narrator orders "some lotion that would restore her youth," and Gwen promises to drop it off next time she comes around. When Franklin comes home, she tells him all about Gwen and then dislikes herself for admitting, " . . . it's another world. I rather enjoyed it," suggesting the depths of her boredom and her curiosity about someone different from herself, and potentially her pleasure in perceiving herself as an unmarried woman who strikes up unusual conversations. Rather than showing any curiosity, Franklin suggests she needs to get out more and should apply to be a substitute teacher.

On Gwen's return visit to deliver the lotion several days later, the two women chat, and the narrator is again embarrassed by her acute discomfort with Gwen's grammatical mistakes and her obvious awe at speaking to a writer. She feels, she says, "as if I had no right to be so superior," but we also sense her enjoyment of the attention. She gives Gwen a copy of the novel by the author whose biography she is writing and is startled when Gwen says she has never read a book through but will read this one. The narrator feels flattered and then a bit embarrassed and cautious, as she once did when a student had a crush on her. Through the exposition to this point, Munro's tone is conversational and her pace is slow, as if the narrator is still pondering the significance of the visit, what she learned about herself through the event.

Only later in the story, when we learn that Gwen is the Dolly of Franklin's poem (a poem about which Gwen knows little), do we begin to understand the significance of the scene that has unfolded between Gwen and the narrator, and yet Munro invites us to see the import of the exchange even before the narrator is (or we are) aware that her heightened emotional response will soon be pushed to uncharacteristically dramatic heights.

In the period before Gwen is revealed as Dolly, we learn that, after their long conversation, Gwen's car will not start and is blocking the driveway when Franklin arrives home after dark that evening. Without coming in to meet the owner of the car, he tries unsuccessfully to start it and calls the village garage only to learn that it is closed until morning. Reluctantly, and with a sense of good manners, the narrator invites Gwen to stay for supper and overnight. She worries about Franklin's reaction to the stranger, fearing that polite conversation with Gwen will mean upsetting Franklin's usual routine of quietly watching the news, and she speculates whether Franklin will remain in the room and eavesdrop or whether he will slip away upstairs. She suggests Gwen call home and secretly hopes someone will come and get her.

When Franklin finally enters the kitchen and sees Gwen, the narrator vividly recalls that "both she and Franklin . . . were struck at the same time." Gwen blurts out, "Oh my Lord," to which he responds, "No, it isn't . . . It's just me." They recognize each other, are uncomfortable in the narrator's presence, and repeat each other's names in tones of mockery and dismay:

"Frank."

"Dolly."

The narrator shares her sense that, if she were not present, they would have immediately fallen into one another's arms.

She remembers that Franklin's voice "insisted on going back to normal," while Dolly/Gwen emphasizes the enormous or even supernatural joke of their finding each other. In retrospect, the narrator realizes the oddity of her own participation in the general merriment of that evening, bringing out a bottle of wine, though Franklin no longer drinks. Dolly explains that she had been working as a nursemaid in Toronto when she met Frank on his last leave before he went overseas during World War II. They had "as crazy a time as you could imagine," and then lost track of each other. She makes vague references to being too busy to answer his letters and then marrying a young man she met on shipboard after the war while accompanying two evacuated children back to Europe from Canada.

Until that evening, the narrator had not known anything about this part of Franklin's life other than the erotic details of his poem. In it, he is enthralled by Dolly, enraptured by her lavish lovemaking during their adventurous two weeks together and fascinated by all her superstitions, such as her belief that she is protected from pregnancy by wearing "her dead sis's hair in a locket" around her neck. The poem recounts that she gives him a magic tooth to protect him during the war. Years earlier, the narrator had teased some details out of Franklin and had somewhat hoped that Dolly might have been made up, but even then, she thought that unlikely given the particularity of her poetic representation and how foreign her qualities seem to the Franklin she knows.

In contrast to her earlier uneasy feelings of superiority to Gwen/Dolly, we can tell the narrator's discomfort now stems from a sense of failed competition. Her assumptions have been thrown off course in ways both big and small. The narrator recounts in detail each "abnormal" behavior of the never-to-be-forgotten morning after their visitor stays the night. She dresses and does her hair—which she would not normally do so early in the morning. Franklin uncharacteristically offers to make her breakfast. She notices, with discomfort and annoyance, that Gwen not only cleaned up the dishes she had been too tired to do the previous night but also washed a row of long-neglected dusty jars that formerly sat on a high shelf. When Franklin goes outside to prepare Gwen's car for towing, the narrator is convinced Dolly follows him "as if she didn't want to lose sight of him for a moment."

Recalling the full force of her anger and jealousy, the narrator admits she wanted to run after them and "pound them to pieces" as they drove off together. Usually complacent, she is overtaken by a sense of "grievous excitement" and rashly determines to leave Franklin. Flushed with feeling, she leaves him a terse note about going to check facts on her current novelist. She then packs a suitcase, drops her house key through the mail slot, and drives off in her car. She had written a longer note but then takes it with her, not wanting Gwen to see it "when she came back with him as she surely would."

In that letter, she writes, without dignity or grace, about his deception and self-deception, using words such as *lies* and *cruel* and *puke*. She had planned to rewrite it but ends up mailing it without revision. The intensity of her letter and the rashness of her departure reveal how much she has tamped down her emotions during her years with Franklin. They seem to have taken each other for granted, settling mostly into his routines. Her jealousy appears to remind her of a time she and Franklin were passionate rather than simply careful with one another. Munro suggests through this rekindling of emotion, even if negative, that there was once passion between them, and a non-narrated and buried history when feelings were not so carefully managed.

Dolly's visit shows the extent of the narrator's docile adaptation to Franklin's whims, such as not eating in restaurants or rarely purchasing anything for herself. In her one night away from Franklin, sleeping alone in a strange motel after dining in a restaurant and nearly purchasing a silk scarf, she recalls herself as a young student teacher spending the night with a married man in a cheap motel, when she was reckless and unconcerned about anything but her pleasure. The contrast between her youthful, passionate self and her present dull routine is sharp.

The narration of the aftermath of the Dolly visit has the urgency of present tense although it is a recollection. By 6:00 the next morning, she knows she made a "terrible mistake." Driving home, she is slowed by an accident on the highway, and she realizes that she or Franklin might, too, have an accident and never see each other again. She is eager to get home to him. When she arrives home, she argues passionately with Franklin about Dolly, who has left. After reassuring her, he remarks, "We can't afford rows." She realizes she had temporarily forgotten "how old [they] were, forgotten everything. Thinking there was all the time in the world to suffer and complain." She decides she does not want to fight, does not want to engage the jealousy or bitterness, and that she would have to be on the lookout for the letter she had mailed the previous day, since "you can think yourself in reasonable shape and then die, just like that."

Munro implies that the narrator's decision to stay, to choose a life with Franklin that is peaceful, kind, and without rancor is not the same as her previous, more passive acquiescence but suggests a different sort of conscious appreciation and desire. As a result of their unexpected visitor, they realize the value of their days together, in contrast to the opening explanation of such days as unworthy of life itself. They realize they have to appreciate what little time they have left together.

I chose to include this story in this chapter about sexuality because of Munro's portrayal of the awakening of the narrator's anger and jealousy brought about by Dolly's visit—proof of the existence of the sexuality celebrated in Franklin's poem and of the narrator's own repressed desire. Dolly's appearance stirs in both of them a suppressed love, a passion long forgotten. The story reminds the reader that our relationships define us, that there is some balance between choice and accommodation, useful passion and hurtful rows, partnership and loss of self. The story is not upbeat, nor is it bleak. We sense that the narrator is more self-aware and will no longer compare herself to the Dolly of the poem who has always haunted her imagination. Franklin is no longer the inexperienced service man, and the narrator is no longer the young graduate student who had an affair with a married teacher. They are now in their eighties and nineties—still capable of strong feelings and also more capable of kindness, of quiet choices, and of care. Dolly's visit was an anomaly for both of them, jarring them out of their comfortable indifference, and suicide is now untenable. Munro reveals the ways in which aging people have the capacity to redefine their attitudes, subtly but significantly recalibrating the emotional tenor of their lives in ways that fundamentally shift their vision of themselves, of time, and of life itself.

## CONCLUSION

The stories in this chapter begin with the mistaken notion that erotic desire is meant to disappear along with youth and is either a matter of embarrassment or ridiculous humor in women of a certain age. From tales of childish crushes to near-death memories of past entanglements to regrets for missed experiences, desire, passion, and sex permeate literature and life. While women are consistently the objects of a male desire, which is treated as normal ("wild oats," "boys will be boys," etc.), female sexual desire is often portrayed in literature as dangerous and even monstrous. From Eve's first bite of the apple, to the insatiable appetite of the Lady of Bath, to Shakespeare's erotic Cleopatra, to the lusty or languid women of the eighteenth-century seduction plot, women's erotic passions may result only in marriage or death, and the sexier the passion, the more likely death is the answer!

Even in contemporary fiction, erotic love and lust are usually assumed to be dead in women over sixty. Long after medical research has revealed the falseness of such notions, noting that women do experience orgasms well into old age, outlasting the common erectile dysfunction often experienced by men and treated with drugs such as Viagra, outmoded ideas about the death of women's erotic passion persist. We see this both in cultural narratives and in the internalized notions of women themselves.

This chapter opened with two novels set in boarding homes for the able-bodied, well-off, elderly residents who have outlived their partners and cannot live on their own. In the first novel, we learned that the residents all retained some desire or passion that was unfilled. Underlying all the various sexual proclivities was a desire to continue to matter as a person, to be viewed in a positive light, to exercise some individual control. Similarly, in the second novel, Mrs. Palfrey continues to care about appearances as well as to long for tenderness. Reading these two novels heightened my sense of the importance of maintaining friendships with younger people throughout our lives and of learning to live with one's self before one becomes elderly. None of the characters in either novel has a spiritual life or a deep set of beliefs. They are not comforted by art or music or literature. They do not have an internal store of imagination, fascinations, or beliefs to comfort or bolster themselves.

In comparison, the second set of stories is entertaining and upbeat. Both stories portray the discomfort adult children feel when confronted by their mothers' sensual behavior. Miss Hazel and Julie are far less imprisoned in stereotypes of maternal behavior than are their children. Whether or not Miss Hazel goes to bed with the old blind man, she is happy to dance in public and to enjoy her body. Although she cares about her children and will cook for them the next day, she will not repress her enjoyment at the community meeting. And, after years of being a proper divorced grandmother who is available to babysit on a moment's notice, Julie allows herself to experience her own dormant passion and, in the process, frees her daughters to follow their own hearts.

In the final set of stories, two long-married women who have settled into predictable patterns over decades are shaken out of their habits and reconnect with their submerged desire in time to enjoy their final years. The protagonist of "The Liar's Wife" is able to appreciate how much she has matured and how repressed she had become, and the unnamed first-person narrator of "Dolly" is able to lose her sense of competition with the Dolly of Franklin's early erotic poem. We leave these stories with a sense that each woman may continue to discover some of the unexplored parts of herself that she gave up in her youth.

Running through all six stories are portrayals of the persistence of desire and passion beyond any arbitrary age limit. We all want to love and be loved, to experience ourselves in new ways, to continue to matter as individuals. We need to nurture interests and friendships throughout our lives if we do not want to be bored and lonely in our old, old age. Our age does not prevent self-discovery or preclude happiness.

## Chapter 3

# Altered Realities

*Memento Mori* (1959) by Muriel Spark

*The Girls* (1999) by Helen Yglesias

*Missing* (1990) by Michelle Herman

*As We Are Now* (1973) by May Sarton

*The Hearing Trumpet* (1974)
by Leonora Carrington

*The Madonnas of Leningrad* (2006)
by Debra Dean

While I appreciate stories about desire that persists after youth, I also want stories that deal with the more difficult realities of aging. I was pleased when I discovered novels that portray old people as old, with their anxiety about losing independence and needing care as they age second only to their fear of losing their minds. In reviewing my growing pile of books for this chapter, I winnowed the ones I like best into three distinct pairs. One pair includes books about confronting mortality and the loss of independence. A second pair of books focuses on loneliness and dementia. My favorite pair of books, unlike the others, moves beyond conventional assumptions about dementia and imagines alternative realities that replace the usual dread with laughter and uplift our spirits.

Muriel Spark's *Memento Mori* and Helen Yglesias's *The Girls* are in my first pair. Both novels include ample humor, and their elderly characters feel realistic. *Memento Mori*'s elderly friends reveal no fear of death; instead they either take its eventuality in stride or deny it entirely. Spark holds her characters at arm's distance from us with her omniscient narration and wry humor so that the final accounting of their various deaths has a journalistic tone rather than touching us emotionally. I include this book for its convincing portrayals of eccentric, realistic old people whose antics amuse rather than depress the reader. Yglesias similarly combines levity with reality in her novel about facing decline. She brings the four women of *The Girls* to life on the page, as the two younger sisters, ages eighty and eighty-five, prepare their elder sisters to move into an expensive nursing home. Despite their affluence, all the sisters' fears of the nursing home and the fairly imminent deaths of the two eldest ones is palpable by the novel's conclusion. Nevertheless, I recommend the book as a "good read," and I imagine it will resonate with many readers who not only share the sisters' anxiety about losing their independence but also appreciate seeing them portrayed as vital and feisty.

The lively tone and humorous misunderstandings, antics, and quirks of characters in the first two books are nowhere to be found in Michelle Herman's *Missing* or May Sarton's *As We Are Now*. Both of these slim novels confront the intense loneliness and fear of mental decline that haunt their older characters, and we begin to feel as imprisoned as they do within their narrow spaces. Revke of *Missing* thinks she has been robbed of the beads she has misplaced as the novel opens, but as we observe her memories over the course of the day, we gradually realize along with Revke that she is in the early stages of dementia and is terrified of forgetting everything. The novel portrays her with respect and sympathy, but it offers us no comfort. Caro, although only seventy-six in comparison to Revke's eighty-nine, may be going mad rather than suffering from dementia in *As We Are Now*. Sarton's riveting novel evokes our concern, our horror, and our astonishment as we read Caro's journals to their surprising end. Both novels force us to think about the unexpressed loneliness and anxieties old women hide from friends and relatives for fear of being thought mad and committed to institutions.

The books in the third pair are the ones I give to my friends and urge my family to read. Both Leonora Carrington's *The Hearing Trumpet* and Debra Dean's *The Madonnas of Leningrad* are a pleasure to read. Although their protagonists are neither reasonable nor lucid, reading these novels does not leave me with a sense of obligation to take any action, whether to ease the loneliness of old people, to visit nursing homes, or to support research into Alzheimer's. Rather, because both authors go out on a fictional limb and imagine for their protagonists altered realities beyond our usual fears of dementia, their stories surprise and entertain us. Carrington's Marian delights in her unconventional personal attributes—such as her toothless gums and "gallant" beard. In *Madonnas*, Marina's confused sense of time and place is countered by her intense responsiveness to beauty and her secret Memory Palace. Both of these novels astonish me, and each presents possibilities for opening our eyes to alternative ways of seeing.

All six of these books provide windows into the ways we imagine the end of life, beginning with the amusing reminder of mortality that haunts *Memento Mori* and the compassionate portrayal of the elderly sisters in *The Girls*, who need no such reminder. The nearly visceral portrayals of loneliness and fear in *Missing* and *As We Are Now* prepare us to appreciate the imaginative accounts of altered realities in *The Hearing Trumpet* and *The Madonnas of Leningrad*. Together these books allow us to examine our own fears of mortality and possible loss of memory as well as to consider the limitations of our assumptions and to entertain expanded imaginations about life after lucidity.

# MEMENTO MORI

## by Muriel Spark

The first of the amusing and realistic novels I include in this chapter, *Memento Mori* (1959), may be the most humane of these books about decline. Muriel Spark portrays her elderly characters, aged sixty-nine to eighty-seven, in their present lives, in which memory is present but not central; in which yearnings, jealousies, appetites, small daily inconveniences, and large concerns about wills, bequests, old secrets, and self-importance are individualized, and elderly persons remain individuals rather than stereotypes. The plot: everyone dies. The novel's opening pages report the first of the many mysterious telephone calls that deliver the same message to multiple characters: "Remember you must die." No two characters hear the same caller. Some hear a young man, others a woman, and the voice of each caller differs from that reported by others. Although the surface plot focuses on the mystery of the unidentified callers, the latent plot of the book seems to be the effect of the mysterious calls on a small group of elderly friends, an inquiry into how elderly persons respond to the awareness of their mortality. How do people live when it is no longer possible to deny their impending deaths? I include the novel in this chapter as an introduction to perceptions of characters with altered realities along a continuum from post-stroke muddle to extreme dementia.

Unlike the more isolated characters in "Tell Me a Riddle" and *Mrs. Stevens Hears the Mermaids Singing*, from chapter 1, the characters in *Memento Mori* have grown old together, maintaining their friendships as they aged. And although we see Mrs. Mortimer, the contented wife of retired Inspector Henry Mortimer, enjoying her grandchild, the novel focuses on the elderly themselves, without many younger characters. Major characters include Godfrey and Charmian Colston and Jean Taylor, who was Charmian's companion until her retirement two years before the events of the novel. They are all fully alive in their present states, aware of the past but not fixated on it as in chapter 1's "Jilting" or *Evening*. The reader experiences them as surprisingly unstereotypical, slowed down by various physical ailments and unreliable memories, but still individual and lively in their emotions and degrees of insight. I was pleased at the ways in which their distinctive characteristics and active plotlines continue from youth into old age—romantic affairs, secrecy and lying, sexual urges (however restrained), ties of friendship, dignity, and pride in the face of physical and mental decline. Their sexual and emotional needs continue without being caricatured by the narrator. For example, the emotional balance of a long-lived marriage in which each partner spars with the other for dominance is revealed as rather ordinary, with surprising flashes of genuine caring even after decades of sexual infidelity.

Two mysteries haunt the novel. One is the validity of a character's will, drafted just a year before her death, bequeathing her entire fortune to her "husband if he survives me," and otherwise to her housekeeper. Since her first marriage had been dissolved, and she had kept secret another husband who surfaced only after the will was made public, surviving family members threaten a lawsuit, until finally the supposedly dead second husband is discovered in a mental hospital, where he has been a resident for over forty years. The housekeeper eventually receives the inheritance, solving that first mystery. The other mystery is the identity of the callers. Whether the multiple phone messages actually occur or are a literary device, the characters' differing responses to being made aware of their mortality reveal their personalities and beliefs. While I, as a reader, join them in their curiosity about the identity of the mysterious callers, an equal mystery for me is why these elderly characters focus their attention on identifying the callers rather than taking for granted the truthfulness of the message, which is presented not as a threat but as a reminder. In contrast to those characters who focus not on the calls as a reminder but rather on the responsibility of the police to apprehend the caller, a futile misdirection of energies, the most positive responses to the phone calls are those of Charmian Colston, Jean Taylor, and the Mortimers.

Charmian has survived a stroke and has many symptoms of dementia, and her husband, Godfrey, considers her "out of it." She calls familiar friends by the wrong names and addresses the current housekeeper as Taylor, long after Jean Taylor has moved out of the household. However, she still has occasional surprising insights, and in certain areas—such as in the books she has written—her memory is accurate even though she confuses the names of things, places, and people from the past. Charmian, a once prolific and successful novelist, is revealed as a woman of immense charm. Her fifty-five-year-old son, Eric, like his father, Godfrey, is jealous of his mother's talent and the fame she enjoyed throughout her life. Charmian, following the stroke, is initially muddled, but then begins to revive as she is courted by admirers and buoyed by the renewed interest in her novels after they are simultaneously republished. She adores company. Yet as she thrives and seems to be increasingly aware of her present surroundings, her husband feels as if his powers are diminishing, and we learn that they have been highly competitive throughout their marriage. As she gained literary attention, he always felt at a loss, as if he were less accomplished than her as he merely inherited his business, the Colston Brewery. She, on the other hand, is a self-made writer.

Because of the complexity of her mind and her feelings, Charmian complicates the stereotypical portrayal of the character with dementia. She is still capable of surprising her husband, her son, and her housekeeper. She does not reside primarily in past memory. She is astute in her awareness of the current feelings of her husband of many years. She appropriately trusts and mistrusts others, particularly the blackmailing housekeeper. She wears her life lightly, is not obsessed with her future, and is amused rather than upset by the mysterious phone calls since she does not consider the reminder threatening or newsworthy. She reports that the caller is "a very civil young man." She lives in her present, and when life at home becomes too unpleasant, she makes her own arrangements to enter the rural retirement home with which Godfrey had threatened her whenever she resisted his overpowering control.

Jean Taylor, Charmian's longtime employee prior to Charmian's stroke and Jean's failing health, is the most reliable source of information in the novel. Rather than allow her wealthy former employers to pay for her residence in a private retirement home, she chooses to reside in the state-provided old women's home. The state-supported home allows Jean to maintain her fierce sense of independence, and also allows her to continue her conversations with her old employers and their circle of friends. She knows all of their secrets, and they turn to her for moral support and affirmation, even as they feel financially superior to her. The Maud Long Medical Ward, where Jean Taylor is one of twelve female residents, is noisy, desolate, and humiliating, and the "lacerating familiarity of the nurses' treatment merged in with her arthritis." Yet its residents maintain their individuality, class-consciousness, and personal pride, dignity, and outrage at the many ways in which they are dehumanized. The residents are constantly patronized by the doctors and nurses and indiscriminately called "grannies" over their vehement objections. Spark portrays each of the women by name, and does not rob even the most senile residents of individual interests and quirks. Jean Taylor's lucidity and reliable memory distinguish her from the other residents. Still intelligent and reflective with a strong sense of reliance on the "Will of God," she muses upon old age in general and wonders why some people lose their memories, some their hearing. She thinks with fondness about "poor Charmian, since her stroke. How muddled she was about most things, and yet perfectly sensible when she discussed the books she had written."

Jean Taylor's former suitor, Dr. Alec Warner, a retired sociologist who focuses on age and prides himself on his scientific study of the elderly, frequently visits Jean; he keeps copious notes on the physical reactions of their many shared friends and even strangers, such as the local night watchman, treating all of them as objects of study. He even studies the geriatric cases at the "noisy end" of Jean's ward, and notes that "the interesting thing is senility is somewhat different from insanity" and that the "really mad old people have had more practice in irrational behavior." His methods of asking people to record their temperature and take their pulses after receiving various types of news contribute to the novel's humor and remind the reader to differentiate elderly people from the so-called scientific data that turns them into objects.

In her sage voice, Jean tells Alec Warner that "being over seventy is like being engaged in a war. All our friends are going or gone and we survive amongst the dead and the dying as on a battlefield." To Godfrey's older sister, she insists that it is "difficult for people of advanced years to start remembering they must die," and that it is "best to form the habit while young." Jean says the reason "we all appear to ourselves frustrated in our old age [is] because we cling to everything so much. But in reality we are still fulfilling our lives." This sense of fulfilling our lives in old age contrasts with notions of diminishment, and is an important note of wisdom in the novel. Jean recognizes the importance of continued mental and spiritual growth that is still possible until death.

Henry Mortimer, the retired inspector, provides another source of wisdom and perspective in the novel. After disappointing the gathered group of friends who hired him to discover the identity of the mysterious phone caller by telling them their accounts differ so greatly that it would be impossible to identify a single culprit, Mortimer tells his wife he thinks "The offender is Death himself." He gives the group of friends what he calls a little sermon: "If I had my life over again I should form the habit of nightly composing myself to thoughts of death . . . There is no other practice, which so intensifies life. Death, when it approaches, ought not to take one by surprise. It should be part of the full expectancy of life. Without an ever-present sense of death life is insipid. You might as well live on the white of eggs." His words fall on deaf ears as they continue to insist, "We've got to find the man." The group of friends considers the afternoon meeting with Inspector Mortimer pointless, and later that evening, when Henry Mortimer receives the by now familiar call, he muses that his caller is "always this woman, gentle-spoken and respectful," and is unconcerned.

The novel is frequently taught in colleges as a reminder to the young of the truism that no one lives forever. However, my students disliked the characters, were annoyed by the mysterious phone calls, and felt duped by a mystery that they felt was never solved. The omniscient third-person narration with its sharp humor and witty dialogue creates distance, allowing students to maintain their unexamined notions about old people even as they felt discomfort in considering their elders as people who still maintain desire and individual longings, qualities that make the portrayals feel most realistic to older readers.

In Spark's novel, we are not in the mind of a dying person obsessed with repressed memory. Death is normalized. Everyone dies, although the causes differ. Although Charmian has lost much of her former lucidity as the result of her stroke, she lives in a network of family and friends her age and is not worried about her reputation. She is not isolated or lonely. She does not seem troubled about her past nor does she complain about the limits that persist after her stroke. Jean Taylor is not, like Caro in *As We Are Now*, discussed below, depressed by her surroundings and the lack of amenities in a home where most residents cannot carry on a coherent conversation.

*Memento Mori* portrays complicated old characters that surprise readers with their variety and complexity. Although the novel may be taught as a lesson to the young who may find its portrayal of feisty elderly people unappealing, older readers may discover a satisfying story. The novel challenges a reader's sense of old women and men and suggests that their minds and memories are varied and differentiated, their lives intense and engaged, and that it is our orientation and attitude toward the shared end—the burial plot—that make the difference, not the resolution itself.

## *THE GIRLS*

### by Helen Yglesias

Like *Memento Mori, The Girls* blends humor and seriousness in its story of facing mortality. Helen Yglesias published the novel in 1999, when she was seventy-nine years old, just a year younger than Jenny, the protagonist and youngest of four sisters. Jenny, whose perspective governs the novel, has been summoned from New York to help her sister Flora, age eighty-five, comfort and make new living arrangements for their two older sisters, Naomi, age ninety, who is riddled with cancer, and Eva, age ninety-five, who is healthy but also in need of increased care. The novel begins with Jenny's arrival in Miami and ends when she and Flora accompany Naomi and Eva to their new apartments in an exclusive assisted living facility, their final home. Despite the proximity of death, *The Girls* is often funny and contains more laughter than tears, making it an appealing introduction to a difficult topic.

The novel provides an unusual up-close portrayal of four elderly sisters who have outlived their brothers and husbands, who are sharp-witted and sharp-tongued, and who are determined to avoid involving their busy children and grandchildren in the most important end-of-life decisions. They are affluent, and so they have more agency with regard to how they determine their end-of-life care. The four sisters are feisty, vital, and entirely credible as they hold on to their unique senses of self, maintain their sisterly ranking and rancor into old, old age, and preserve as much independence and dignity as they can even when forced to face their increasing dependence on paid assistants.

*The Girls* initially impressed me as somehow getting the fact that old people maintain their essential selves throughout their lives. The four sisters carry into old age the qualities and characteristics of their younger and middle-life selves. They all cling to shared memories as well as individual secrets and grudges. Memory in this novel is a backdrop but not a compelling central narrative. The focus is on the old women in the present tense. As they gather to face the impending death of Naomi and the advanced age of Eva, they are fragile and frightened, not humorous caricatures of their former selves.

The novel depicts the sisters' intimately linked reliance on one another into their eighties and nineties, a bond even more powerful than that with former spouses. Their shared family identity seems to be due to their shared memories and to the losses they have all suffered—of their parents, of all three brothers, and of their husbands. Perhaps the absence of close female friendships in the novel is because of the bonds of biological sisterhood. They are alone together, and they rely on one another in the face of death, which is not only inevitable, as in Spark's novel, but imminent for Naomi, with her advanced cancer, and certainly soon for Eva, who can't expect more years than she can number on her fingers, if that many.

Each of the sisters retains her sense of place in the hierarchical structure of family, and even at eighty, Jenny is forever the little sister to Flora, Naomi, and Eva. In my own life I observed similar behavior in my elderly aunts, so it seemed natural to see sibling ranking portrayed in this novel. There was such self-awareness on the part of the characters that even when they acknowledge the major changes that have occurred in all of them, they cannot avoid their childhood ways of seeing each other, in which Eva is the motherly big sister and Jenny is the baby.

Similarly, the old jealousies are retained into old age—differences of value remain unchanged; pride, shame, and embarrassment persist like faded stains on much-laundered linen. Jenny, the only one to pursue a career, determined to avoid the old-people culture of Miami, nevertheless recognizes that to the outsider she is just another wealthy old Jewish lady—even if she has a PhD, speaks Spanish, and has westernized her name to escape that very identity.

*The Girls* acknowledges the full range of emotions of its characters rather than limiting them to partial stereotypes. It recognizes their continued sexual and sensual longings, on a continuum from Flora's insatiable demand for raw sex with any man who can "get it up" to Jenny's unexpressed longing for the physical closeness of her husband a decade after his death. Jenny feels "horny." "Eighty-year-old women weren't supposed to feel horny. They were supposed to be serene, wise, resigned. But here she was, raging in bed, for love, for lost love."

Appearance still matters to each of them. Each in her own way tries to hold on to her physical appearance, and we get the sense that freedom from poverty as well as good genes have allowed them to have nearly wrinkle-free complexions and lovely full heads of hair, whether dyed boot polish black by Flora or allowed to gray naturally by Jenny. We are told Flora has "wonderfully alive black eyes flashing under the heavy black eyebrows," and she dresses in bright purples and oranges. She informs Jenny that she will continue to dye her hair until death and boasts, "I'm living and looking good right up to the minute they put me in my coffin." Well-cut clothes in luxurious fabrics still give the sisters pleasure, even at Eva's advanced age of ninety-five and in Naomi's last months of dying from cancer. Because of their affluence, they can indulge their lavish tastes in dress and comfort themselves with beauty salon pedicures and hairdressing.

Yglesias has an eye for apt detail, and the novel's tone is somewhat light—perhaps as a way to balance its serious portrayal of deteriorating bodies, failing memories, and the ultimate solipsism that results from being invisible to others who read only the most external codes of age. The strength they feel together within the family structure, and that Jenny is accustomed to in her normal New York setting, where she is revered as a professor, is quickly undercut in public. Whether hailing a cab or dealing with institutional personnel, they are viewed stereotypically as old and out of it and not worthy of personal attention. Even caretakers and institutional assistants, whose jobs are to attend to the old, appear to be frightened of them or dismissive, unkind, or supercilious. Miami's artificial playgrounds and final resting places for the elderly and dying diminish them as human beings regardless of their wealth. The book rings with truthfulness.

Although none of these sisters lives in the general ward of a state-supported institution such as Jean Taylor in *Memento Mori*, or is forced to live in an undesirable rural board and care home such as Caro in *As We Are Now* due to limited funds and lack of involved family members, they cannot escape the nearby presence of persons their own age who are wizened or demented, and their surroundings are dotted with wheel-chairs, walkers, canes, and attendants. In addition, the sisters are prey to the machinations of those who wish to swindle them out of their money, and they each hold strongly differ-ing opinions about the money each of them possesses. They mistrust one another, for example, in terms of who would best serve with power of attorney for the dying Naomi—Flora, who is frugal to a fault but lives near Naomi, or Jenny, who mistrusts and is constantly in a power struggle with Flora.

The novel ends with Jenny and Flora accompanying their sisters, "strapped into their wheelchairs in the medical van," taking them on their move to different floors of Serenity Villa, an expensive nondenominational nursing home selected sight unseen by Eva's children. The sisters "looked fine," with new hairdos, lovely clothing, their fingernails gleaming red on the pocketbooks clutched in their laps, their painted toe-nails shining red through their open-toed sandals. They burst into song in the van as it carries them to "Eva and Naomi's final home, and in time, Flora's, and in one way or another, Jenny's too."

Although they have sufficient financial means to ensure care in an expensive nursing home, they are terrified of losing the ability to care for themselves. As the youngest, Jenny realizes not only that her elder sisters are headed to their last home but also that a similar fate awaits her. Unlike Eva and Naomi, she has no younger sister to assuage her fears or to help her face her own mortality. Yglesias portrays the humor in their relationships and often makes readers laugh, but the novel ends on a somber note, contrasting their impossible yearning for a triumphant escape into "the perfection of the painted Fontainebleau" rather than "the real horrors to come." Although I enjoyed reading the novel and recommend it to others, I wish the author had imagined a possibility between these two extremes, in which the sisters could appreciate beauty, savor their good memories, and face their mortality, not with fear and resistance, but with the Mortimers' acceptance and Jean Taylor's serenity.

# *MISSING*

## by Michelle Herman

Though not as enjoyable to read as the previous two stories, the next two in this chapter provide the most unvarnished look at the mental and physical deterioration of old age. In the first of these two, the slim novel *Missing* (1990), Michelle Herman takes us into the present-day reality and memories of eighty-nine-year-old Rivke, a first-generation Polish immigrant who lives alone in her Brighton Beach apartment. She had shared this apartment with her husband for seventy-two years, until his sudden death two years earlier. Rivke's only close relationship is with her beloved granddaughter, Rachel, a single young photographer whose most recent project is a documentation of Rivke's life. The plot follows Rivke's thoughts as she tries to remember when she last saw her missing beads, carefully removed decades ago from her one good black dress and saved in a box, perhaps eventually to be made into a necklace for Rachel. Rivke speculates about who might have stolen them, eventually finding them where surely she herself must have misplaced them. Rivke's acute sense of loss about the missing beads prefigures her even more poignant loss of visual memory. In just six short chapters, Herman gives us Rivke's history from childhood to almost ninety and makes us care about her with exasperation and tenderness.

The omniscient narrator's perspective is so close to Rivke's memory that reading this novel feels like seeing the world through Rivke's eyes. Nothing beyond her perspective enters the text; even present-tense dialogue is rendered through her mind. She is stuck in her small apartment, and the reader feels similarly caged, as the entire novel takes place within its walls. Her only human contact is with family members who make occasional visits back to the city from their new lives in the suburbs and her daily phone calls, from her daughter Myra in the morning, and from Rachel in the evening.

After decades of being in constant motion, Rivke is no longer able even to leave the apartment on her own. Her heart and knees are wearing out, and the combination of dimming eyesight and arthritic hands makes it difficult to sew or mend. All her actions are now in slow motion, from brewing tea to dialing a telephone number, and taking a bath is a grand accomplishment that requires carefully choreographed movement to avoid losing her balance. She depends on others to bring her groceries, longs for the days she could care for herself, and is troubled by the disrepair of her apartment now that she can no longer scrub and clean to make it a pleasurable place in which to live. Living alone for the first time in her entire life after her husband, Sol's, sudden stroke, Rivke is profoundly lonely. She had not expected to live alone, not taken in by her daughter Myra, who we learn has suffered from mental illness throughout her life and whose own daughter, Rachel, was primarily raised by Rivke until the family moved out into the suburbs.

Rivke is strong-willed and harsh in her judgments of others. "Rachel is the only one of her grandchildren who was of importance to her," and she excuses her preference by assuming she is no more than an idea to the many grandchildren. None of her adult children's spouses pleases her, and she considers all five of her children failures. She is constantly sorting through her accumulated belongings, stripping her apartment in her determination to give away her possessions while she is still alive rather than allow them to be distributed after her death to people who might not appreciate them.

The story echoes many of the themes from Tillie Olsen's "Tell Me a Riddle," in that Rivke, like Eva, is a first-generation Jewish immigrant woman who has lived her entire life in service to home and family, always making do with limited resources, and never being seen as an individual person by her children. The children who were raised in America never really understand their parents' hardships, never know the emotional and spiritual cost borne by mothers who seldom had a moment to consider their own unfulfilled promise. But unlike Eva in "Tell Me a Riddle," whose family eventually tries to respond to her needs, Rivke's adult children come to her only to tell her their own problems. Unlike Eva, Rivke has no inner wealth of literature or music to express her feelings or to bring her joy. Rivke can barely puzzle out the content of a newspaper's articles, having never been formally educated in reading English. She and Sol were orphans when they married as teenagers, and their entire lives were built on inventing their own family life along strictly defined gender lines. He worked outside the home as a barrel maker; her work was within the home, and he refused her request to attend night classes to learn English. Their Jewish kosher home and their ritual celebrations were cultural rather than religious, and they were not members of a synagogue.

Rivke's granddaughter Rachel prompts Rivke's memories by insisting on sorting through and organizing her hundreds of photographs, and then asking questions about her child-hood, her coming to America, about aunts and uncles, as well as unidentified photographs. It's in her answers, as well as in silent memories, that we gradually become acquainted with Rivke. As she goes through these photographs with Rachel, Rivke carefully cuts out disliked folks from family photographs so that Rachel chides her: "You think you can change what was by ignoring it? You want to rewrite your own history? What are you, a Communist country?"

Rachel chooses photographs to hang in her own apartment. Pictures of Rivke at fourteen, newly arrived in the country, clash with pictures of her at age fifty, posing with a frown on her face on the boardwalk, and at sixteen, in a hand-tinted, elaborately framed copy of her wedding portrait. Rachel mingles the old photographs with her own photographs of Rivke, ranging from portraits in which Rachel has allowed Rivke to "dress up and pose properly, brush her hair and remove her glasses" to Rachel's favorite, which Rivke dislikes, in which Rivke looks "harsh and unyielding" and is "wield[ing] a long spoon like a weapon" by the kitchen stove, where she "stood glowering." Caught by surprise, Rivke looks "a little terrifying," according to Rachel, who teases her grandmother about the image and insists it is her favorite picture except for the formal portrait in Rivke's bed-room because that portrait "told a story that could not be easily explained in words or be understood by a stranger who was tak-ing a casual look." That is the portrait in which Rivke also looks severe, but she thinks she looks attractive because she is wear-ing the exquisite black dress with its embroidery of black crystal beads—the beads Rivke believes have been stolen from her.

I wondered whether or not to include this novel in my selection of novels about altered realities because of its stark portrayal of Rivke's loneliness and her gradually encroaching memory loss. Some of my students found this novel particularly depressing. It is not so much because Rivke has slowed down or hates living alone, or is housebound at her advanced age. Beyond Rivke's loneliness for Sol, her one best friend in her entire long life, is her frightening sense she will soon be deprived of her own most cherished memories. It is commonplace for older people to misplace items in their homes and to have somewhat unreliable short-term memories even when memories from decades earlier retain almost perfect recall. So Herman's portrayal of Rivke's unreliable memory of moving her beads from their familiar place on her bureau is not particularly surprising or unusual. However, when Rivke is not able to call into memory a visual image of Sol, to whom she was married for over seventy years, the reader shudders. This failing of memory sometimes occurs after severe brain injury and also precedes the better-known symptoms of dementia. Such visual memory loss upsets a person's entire sense of self. To see only a blank canvas where once she could envision her best friend is catastrophic loss.

The fleeting joy of finding her lost beads is destroyed profoundly by Rivke's inability to visualize Sol, so much so that she avoids retracing her steps into the bedroom to look at the gilt-framed photographs, grasping the severity of the loss and the grim future in which she will eventually not recognize his image even in the familiar portrait. This premonition of total isolation from past memory is terrifying and haunts the reader long after reading the last page of the book. This unflinching portrayal of loss is disturbing, but it is a valuable glimpse into a harsh reality.

# AS WE ARE NOW

## by May Sarton

"I am not mad, only old," insists Caro Spencer, protagonist of May Sarton's *As We Are Now* (1973), writing in her journal two weeks after being dumped "in a concentration camp for the old . . . as though it were a trash can." Critics describe the novel as harrowing, indignant, and a powerful indictment of our treatment of the old, what Madeleine L'Engle calls the "problem we'd all rather close our eyes to." This novel directly confronts unsettling realities, like Michelle Herman's *Missing*, but its realities are even more disturbing. Sarton's novel, like Herman's, focuses on a woman, her loneliness, and her despair. But unlike Rivke of *Missing*, Caro has no children or grandchildren and is not surrounded by beloved objects in a familiar setting. Her elder brother and his wife, with whom she could not live on good terms after her heart attack, place her in a nursing home whose other residents are primarily senile old men and whose "caregivers" are undereducated, overworked, and hateful. Sarton's title comes from the epigram she quotes on the novel's opening page: "As you are now, so once was I; Prepare for death and follow me." Unlike Spark's *Memento Mori* with its deadpan humor and warning to the young, Sarton's warning is to the old. Her horrifying portrayal of the powerlessness of one intelligent and increasingly desperate old woman explores the violent building of rage as an alternative to despair.

Only in the novel's final pages do we discover we have been reading Caro's journal, published posthumously after Caro has burned down the Twin Elms Nursing Home. The manuscript, salvaged from the Frigidaire where Caro hid it before her death in the fire, provides evidence of her gradual deterioration during the months of incarceration and the circumstances that lead to her violent act. The novel echoes the trope of madness/suicide as an escape, one common in feminist fiction and poetry since the mid-nineteenth century—most famous in texts such as Charlotte Perkins Gilman's "The Yellow Wallpaper" and Kate Chopin's *The Awakening*. Here the figure of the "madwoman in the attic" is fueled by erasure because of so few choices for women when they are not only old but also dependent on others for their personal care. Sarton's only imagined escape for Caro is suicide.

Caro's journal shows us evidence of a life well lived, in which her current imprisonment is not due to personal failure but to inadequate social structures. Her memory is failing, and she begins writing in her journal as an attempt to remain sane in her new location, in which she has lost all independence and is afraid she may be losing her mind. Caro, a retired math teacher, is starved for human compassion, conversation, and beauty. She reflects on her life, never married, different from her family, and eventually moving from old maid to eccentric in the eyes of her colleagues. We get glimpses of her pleasure in music and poetry, of her twenty-year romance with a married man, of her determinations to hold on to her independence, body, and soul. She questions her lucidity, wondering if she is becoming senile, and reflects that "old age is not interesting until one gets there, a foreign country with an unknown language to the young, and even to the middle-aged." She is amazed at how much time she can spend "apparently doing nothing" when she is "extremely busy with this kind of dreaming-awake" that sustains her. Occasionally she nourishes herself with happy memories of her lover, her passion for teaching math, and thoughts of special students who blossomed under her mentoring.

Caro's astute self-questioning and reflection reinforce our awareness that she is lucid, and that the onset of "madness" is created by the context of the nursing home. She craves understanding and kindness, and her initial journal entries, with their insistence on her sanity, describe the nursing home in strong language that indicates a lack of community and care: "solitary confinement," "cage," "jail," "prison," "old people's home," "concentration camp," and "Hell." She describes her treatment as "punishment" and tries to dredge up explanations of personal guilt to justify such meanness by her caretakers, Harriet and Rose. She wonders if she is a snob, if she is somehow guilty because of her inability to empathize with the other residents, whose lewd jokes and sexual fantasies fuel her distaste and hatred. She painstakingly records her attempts to avoid internalizing the attitudes of Harriet and Rose, whose care of the residents is harsh and devoid of human kindness. Their view of the residents as "mental," as moral lepers, as untouchables, is demoralizing. She turns for escape from their complete control to the view out her window, the landscape, the sky, memories of literature and music. Lacking human comfort, she feels connected to animals and finds comfort in the nursing home cat when it surreptitiously sneaks into her room at night.

Accustomed to seeing life as orderly, Caro often reflects on evil and its causes, searching for some rational explanation for the horrors she endures. She remembers as a little girl seeing her father weeping and his explanation to her that he was thinking of prisoners in concentration camps. She writes, "There is a connection between any place where human beings are helpless, through illness or old age, and a prison," and adds that "it is not only the heroic helplessness of the inmates, but also what complete control does to the nurses, guards, or whatever." She wonders what might result if anyone took the trouble to "sense things, to observe, and to keep an outsider's eye on our keepers," but supposes people just assume old people are naturally depressed and need drugs rather than imagination or kindness. Sarton's keen social critique indicts all of us, moving far beyond the attitudinal focus of *Memento Mori*.

We observe Caro's lucidity in her intelligent observations and glimpse her snobbery in the ways in which she attempts to ground her observations in the details she selects. Lacking her previous setting, without clocks, newspapers, radio, or a calendar, Caro records time in her journal in terms of how long she has been in the nursing home. After two weeks of confinement, when she finally obtains paper and pencils, she begins her journal, noting lapses of days or weeks that give the reader scaffolding for her writing. She also describes the change of seasons as noted in the color of leaves, the quality of the air, the temperature as warm or cold outdoors. As the hours, days, and months go by, she sets herself mental challenges and tasks in her attempt to discipline her mind and maintain her sanity.

Caro aligns herself emotionally with the one other resident, Standish Flint, who like her also has a private room, unlike the other residents, whom she presumes are on welfare. Early in her stay, she admires his attempt to starve himself to death but quickly reminds herself that she wants to protect her soul from such thoughts of suicide. Yet she feels a kinship with him as a rebel and applauds his determination not to "be beaten down." She senses that both of them are determined to hold on to their minds. While she shares his rage, she is also afraid of her anger, afraid that she will eventually lose control and be punished even further by Harriet.

Sarton's novel traces Caro's descent as she increasingly sinks into self-hatred, internalizing the pervasive social dismissal of her very being—an old, single, nonreproductive working woman without sufficient means to avoid the nursing home. As the journal progresses, Caro increasingly writes about losing her mind. She fears writing letters to anyone and sounding desperate for fear of being seen as mad. "I am learning that any true cry from the heart of an old person creates too much havoc in a listener, is too disturbing, because nothing can really be done to help us on the downward path." Her assumption that growing old eliminates any possibility of true communication or of spiritual, psychological growth is heartbreaking. She continues, "Old age is really a disguise that no one but the old themselves see through. I feel exactly as I always did, as young inside as when I was twenty-one, but the outward shell conceals the real me—sometimes even from itself—and betrays that person deep down inside, under wrinkles and liver spots and all the horrors of decay." Her belief in an essential self, a "real me" that is changeless and that is betrayed by her external appearance reveals the extent to which she reflects the societal distaste for her aging body and also her decreasing kindness to herself.

Caro notes that because people assume the old to be serene, their anger is considered a sign of madness or senility. This assumption might lead readers to detect madness in Caro's increasing anger if Sarton had not included Caro's records of her visitors and their conversations with her, lending by contrast credulity to her account of cruel remarks and rough treatment from Harriet. Reverend Thornhill, a young Methodist minister, pays the first visit to Caro. She admires his silence in response to the nasty outburst of Standish, and she appreciates the minister's respectful listening to her. In response to his inquiry about what he can do to help her, she requests a thick novel. When he is not able to return immediately, he sends his teenage daughter, Lisa, with several books and a bouquet of garden flowers. Later gifts of books and a transistor radio suggest he and Lisa find her lucid.

The importance of even one person's kindness is revealed in Caro's account of the difference Mrs. Anna Close makes when she takes over the nursing home during Harriet's two-week vacation. During that respite, Caro recognizes the importance of "being cared for as though I were worthy of care." Caro writes, "The whole atmosphere has changed radically since this angelic person made her appearance in a clean white apron over a blue and white checked dress like some character in a Beatrix Potter book." A thorough house cleaning, a single pink rose on an attractive breakfast tray, gentle touch, and shared silence arouse in Caro a long-dead sense of love that makes her dread Anna's departure.

Three days before Harriet's return, Caro writes, "I am about to die." She has a flash of insight that once Anna leaves the only way to change things is to "burn the place down some day." Even Lisa's return with a promise to bring Caro's friend

Eva for a visit and the reverend's intention to get her "out of here" are not sufficient to deter Caro from her developing plans to set fire to the nursing home. Before ending her life, Caro composes a draft in her copybook of an intended letter to Anna, telling her how much she loves her. But before she can copy it out for sending, Harriet reads it, calls Caro filthy, and threatens to commit her to the state mental hospital. As matters worsen, Caro notes her deterioration in the six months since she began her journal, and she dutifully records her actions: collecting matches, lighter fluid, and other combustibles. She writes, "I want my death to be something more like me than slow disintegration," and she quotes Dylan Thomas, "Do not go gentle into that good night." Waiting for January snows, she writes that, having made her decision, she feels "free, beyond attachment, beyond the human world." In preparation for death, she listens to music, looks at the bare trees, drinks in the sunset like wine, and reads poetry, "gathering together all that matters most, tasting it for the last time."

Caro's decision to act fills her not only with newly seized freedom but also with tenderness toward others and a heightened sense of vitality. After Lisa takes her for a final visit to Anna, Caro makes plans for dying, the only escape she could see from madness. In December, she admits, "I do not want to die." However, when she discovers Harriet reading her last copybook, Caro feels a flood of "fierce strength," lunges, seizes the copybook, knocks Harriet to the floor, and locks herself in the bathroom, where she finally feels at peace, and writes the final words of her journal, "THE important thing I must manage to do is place all the copybooks in the Frigidaire. To you who may one day read this, I give them as a testament. Please try to understand." Is she pleading for the understanding she was denied in those final months or for an understanding of her entire being? Is she indirectly asking her readers' forgiveness, assuming that her testimony as a witness to "Hell" is worth the destruction?

I first responded with relief and vindication at Caro's act, as her actions feel like the only possible escape to the reader. Only later did it settle in that an act of suicide and murder is never justified, no matter the horror and hopelessness of her situation. However, soon I wondered if Caro really has gone mad in choosing to kill all the others rather than accept the minister's offer to get her out of the nursing home. But his offer comes too late, and even in hindsight does not seem realistic. The nursing home is a symbol, like Charlotte Perkins Gilman's yellow wallpaper, of a stultifying "pattern" to which the only "sane" reaction is madness.

Sarton's novel raises questions at an individual level, but the questions pale in comparison to the meta critique of the brutality of our social system. I wonder why Caro, like Eva and Naomi in *The Girls*, allows others to choose where she will live the rest of her life. Why do her brother and his wife place Caro in a remote nursing home, isolated from former colleagues, friends, and students? Sarton's critique of society's attitudes and treatment of the old reveals the systemic failure of families and communities even to *see* old people as fellow human beings, yet alone to treasure them. Caro, a self-supporting retired teacher, is only seventy-six years old when her heart attack catapults her from independence into a dependency for which there is no state-supported home similar to the one chosen by Jean Taylor in *Memento Mori*.

Not until I reached the final page of the book did I realize I had been reading Caro's journal and had unconditionally accepted her account as accurate. Without any intervention of an outside narrator, it is difficult while reading the novel to differentiate lucidity from madness. My sympathetic concern for Caro temporarily overpowered my strongly held commitment to nonviolence. Only in retrospect did I wonder if Sarton wanted her novel to be a call for social change that goes far beyond any personal reminder to plan ahead and to treasure old people.

# THE HEARING TRUMPET

## by Leonora Carrington

In contrast to the stark realism of the previous pair of books, the last pair of books in this chapter explores the fantastical possibilities of old age. Leonora Carrington's 1974 novel, *The Hearing Trumpet*, is the most surreal of the books I have included, and I loved reading it primarily because of its lively imagination. Narrated in the first person by ninety-two-year-old Marian Leatherby, the engaging story requires a suspension of disbelief with its introduction of an old-fashioned hearing trumpet into a historical setting that includes television, automobiles, and airplanes. Yet we are caught up in Marian's reality, which is compelling and wonderful and somehow believable even when we know it has crossed into surreal territory.

The novel's plainspoken prose suggests a realistic tale written after Marian's move into a most unusual institution for old women, even though the tenses frequently vacillate between present and past. Marian is rather odd, but her attention to detail and her personal description fit easily into our notions of an elderly woman. Although she is acutely aware of normal conventions, she no longer cares about satisfying them. She admits that the hearing trumpet, a gift from her friend Carmella that amplifies sound when held against a wall, allows her to eavesdrop on others and then insists that her other senses are not impaired. Her eyesight is excellent, although she needs reading "spectacles"; her posture is bent, but she can still take walks in clement weather; and she sweeps her room weekly. She remarks that she is "still a useful member of society" and "still capable of being pleasant and amusing when the occasion seems fit." I like Marian's confidence in herself, her outrage at inhumanity, and her sense of dignity. Although she is not always sure what is reality and what is imagination, she is unapologetic and extremely likable.

Assuming her audience will pity her for having no teeth and not being able to wear dentures, she insists that she is not discomforted. She says she does not "have to bite anybody and there are all sorts of soft edible foods." She explains that she never eats meat as it deprives "animals of their life when they are so difficult to chew anyway." She introduces her beard parenthetically in a sentence about her mother's valet, saying her blind mother does not have a beard. Which is followed by the wonderful statement: "Indeed I do have a short grey beard which conventional people would find repulsive. Personally I find it rather gallant." As if aware of an audience, Marian comments on having digressed and insists that although her mind wanders, it never wanders "further than I want."

Marian had settled into a quiet routine over twenty years of living with her son, Galahad, his wife, Muriel, and her grandson, Robert, and she provides no detail about her life before age seventy-two. Using her new hearing trumpet, Marian overhears the family discuss moving "the old lady" into an institution with their recent inheritance. In response to Galahad's assertion that "institutions here are not fit for human beings," Robert replies, "Grandmother can hardly be classified as a human being. She's a drooling sack of decomposing flesh."

Muriel insists, "Old people do not have feelings like you or I. She would be much happier in an institution where there's proper help to take care of her." Because of our easy acceptance of Marian as an amusing and appealing human being with feelings and opinions, the family's comments register as cruel, and we tend to believe her rather than them even when she makes fantastic assertions, such as wanting to visit her 110-year-old mother in London.

The account of a conversation between Marian and her friend Carmella about the family's decision to send Marian to Lightsome Hall, run by the Well of Light Brotherhood, is a mixture of realistic fact and complete fantasy. At this point in the book, my graduate students often decide that the entire narrative takes place in a home for the mentally ill. Marian is clearly writing her account of past events at a later date from within the institution, for she explains, "At that time I do not think I attributed any ominous interpretations" to the event (of her son's unusual gift of a bottle of port before telling her of the move), "I was merely curious and surprised." Marian wonders how her family could possibly know that she would be better off dead, and she is terrified of any institution "with the grim knowledge of what is better for other people and the iron determination to better them whether they like it or not." She and Carmella agree, "the Well of Light Brotherhood is extremely sinister" and try to come up with an escape plan— perhaps to Lapland. She often mentions Lapland, but the novel provides no explanation other than her desire to return to the far north, and Lapland is further north than England, where she once lived.

Marian's insights are important, regardless of her suspected senility. Reflecting on her attachment to her home, she writes,

"Houses are really bodies. We connect ourselves with wall, roof, and objects just as we hang on to our livers, skeletons, flesh and bloodstream . . . This is true of the back yard and the small room I occupied at that time, my body, the cats, the red hen all my body all part of my own sluggish bloodstream." She observes, "A separation from these well known and loved, yes loved, things were 'Death and Death indeed.'" She acknowledges that escaping to Lapland "would also be a fine violation of those cherished habits, yes indeed, but how different from an institution of decrepit old women."

Marian moves between fantasy and reality in her account of her time before Lightsome Hall. She describes herself as "crushed with despair" and says she "could not think coherently" because of the "horror of the situation." She tells us, "Strangely enough I was in England and it was Sunday afternoon," and I assume she is in a dream in which the horror of the coming move to the institution and the need for a solution somehow transmutes into a fairy-tale reverie in which she has a sense that she must solve her problem alone, without the help of the Snow Queen. The dreamscape continues until her son Galahad awakens her, insisting he has something "very agreeable and important" to say. When he tells her she is going on holiday, she counters by confronting his lies. "You are sending me away to a home for senile females because you all think I am a repulsive old bag and I dare say you are right from your own point of view." She tells him that rather than being lonely living with his family, she is afraid of having her loneliness "taken away . . . by a lot of mercilessly well-meaning people" and insists that rather than persuading her, he is forcing her against her will.

From such a lucid conversation, she digresses into an account of packing her ancient tin trunk for an expedition to the far north. She lists the contents: her seven-year-old sleeping potion, her hearing trumpet, and her various collections of odds and ends. She remarks that "one has to be very careful what one takes when one goes away forever" and then packs "a screwdriver, hammer, nails, birdseed, a lot of ropes that I had woven myself, some strips of leather, part of an alarm clock, needles and thread, a bag of sugar, matches, coloured beads, sea shells and so on."

When Marian arrives at Lightsome Hall, run by Dr. Gambit and his wife, it is so strange that even she doubts the accuracy of her observations. She describes a large oil painting in the dining room that showcases a nun with a malicious face that seems to be winking with a mixture of mockery and malevolence, undercutting Dr. Gambit's insistence on the various principles, exercise routines, and dietary habits he imposes on the ten inhabitants of the institution. Marian describes each of these women, aged seventy to ninety-eight, and though they all seem a bit addled, they make occasional sensible remarks: "People only ever like whatever concerns themselves and I am no exception"; "We old people get a lot of simple pleasure from eating"; "Old people do not sleep much." Residents of Lightsome Hall live in their own separate mental realities, and when they interrupt each other's solipsistic comments, they sound as if they are carrying on normal conversations. When Christabel Burns, a daughter of a chemist from Jamaica, loans Marian a book that purports to be the life of the abbess in the painting, the winking nun, the novel becomes increasingly strange and symbolic. The contents of the small book are inserted into the novel, interrupting Marian's narrative without commentary for thirty-five pages.

After her "perusal of the history of the Abbess," Marian tells of being shaken awake by Anna Wertz, who informs her that Maude died during the night and that Natacha is so upset she had to be given multiple sleeping tablets. Marian recalls seeing Natacha add something to a batch of brownies the previous day and feels guilty for not warning Maude when she saw her emerging out of Natacha's igloo. The two old ladies climb up on the roof to look into Maude's bungalow and discover that the corpse of Maude is actually that of an old gentleman, Arthur. Marian confides the whole story to Georgina, who realizes the poisoned dessert must have been intended for her. When they tell their story of poisoning and cross-dressing to Dr. Gambit, he immediately disbelieves them and prescribes them sedatives and new work to do. Is he accurate? Did they dream up the whole incident? All we have is Marian's narrative. Even if the story were true, it would be normal for him not to believe such a story told by senile old women.

Marian's account wanders beyond any listener's suspended sense of disbelief and is a wonderful diatribe against power and governments, against men and their institutions. The poles of the earth somehow reverse, and snow falls below the equator. The novel grows more surreal and exciting as it moves toward its conclusion and the account of the ice ages. It ends with Marian's pronouncement: "If the old woman can't go to Lapland, then Lapland must come to the Old Woman."

I love seeing the Gambits exposed, watching the old women insist on their freedom, and following the account of justice, escape, and an overturning of the institutions that have shackled them throughout their lives. None of them yearn for the past, bemoan a lost lover, or miss their relatives. Instead, they seize power over their own lives, insist on preparing their own food, and break away entirely from the rules of the institution run by Dr. Gambit:

> Because we have absolutely no intention of letting ourselves be intimidated by your beastly routine ever again. Although freedom has come to us somewhat late in life, we have no intention of throwing it away again. Many of us have passed our lives with domineering and peevish husbands. When we were finally delivered of these we were chivvied around by our sons and daughters who not only no longer loved us, but considered us a burden and objects of ridicule and shame. Do you imagine in your wildest dreams that now we have tasted freedom we are going to let ourselves be pushed around once more by you and your leering mate?

Whether or not the rest of the story is hallucinatory, it is compelling, and it continues in Marian's recognizable voice even though the incidents are impossible in the world as we know it. I love this novel because of Carrington's imaginative leap into Marian's reality, with her lack of fear and her defiance of ordinary clichés and expectations of apparently senile women. Its wonderful portrayal of the women's agency and power is celebratory. In sharp contrast to Rivke's poignant loneliness and fear of memory loss and the even greater horror of Caro's incarceration in a nursing home, Marian's acute sense of self and ability to join with the other women in confronting the Gambits and all policies of control over women's lives make this book an enjoyable read. Instead of cringing, I laughed as I read it.

# THE MADONNAS OF LENINGRAD

## by Debra Dean

The last book in this chapter, like *The Hearing Trumpet*, finds wonder in what might otherwise be horror. Debra Dean's 2006 novel, *The Madonnas of Leningrad*, is as much about the siege of Leningrad in the 1940s as it is about its protagonist, Marina, who as a young woman was a tour guide at the Winter Palace, part of the State Hermitage in St. Petersburg, Russia. Her acute long-term memory of those years of starvation and deprivation and her photographic memory of the paintings in the Winter Palace contrast with her frail short-term memory, ravaged by Alzheimer's in her old age. In the novel's present tense, Marina lives with her beloved husband, Dmitri, loving family surrounds her, and the plot includes attending her granddaughter's weekend wedding on Drakes Island, where the setting's unfamiliarity exacerbates her dementia. Like *Evening*, the scenes set in the past are often more vivid than the present scenes, but that past is not the familiar romance tale. *Madonnas* portrays not only memories of the past but also the ability to celebrate and to really see what is in front of one's eyes in the present.

Debra Dean allows an elderly Marina her long-term memory, and the third-person narration in the present alternates with detailed flashes from her past. Our credulity somehow is not stretched, perhaps because of the convincing account of the aged Anya teaching a young Marina to look and truly to see, to memorize each painting in the Hermitage during the siege, and to create within her mind a Memory Palace to equal the external Winter Palace. Anya teaches Marina how to furnish that internal palace, using the structure of an actual building, and that legacy remains until Marina's death. The most vibrant accounts in the novel are of the paintings she committed to memory prior to helping remove them from their frames and hiding them in the basement of the museum when she was a young unmarried girl in Russia before fleeing to Germany, marrying Dmitri, forging a new identity as a Polish Ukrainian, and eventually coming to America.

The narrative is engaging, and the protagonist matters to the reader, who is caught up simultaneously in the vivid memories of spectacular paintings and of Marina's starvation and near death during the siege. Marina is not caricatured or placed on a pedestal. She comes across as fully human not only because of our glimpses into her Memory Palace but also because of Dean's respectful and poignant portrayal of Marina's present reality. I feel affection for Marina because of the narrator's respect for her.

In her old age, Marina moves seamlessly between her inner Memory Palace and her confusing daily life, in which "it is as though she has been transported into a two-dimensional world, a book perhaps, and she exists only on this page. When the page turns, whatever was on the previous page disappears from her view." We are told, "whatever is eating her brain consumes only the fresher memories, the unripe moments. Her distant past is preserved, better than preserved." We learn that she no longer cooks or even makes tea, because she omits

essential ingredients or forgets to turn off the burner. Her husband Dmitri now does all the cooking, chooses the clothes she
will wear, and helps her dress. An example of her confusion is
apparent in a scene where Marina does not know why she is
in front of her kitchen sink, holding a saucepan of water. She
thinks she must be hungry and is about to cook eggs, when her
husband enters the kitchen carrying the dirty breakfast dishes,
"evidence that she has eaten already, perhaps no more than
ten minutes ago."

We see her confusion again on a visit from her daughter
Helen when Marina offers her coffee and then asks her daughter generic questions such as "how is your family?" She then
comments that she is sure her divorced daughter is a good wife.
Although she does not initially recognize Helen as her daughter, Marina says that she remembers telling her she did not
need to follow through with the marriage even if already preg-
nant in 1970. "I didn't say this because you were a mess. I said
this because you didn't need this boy. Babies need only their
mother's milk and clean diapers." Reading this novel affirmed
my sense that people with dementia recall more than they can
communicate and that they are more "there" than most people can recognize. Some essence continues even when their
actions and words may initially seem incomprehensible.

In the unfamiliar setting of her granddaughter's island
wedding, away from her own home in Seattle, Marina is initially unable to follow instructions about the location of the
bathroom in her son's house, and then in relief, she delights in
finally "making water after holding it for so long." The narrator explains, "one of the effects of this deterioration seems to
be that as the scope of her attention narrows, it also focuses
like a magnifying glass on smaller pleasures that have escaped

her notice for years." It is as if we have insight into Marina's thoughts, because we read that she has learned to keep these observations to herself after trying to explain them to Dmitri and asking herself the question, "What would he say if she told him her pee sounded like a symphony?"

At the wedding rehearsal, Marina's comments and odd associations between present and past make her advanced dementia apparent, and Dmitri is no longer able to hide her confusion from their adult children. For example, Marina's response to seeing an eagle gliding by is to mention a bluebird nest, an observation that makes no sense to those around her. She repeats herself, ignores her melting ice cream, and then compares the melted dessert to jelly made from joiner's glue during the war. She refers to her son as having been fathered by a golden-haired god, and she tells her daughter-in-law, "I am becoming just like the museum. Everything, it is leaking. It is horrible." The narrator tells us, "More distressing than the loss of words is the way that time contracts and fractures and drops her in unexpected places." The text slips between citing of the wedding vows and memories of a long-ago celebration in the cellar, the music and words making a seamless connection in Marina's mind. A mention of her granddaughter Katie's beauty as a bride leads to memories of a girl in a painting in Leningrad.

After the wedding, Marina disappears from the inn where the family is spending the weekend, and she is not found until nearly thirty hours later. In Marina's consciousness during her many hours alone and lost, she senses that she must stay awake and recognizes that the cold and hunger are familiar to her. She remembers her past and the discovery of her pregnancy. The text moves from Marina's intense memory to the present:

"Green. The word doesn't begin to describe this," and "she forgets she is lost, that she is weak and chilled." We learn that "this slow erosion of self has its compensations. Having forgotten whatever associations might dull her vision, she can look at a leaf and see it for the first time. Though reason suggests otherwise, she has never seen this green before . . . The world is so acutely beautiful, for all its horrors, that she will be sorry to leave it."

In *Madonnas,* dying is part of daily life, made common and familiar throughout the siege of Leningrad and finally rendered quietly in Marina's cessation of breathing after she has already become lost to her family through Alzheimer's. In the final chapter, Helen sketches her mother as "Marina's body is finally winding down" and "Marina herself has left, though no one is able to pinpoint exactly when that happened, only that at some point she was no longer there." The narrative flashes back to the morning on the island when the roofer found Marina curled up in the fireplace of a mansion under construction after she had been missing for so long. She told him "Look." And pointed: "It is beautiful, yes?" When asked by Helen what was beautiful, the young man replied, "Everything, man. That's what was so amazing. There's a killer view of the straits, but she was pointing at everything, you know, this dead madrona tree out back, and these bands of sunlight coming through the roof in the garage . . . It was like she was saying everything was beautiful."

In this novel the old woman evokes our respect, she remains human, and she is not dismissed as crazy or worthless, although her reality has certainly been altered. A reader is grateful that Marina is not shut up in an old folks' home, that she is not drugged into a stupor or dependent on the ministrations of experts such as the doctor who would pin a label on her rather than see the world anew as the young roofer does. Her children do not know or see her reality. Unaware of her youth as a tour guide and the privations she endured during the war, they do not understand her occasional references, and they do not ask—or perhaps they do not care to know—until it is too late. Marina's Memory Palace provides her dignity and allows her to see beauty as a shield not only against the ravages of war in her youth but also against those of dementia, so that we as readers experience her death not as a tragedy but rather as ordinary, and we, too, are enriched by her life. I appreciate Dean's portrayal of a hidden possibility behind the surface deprivations of dementia. I love the concept of creating our own Memory Palaces throughout our lives, collecting beauty, whether in paintings, music, or nature as a shield against the inevitable losses of our lives. Instead of denying aging or fearing loss, we can grow older with courage and optimism if we can learn to *see* the world anew.

# CONCLUSION

When considering what wisdom these novels offer us as we anticipate facing old age, we see the importance of strong memories, self-respect, human dignity, and reliance on internal resources developed over a lifetime. Qualities we admire and that ease our reliance on others—patience, kindness, a sense of humor, or serenity—do not suddenly appear in old age. When we can no longer escape facing ourselves through being busy or entertained, we must sit with ourselves and accept our situations. Part of the experience of the characters in this chapter is that because of physical or mental decline, separation from family or friends, or a move into assisted living or a nursing home, the lives they once enjoyed are no longer possible. With such major physical and mental losses, they need to rely on others. Family and friends can be comforting and offer genuine respect, regardless of age, if those ties have been nurtured.

Although there is no single template for facing decline well, there are internal and external resources that can make life bearable and even joyful until its end. These books offer humor and words of wisdom along with cautionary lessons, such as the reminder that life does not last forever. In *Memento Mori*, *The Girls*, and *The Madonnas of Leningrad*, family is an asset, while in *Missing*, *As We Are Now*, and *The Hearing Trumpet*, family is of little or no help. Yet even in these books, a single granddaughter, a kind neighbor, or a loyal friend makes a positive difference. The authors all imagine old women who, even near the ends of their lives, are still capable of responding to kindness and of surprising us. They do not fit into tidy stereotypes; rather, they are as differentiated from one another as from younger characters. Charmian's ability to recall the details of her novels even when she cannot recall the day of the week, Marian's fantastic tales of life at Lightsome Hall, and Marina's heightened joy in the color green remind us that even when a person appears muddled and we cannot comprehend much of what she tells, her internal landscape is not necessarily blank, and she is worth our attention.

### Chapter 4

# It's Never Too Late

*Olive Kitteridge* (2008) by Elizabeth Strout

*The Seven Sisters* (2002) by Margaret Drabble

*Spiderweb* (1998) by Penelope Lively

*Visitors* (1997) by Anita Brookner

*Broken for You* (2004) by Stephanie Kallos

*Astrid and Veronika* (2003) by Linda Olsson

n the previous chapter, I looked at stories in which women face the ends of their life stories while living in the present. In this chapter, older women make fresh starts and look toward the future even after dreadful losses and irretrievable decades of life. Not all of the characters in these six novels are likable; I did not choose them particularly as role models. Each character has lived out some sort of scripted life in which she has hardened into familiar and often unexamined routines until a crisis forces her to question her identity. Each character taps into unknown parts of herself and experiences an internal catharsis or change, surprising us as readers, and allowing us to wonder at what is possible in the latter years of our lives.

In Elizabeth Strout's *Olive Kitteridge* and Margaret Drabble's *The Seven Sisters*, women make new lives for themselves after losing their partners. Olive Kitteridge is a complicated, smart, flawed person who takes for granted her gentle husband, Henry, until his sudden stroke and the loneliness that follows his death. Similarly, Drabble's Candida Wilton seems to have spent the thirty years of her marriage in arrested development prior to her husband Andrew's adultery and divorce. Both have estranged their adult children and they are each unkind. Olive is often entertaining in her ridiculous remarks, and her sadness eventually makes me feel sympathy for the wounded self under the brash exterior. Candida initially seems dull and self-pitying, but Drabble choreographs her subtle transformation in this intellectually engaging novel. As I follow their experiences and watch them take risks and become increasingly self-reflective, I grow to care about them.

Penelope Lively's *Spiderweb* and Anita Brookner's *Visitors* deal with the ways women adjust to altered life circumstances. Lively's Stella has been forced to retire after a successful career as an anthropologist. Defined by her profession, she is catapulted into a late-in-life coming-to-age story in which we watch her initial steps toward settling into a small village for which she holds a naive sense of nostalgia, but where she does not fit in. The novel's conclusion is open-ended as we observe her lack of intimacy and her refusal of two quite different options for partnership. Brookner's Dorothea May has been comfortably on her own for fifteen years since her husband's death. Thea's rather ordinary challenge of entertaining a wedding guest for a week would be amusing, except for the internal impact it has. Brookner's prose is elegant, and much of the pleasure of reading the novel is in the telling. By the novel's end, I exult with Thea in the sea changes of her sense of self and her discovery of hope and of how much she matters as a person.

In Stephanie Kallos's *Broken for You* and Linda Olsson's *Astrid and Veronika*, women with tragic pasts learn to open their lives to others. Both remind me of fairy tales in the satisfaction they provide, wrapping up loose ends, allowing their protagonists, Margaret Hughes and Astrid Mattson, a second chance late in life to heal old wounds and escape from their self-imposed isolation. Kallos's Margaret at the age of seventy-five learns she has an inoperable brain tumor. As she makes drastic changes by inviting strangers into her home, it is a joy to watch her come fully alive and create a surrogate family of other broken persons whose lives together allow them to develop in surprising ways. Olsson's Astrid harbors dreadful secrets from her youth, yet as she begins to care about her new neighbor, she experiences her own capacity for love and for generosity at the age of eighty. Both of these amazing protagonists experience late in life their capacity for friendship, and each leaves her home as a legacy to the next generation.

In my own seventies and as I grow older, I am nourished by these stories in which love and family are redefined, in which the sixties, seventies, and eighties are decades in which loss and crisis not only can be endured and survived, but can provide the catalyst for growth, for development, for hope.

# OLIVE KITTERIDGE

## by Elizabeth Strout

I began to read Elizabeth Strout's Pulitzer Prize–winning collection of thirteen short stories, *Olive Kitteridge* (2008), in response to the urging of a student who promised I would love it. The eponymous protagonist, Olive, links the stories even in those where she is not central. Olive is not a particularly nice person, not anyone's role model, and yet she lingers in my memory as a real human being, vulnerable beneath her harsh exterior. As the stories progress, she deals with the death of her husband, and starts to reexamine her life. Her ability to change, to stretch beyond who she thinks she is and to look ahead not only with regret, but with hope, suggests that an old woman is still capable of new insights and can "wake up" and enjoy herself beyond her losses and regrets. As Olive begins to change, however painfully, she does so with newfound honesty. Elizabeth Strout allows us to see the complexity and depth of Olive—and the other characters—precisely and with an understanding and empathy that develops throughout this beautifully crafted text.

Rather than a sweet little old lady, a selfless saint, or an eccentric crone, Olive Kitteridge is a complicated, smart, flawed person. Her interference in people's lives vacillates from caring concern to oblivious disregard, from conscientious adherence to community standards to nasty revenge when her feelings are hurt. She often dismisses people as hellions, morons, or flub-dubs, and she makes flamboyant and insensitive assertions about people's beliefs. Even her patient husband, Henry, sometimes finds their marriage a burden as well as a blessing, and their thirty-eight-year-old son, Christopher, marries a woman after knowing her just six weeks and moves as far from home as possible to escape her controlling nature. In her loneliness after Henry suffers a stroke, Olive gradually realizes how much she has taken him for granted over the decades of their marriage. And as Christopher learns to confront her with her fault-finding and unkindness, she takes her first steps toward self-awareness, friendship, and intimacy. She disproves the old saying that "you can't teach an old dog new tricks," and we watch her move from absolute rigidity and disappointment in life to an unfamiliar sense of vulnerability and an awareness that she wants to keep on living.

While we wish Olive would "wake up and smell the coffee," we also sympathize when she is "abandoned" by Christopher and then loses Henry. In spite of her self-delusion and often woefully inaccurate sense of how her words and actions affect others, we care about her when she overhears mean gossip about how her favorite dress exaggerates her girth, or about how difficult she has made Christopher's life. There is gratification in seeing well-meaning but deluded Olive pick herself up and eventually gain some insight after Henry's stroke. Strout's compassionate characterization of Olive and her neighbors is convincing, and her writing makes it a pleasure to read her amazing portrait of a woman who is as lovable as she is frustrating.

In "Pharmacy," the opening story, we get our first glimpse of the invisible emotional scars that can make communication difficult within even the most apparently solid marriages. Henry, a kind pharmacist whose presence others experience as "moving into a warm pocket of air," recalls his quiet joy in working with Denise, his young married assistant. After the premature death of her husband, he treats her like a daughter, teaching her to drive on back-country roads and helping her find an apartment. In contrast to loud, capable, prejudiced Olive, Denise is a simple but intelligent and feeling woman. Henry's yearning for her is poignant, yet he realizes he could no more leave Olive than "saw off his leg." When Denise accidentally runs over the cat he had given her after her husband's death and calls Henry during dinner, Olive tells him, "For God's sake. Go over and comfort your girlfriend." When he returns, Olive snidely asks, "Well, widow-comforter, how is she?" Olive feels superior to what she thinks is Henry's simplicity and willingness to let others take advantage of his kind nature, yet she more than anyone else regularly takes him for granted.

In "A Little Burst," we learn what Olive is like as a mother when Christopher marries Suzanne, a girl from out of town. Olive criticizes everything about her new daughter-in-law, from her "inappropriate" clothing to her independent behavior. The whole town is aware that Olive hates Christopher's well-educated wife, but everyone agrees that Olive's possessiveness would prevent her from liking any wife for her son. When we overhear the bride's critical remarks of her mother-in-law around the edges of the wedding reception, we feel Olive's disappointment, hurt feelings, and mortification even though we have earlier bristled at her arrogance and lack of self-reflection. We also begin to glimpse the disparity between Olive's self-perceptions and the opinions of others, and we start to understand the newly married couple's fierce need to move as far away as possible from Olive's interference.

Several stories reveal Olive's genuine kindness despite her obstinate self-righteousness. In "Incoming Tide," we see Olive prevent her former student Kevin from killing himself; in "Starving," we see her attempts to rescue Nina, an anorexic and deeply disturbed teenager; and in "Basket of Trips," she attends a funeral she knows Henry would have attended before his stroke. We get hints of her glacial change in her halting attempts to alter her behavior with Christopher when he invites her to visit New York, where he lives with his second wife, Ann, after his short-lived first marriage. The flight is a first for Olive, and as she looks out the window, she feels a "sudden surging greediness for life" and remembers what hope is, "that inner churning that moves you forward, plows you through life the way boats plowed the shiny water" now that she has been asked to be part of her son's life. In spite of her fledgling hope, the visit is not a warm-hearted affair, and we see how difficult it is to change one's character.

In "River," the final story, eighteen months after Henry's death, and before Christopher and Ann's baby is born, Olive continues to feel "like a package of vacuum-packed coffee." She has developed a daily routine: coffee and donuts at Dunkin' Donuts, where she reads the newspaper in her car until 6:00 a.m., when she walks three miles in one direction and then returns three miles back along the river. Throughout the day, she frequently wishes to die quickly and avoid the embarrassment of a long illness or ending up in the nursing home like Henry. The account of her meeting with Jack Kennison, a banker she has never met but always despised because of his

Harvard education and his wealth, is comical and poignant. Olive finds him collapsed on the walking path by the river, and when she offers to go for assistance after helping him up onto a bench, he pleads, "Don't leave me alone." They introduce themselves. After he regains his color, she tells him that he might die if she leaves him there, and he replies, "I don't care if I die." Olive tells him she doesn't care if she dies as long as it is quick. But when he replies that he doesn't want to die alone, she reverts to her usual harshness: "Hell, we're always alone. Born alone. Die alone." She gets him to describe how he fell, and after a bit, he begins to cry and tells her that his wife died in December. She drives him to the hospital and makes sure he gets back home safely. After refusing his invitation to lunch, she feels bereft on the way home.

Their friendship develops slowly, and eventually they go out for dinner and discover that they enjoy talking to each other. After more dates, they kiss. Still acutely aware of how differently she is behaving from her usual sense of propriety and astonished at her own desire at the age of seventy-four, Olive lies awake and thinks about Jack's arms around her. She pictures what she has not done in years. Yet, characteristically, she criticizes him endlessly in her head and argues with him when they are together. When she discovers that Jack voted Republican, she stomps off and they quit seeing each other. She calls Christopher and complains that Jack is a nitwit. Christopher tells her that the reason he never calls is because it is hard to talk with her when "everything is someone else's fault."

When a lonely Olive and Jack finally reconnect through e-mail in their mutual misery, she uncharacteristically admits to him that she may be somewhat at fault for Christopher's hatred, and he reveals that he has not spoken to his own daughter since she married a woman. Jack invites Olive over again, and although she feels torn between revulsion and tentative desire, she also feels a freedom, because when Jack had needed her at the hospital he had given her a place in the world. She dismisses her initial concern about what others would think. She considers what young people don't know and she is just discovering—that aged and wrinkled bodies are as needy as their own young ones, and that love is not to be tossed away carelessly.

Elizabeth Strout's storytelling transparently reveals credible human beings that are neither saints nor sinners. Henry's stroke propels Olive into subtle changes he does not live long enough to enjoy. Christopher begins to stand his own ground with his mother. Long-term marriages, however painful and occasionally disappointing, are also protective cocoons, sheltering people like Olive from themselves. I admire Olive's self-reflection so late in life, and I am cheered by a story in which identity and meaning can develop in old age and in which there are second chances, including experiences of desire and intimacy. As Olive learns to be friends even when she and Jack do not see eye to eye, and as she tries to appreciate Christopher and Ann's life—so different from her own—she becomes more self-reflective and aware of her impact on others. Strout ends the story and the book with Olive in Jack's arms: "Her eyes were closed, and throughout her tired self swept waves of gratitude—and regret. She pictured the sunny room, the sun-washed wall, the bayberry outside. It baffled her, the world. She did not want to leave it yet."

# THE SEVEN SISTERS

## by Margaret Drabble

Margaret Drabble's 2002 novel, *The Seven Sisters*, is a narrative of self-invention after public humiliation and loss, in which Candida Wilton starts a new life after betrayal, rejection, and divorce from Andrew, her husband of over thirty years. It is not that Andrew was the wrong person for her; rather, the romance plot of her youth that assumed marrying Prince Charming would satisfy a woman's desire was the wrong plot for her. Therefore, as readers we do not want her to find a new lover; we want her to figure out who she is, apart from the cultural narratives of romance, and we wonder if that will be possible for someone who seems to have been in a state of arrested development since she married. Like Olive Kitteridge, Candida is not initially an empathetic character, but she is another older protagonist whose narrative provides an original, valuable, and ultimately enjoyable read. Candida's journey to create an authentic self among friends with whom she can develop a life of the mind, her new self-reliance in the city after feeling marginal to suburban family life, and the novel's focus on the values of such pleasure combine to make this a book I recommend.

Margaret Drabble's formal choices in this carefully choreographed novel reflect Candida's transformation from Suffolk matron to London survivor. Drabble divides the novel into four parts that we eventually realize are all composed by Candida, although only the initial part, "Her Diary," is in the first-person voice. She writes the second part, "Italian Journey," in an omniscient third-person voice; the third part, "Ellen's Version," supposedly written by her youngest daughter who lives in Finland with her fiancé, reports Candida's suicide; and the final part, "A Dying Fall," moves between first and third person. Entirely taken in by Ellen's account, I was startled when I turned the last page of "Ellen's Version" and began "A Dying Fall," where Candida is certainly still alive and admits to impersonating Ellen as a way to attempt to see things from her daughter's perspective. In retrospect, we realize that Candida had to write a text with literal shifts in point of view that would finally allow for a future tense in which she could begin to see herself more truthfully and be able to reconstruct a workable if not ideal human connection with her daughter. Symbolically, Candida dies and is reborn. While such a move could be glib in the hands of a less capable author, Drabble's complex creation of Candida and the playful form of the text allow us to appreciate Candida's changing perspective and to see it as life-affirming.

The first section, "Her Diary," more than half the novel, becomes Candida's closest confidante. In its pages she reveals her subtle awakening, and we follow her progress from being a boring, conventional, depressed woman who assumes she has no future "at this age," to becoming a more vital woman who takes initiative. Because of an unexpected windfall two years after the divorce, she becomes financially stable and is able to travel to Italy and follow the journey of Virgil's Aeneas with a group of friends she assembles—the seven sisters of the novel's title. However, it is not the inheritance or the trip that leads to Candida's insight: it is her own writing of a text that allows her to see herself, possibly for the first time.

Candida begins "Her Diary" on her laptop two years after settling in central London. She moves seamlessly between present and past, and she sounds as if in spite of aging, she has not outgrown her prim girlish attitudes. Married as a virgin, and living for decades in a mutually disappointing and nearly sexless marriage that impeded her growth as a person, Candida has followed internalized social codes and avoided risks until her late fifties. Andrew's very public affair with Althea, a mother whose daughter had drowned herself in the pond of the school where he is headmaster, leads to divorce; somehow he remains beloved at the school and Candida is the one marginalized by the community as cold and reserved. When Candida moves from her beautiful Georgian house, she takes a courageous step toward figuring out just who she is now that she is no longer the wife of the headmaster of Holling House School in Suffolk and is alienated from all three adult daughters.

Candida is an astute observer, and in her diary we see her new surroundings through her eyes—from the litter under the roadway to the smile on a stranger's face, from remembered dialogue to messages on placards posted on the bulletin board of the Health Club. Candida moves between accounts of her day at the Health Club, how many laps she swam, how long she spent in the sauna, and descriptions of the other women in the changing room to summaries of her marriage, descriptions of her daughters Isobel, Martha, and Ellen, memories of girlhood and adult friends. She tries not to be afraid when she ventures out in her unfamiliar neighborhood, and she is wary of revealing her present life to her old friends both for fear of evoking their pity and to protect herself from the kinds of judgments she clearly makes about other people—including her daughters and friends. She seems to have little capacity for intimacy and to have acquired a generally passive manner of living in the world. We sense no passion or motivation, little depth, no capacity for serious self-reflection. Perhaps the betrayal, the divorce, and the public humiliation have numbed her, so that by the time Candida begins to write in her diary, strangely distanced by that third-person pronoun of its title, she is just beginning to be capable of expressing her feelings. Her alienation from all three daughters, two of whom openly side with Andrew, makes me wonder why she has not been close to them since they were little children. Is she unable to show affection and incapable of intimacy, a dry, cold person, or is she just reserved and undemonstrative?

The first fifty pages of her diary feel as constricted and claustrophobic as her life. As she explains why she joined the Health Club after the adult school was closed, we sense she needed structure so badly that when the Virgil class was canceled, she accepted the reduced price membership in the Health Club just to have something to do. Her descriptions of the ugliness of her neighborhood, her bare flat, and her practical clothes reveal little sense of beauty in her new location. She mentions the lack of chlorine smell at the Health Club pool but omits any account of fragrance or pleasant aromas of food, no tactile sensations. She lives with few possessions and feels a "relief in being so reduced," writing, "we accumulate too many objects, as we grow older. I had some hope that by stripping most of mine away, I might enter a new dimension. As a nun enters a convent in search of her god, so I entered my solitude. I felt fear, and I felt hope." Drabble elegantly shows us the initial period of Candida's development as burgeoning and awkward through rather inept, self-involved prose. Candida uses self-consciously poetic language, remembering the suffusion of anticipation she felt, with a sense of destiny that "shone before me like the diffused radiance of dawn breaking over an unknown landscape." She frequently mentions her age when she wonders about the possibility of something exciting ahead or questions her appearance in clothes her daughter Martha said make her look "mumsy." She so clearly knows she needs to reinvent even her appearance but is not sure how to do so.

Looking back at her two years in Ladbroke Grove, her dreary London neighborhood, Candida contrasts her initial fear with her increased comfort as she became familiar with the "elegant young man with dreadlocks" who lives under the bridge, the short old man who walks the streets and carries a "vast plain white wooden crucifix," and the foreign shopkeepers in the neighborhood. She feels like a seasoned Londoner when she finally allows her childhood friend Sally to visit from Suffolk, and rather than feeling embarrassment about its shabbiness, she is pleased with her "colourful neighborhood." As she begins to feel a sense of connection with the people who live in Ladbroke Grove, she admits that she has always been "an unthinking racist" and she still is. Only by living in the diversity of London does she begin to recognize her formerly unquestioned assumptions about race and class.

As Candida loses her fear of strangers and reconnects with her school friends Sally and Julia, she discovers that they share her desire to travel to Naples and Amalfi, although they each have different reasons. Their visits stir in her a desire to reread Virgil. She contacts Mrs. Jerrold, the over-eighty-year-old Virgil teacher, and the rest of the diary looks forward as Candida,

Anais, and Cynthia—all members of the Virgil class—get back in touch and Candida begins to form friendships and make plans. After receiving a letter from Northam Provident with a check for 120,000 pounds, she determines to go to Italy. Feeling buoyed by the windfall, a confident Candida writes: "One can make anything happen, if one has the nerve. It has occurred to me, over the past weeks, that if I'd been a different kind of person, a person with initiative instead of the kind of person who always waits for things to happen, then I could have organized this trip without coming into 120,000 pounds of unexpected and unmerited lucky money."

Eventually the trip includes Candida, Mrs. Jerrold, Anais, Cynthia, Julia, and Sally plus Valeria, the driver they hire to meet them at the Tunis airport and accompany them on their trip. She proudly informs Andrew that she is "going on an educational outing with my Virgil class to trace the latter part of the voyage of Aeneas," and she enjoys being able to surprise him. The day before the trip, Candida rereads her entire diary and describes her voice as "mean, self-righteous, self-pitying," a voice of which she is not proud. Yet she also writes, "I am happy now. I am full of happy anticipation."

"Italian Journey," only half as long as "Her Diary," in addition to being narrated in third person, also addresses the reader as "you" and appeals to a shared internalized sense of "that magical land" imprinted on the human heart, "where the sky is vast and blue, the sand is golden, and the horizon shimmers with pledge and with promise." No longer depressed, passive, or mean-spirited, Candida revels in their journey. Drabble's knowledge of the Greek text saturates this section, and we along with the seven sisters learn literary history and the parsing of several lines of Virgil. Candida becomes better acquainted with everyone in the group, and Mrs. Jerrold, the wise older woman, offers advice about life as well as Virgil. When Candida receives a message from Andrew that their daughter Ellen is in a hospital in the Netherlands, she doubts his word and is afraid to call Ellen because of their estrangement. Mrs. Jerrold, citing her own similar experience, insists that Candida call the hospital and then Ellen. Ellen seems surprised but glad to hear from her mother, and afterward Candida wonders why she felt such anguish at calling her own daughter. When Candida writes of at last making a solitary visit to face the Sibyl, before the return trip, she writes in third person: "she feels with a new pleasure the ageing of her flesh." She hears the Sibyl repeatedly whisper to her to submit and be still, that she can climb no higher and has reached the last height. But the section ends defiantly: "[I]t is not the last height. And she cannot submit."

"Ellen's Version" comes next and is just twenty pages, in which Ellen reports reading the diary on her mother's laptop after learning of her drowning in the canal. Ellen claims it was her mother's frigidity that drove her father into the arms of other women, leaving her daughters a legacy of sexual fragility, but writes that she no longer blames her mother for her own problems. Such forgiveness may be wishful thinking by Candida, and reading it reminded me of the complexity of relationships between mothers and daughters and the maturity required to see through one another's eyes in adulthood. Ellen reveals a new respect for her mother, commends her for making friends in her crime-ridden neighborhood, and writes: "There are a lot of nice middle-aged and elderly women about, at a loose end, and they are good at setting up little support groups for themselves." She adds that her mother tried to be happy, and she reports that Mrs. Jerrold, Cynthia Barclay, and Anais Al-Sayyab all assured her that her mother had been happy in Italy and Africa, but that Mrs. Jerrold also said that Candida never went to Cumae, never visited the Sibyl.

When we turn the page to read "The Dying Fall," and discover Candida faked Ellen's entire version, including the account of Candida's death, we wonder if Candida also made up the story of visiting Cumae. Why does Candida give us both versions? Which version is accurate? In these final pages, Candida describes herself as being back in her same old life, with nothing heroic or tragic. She echoes the epigraph that appears at the beginning of the novel: "Are not five sparrows sold for two farthings? And not one of them is forgotten by God." Is she suggesting that neither heroic nor tragic stature is necessary for her to possess value and that her life story is worth recording without embellishment?

Candida describes how the exercise in trying to see things from Ellen's point of view made her aware of just how impossible it is to enter another person's consciousness. She admits that she has lied to herself for most of her life. It is only when Candida tries to view herself through her daughter's eyes that she talks about herself as a poor wife and mother because of her distaste for the human body, especially sex. She is harsh on herself, calls the trip to Italy a schoolgirl fantasy, and writes that she must learn to grow old before she dies. She provides brief updates on Julia, Mr. Barclay, the budding friendship between Cynthia and Anais, and notes that she visits Mrs. Jerrold weekly. She describes a pleasant trip to Ellen's small wedding in Finland, where she connects with Ellen and her husband intellectually around language and they begin to enjoy each other's interests. Candida meets two interesting older men—one a philanderer and the other a widower— and experiences herself as still attractive to men, though she laughs with Ellen about the unsuitability of the philanderer. She enjoys the company of the widower for an occasional theater outing or dinner when she returns to London, wonders whether he and she could create a nonsexual partnership such as Cynthia and Mr. Barclay (a gay man) have done, and then ends her diary and the novel with a note of expectation: "What is it that is calling me?" followed by the italics that appear as marginal notes throughout the diary: "*Stretch forth your hand, I say, stretch forth your hand.*"

Without the catalyst of her public embarrassment and divorce, Candida could be merely a secondary character in someone else's novel. If her windfall and travel were the only devices that led to her renewal, this plot would be familiar and predictable. Yet Candida's reinvention of herself is a rhetorical one—a shift made possible by her compelling self-narration in her diary two years after leaving Andrew. Drabble uses Candida's fascination with Virgil and her retracing of Aeneas's journey as the template for framing the story as one about stories and their potential. While Drabble's literary allusions enrich the prose, the reader needs no formal literary background to appreciate Candida's newly awakened senses. Language and books, particularly the clarity of classical literature, allow Candida to use her rusty intellectual skills to gain distance on her own life and to begin to change the things that are now within her grasp.

*The Seven Sisters* is not a quick read, nor one that offers an easily digestible happy ending for Candida; however, each reading reveals new pleasures in Drabble's allusions and literary prose, and the novel richly suggests the possibility of creating lives of our own beyond the scripts imagined in our youth. Candida's name nods to Voltaire's Candide, who famously learns he's been sold a bill of goods about the nature of the world in a novel that mocks false pieties in contrast to more individual qualities of character and honesty. Drabble's novel satirizes social assumptions, especially those of marriage and motherhood, and reveals how they can limit individual character development for someone like Candida, who is unsuited for both. In addition to sending me back to Virgil and Voltaire, whom I read as an undergraduate student, the novel makes me think about the ways in which novels in general have such limited plots for women. Candida is an unusual heroine. She had lived a life unfulfilled by romantic love, and the typical romance narrative is inadequate for her. Only in writing her personal journey and exploring differing perspectives does she come into her own as a thinker late in life. In losing her husband and her role, she lost the status and position usually considered a prize for the romantic heroine, yet she gained something more valuable and authentic.

*The Seven Sisters* allows us to consider an alternative path not often explored for women. Rather than ending with "happily ever after," the book reaches out to a future that we cannot predict but that we anticipate will be filled with surprises as Candida stretches forth her hand to receive.

# SPIDERWEB

## by Penelope Lively

Penelope Lively's 1998 novel, *Spiderweb*, like *The Seven Sisters*, makes me think about what we imagine as "good outcomes" in older women's lives and stories. In my search for new narratives—stories that move older women beyond plots of dementia, imminent death, and romance—I cannot recall another novel about an older woman in which the conclusion is as open-ended as that of *Spiderweb*. This novel's sense of possibility for sixty-five-year-old Stella, an anthropologist, is remarkable for its rarity; *Spiderweb* is a coming-to-age novel whose ending resembles those of coming-*of*-age novels in its conclusion that Stella's future includes imaginative possibilities and potential beyond the story.

In this chapter, I examine novels in which the protagonist experiences an involuntary loss that propels her into a new sense of herself: Olive Kitteridge's husband dies; Candida Wilton's husband divorces her. We are accustomed to a tradition in fiction in which a woman changes her status by marriage, and we understand the upheaval of losing a husband and an entire way of life. But *Spiderweb* is notably different in that it portrays the loss of a profession as equally important as a loss of a partner; it is Stella's mandatory retirement that spurs unfamiliar self-reflection and potential change. For the reader accustomed to the romance plot in novels with a female protagonist, a question that runs through this novel is whether Stella will change her opinions about living alone now that she considers the possibility of putting down roots. Stella buys a cottage in Somerset, where she once vacationed with a lover and where Richard Faraday, the widower of her college friend Nadine, now lives. The novel spans a summer, portraying Stella's past primarily through her memories as she connects with Richard and with her longtime professional friend, Judith Cromer. The novel concludes with separate offers from Richard and Judith to combine households, though ultimately Stella rejects both. Lively examines the centrality of work rather than marriage to Stella and Judith and their choice to remain self-proclaimed "unconventional women."

Just as Olive and Candida have been defined by their partnerships, Stella has been defined by her work, and her lack of partnership. She has loved doing background research for her fieldwork, sorting through her notes afterward, and shaping her ideas into lectures and published essays. Stella's mandatory retirement from her teaching position at a Midlands university raises the question of where she should live now that the location is not determined by a field assignment. The irony of her focus on kinship, the spiderweb of the title, and her own relative discomfort with her position in such webs, undergirds the novel. Stella is accustomed by both her disposition and her profession to being a resident observer in villages in places such as Malta, Greece, the Delta, and Orkney. In these locations, at which she stays for no longer than a year, she spins a web of meaning assigned to the webs of kinship she observes, as she keenly avoids being enmeshed in such webs herself, entirely unaware that she is missing essential elements that are key to understanding human connection.

Stella does not require or enjoy traditional attachments to locations or people. She prefers movement and self-determination, qualities familiar to male protagonists, sometimes found in younger female characters but rarely visible in older women, who are often assumed to desire stable community and comfort. Stella resists such domestic tugs. As she remembers her decades-old friendship with Nadine, who recently died of cancer, and her later friendship with Judith since they met at a dig in their thirties, and as she recalls former lovers, we see how determined Stella always has been to resist belonging to anyone and anyone belonging to her. What plots can we imagine for a healthy, attractive, professional woman forced to retire when she has no living relatives, no partner, no children, no home base, when that solitary status is what she prefers? We are so accustomed to thinking of women in relation to other people that it perhaps comes as a surprise that she has turned down proposals of marriage from men with whom she was admittedly in love at the time and has chosen instead to be alone and to focus on her work. *Spiderweb* reveals that not every woman wants a partner for companionship in old age.

In the novel, Lively does not privilege Stella's perspective. She tells Stella's story omnisciently through a pastiche of documents from newspapers, correspondence, and Stella's field diaries, and the narration moves freely between Stella and seemingly unrelated accounts of other characters. Lively's title alludes to the nearly invisible but strong web of connections across time and space that exists just beneath the surface of seemingly random choices and local events. Her novel is mimetic in its suggestion not only that such connections exist but also that we as individuals, groups, and even professions impose patterns of meaning on continuously fluctuating bits and pieces, and that our interpretations, rather than being "truth," are determined by our personal assumptions and perspectives. As readers we may pride ourselves that we have information beyond what Stella is trained to notice, forgetting that we, like Stella, also have limited perspectives.

Stella approaches her rural neighborhood as if she were a short-term visitor on an anthropological field assignment rather than a member of the village. She studies maps, reads background materials, takes long walks, and chats with anyone who is available, though without her customary notebook or tape recorder. She does not, however, connect with anyone on an emotional level. While readers, along with Stella, examine fragments of information and artifacts and try to make interpretations based upon partial evidence, we also have the overview that Stella cannot see. We gradually glean information about Stella's past and present from the many interwoven documents and discrete scenes throughout the novel; in addition, we move beyond Stella's point of view, and it is through these inclusive perspectives that we can see the links between what initially appear as disparate and unrelated parts of the story.

For example, the narrative juxtaposes Stella's plot with that of her neighbors in the village, the Hiscox family of adolescent boys and their mother and grandmother, allowing us to see how Stella misreads them. The novel contains nearly as much information about the Hiscoxes as about Stella, and gives us information she would not be privy to about the adolescent boys' acts of arson, their torment of animals, and their fear and hatred of their mother. We know of their frustration and explosive anger, and we realize they are a threat, not just to Stella but also to the entire community. Stella's few interactions with the two Hiscox boys hint at danger beyond her awareness as they tell her to "piss off" or refer to her as "an old cow." She assumes they are typical disgruntled adolescents, but this, in fact, is not the case. What Stella thinks of this family from the outside is gravely contrasted against what's really going on. She has never questioned her ability to determine relationships between people. Yet in this situation we see that she dangerously misinterprets her nearest neighbors. The dysfunctional and frustrated Hiscox family contrast dramatically with Stella's view of them, filtered through her romantic associations with the bucolic setting. She trusts her first opinions as accurate and holds on to them as if they are not only correct, but also unchanging as they exist in her memory, as fixed snapshots rather than moving films. Her inability to sense feelings or to adjust her fixed interpretations of human behavior after making initial observations not only makes her vulnerable but also makes the reader question the validity of her professional anthropological observations. Lively implies that for Stella, like everyone, perspectives are not neutral; they are colored by our personal assumptions.

What we see of the boys' mother, Karen Hiscox, and their gran is from the boys' perspective. They recognize that like them, Gran has learned not to be caught listening or watching their mother, and they notice that Gran pretends to be asleep and plays more batty than usual at times. They even question, "maybe she wasn't so daft" in spite of the diagnosis of Alzheimer's disease and wonder if the look in her eyes is really one of misery. Ironically, even these "evil" boys see more accurately than Stella. Yet instead of sympathizing with her, they feel that old people, like old dogs, should be put down. Through the boys' eyes we view the contrast between Karen's public performances every two weeks when she takes Gran to withdraw money from the bank and for sweets at the café, making a big to-do over Gran in public, and the abusive treatment at home where Karen shouts at Gran, who sits "huddled up like a dog that thinks you're going to hit it." Although we know the family is postponing Gran's move to the nursing home as long as possible so they can live off her money, Stella, like the social worker, assumes that Gran is "living in satisfactory circumstances in a happy family unit." Lively's novel portrays the unavoidable dangers and limitations of reading situations from a single external perspective not only by individuals but also by trained professionals. Nobody asks the old woman about her life.

Just as Stella misreads Gran as happy and comfortable in her daughter's home, she reveals her inability to pick up on ordinary clues of real life outside her professional role in her conversations with Richard, who had been married to her college friend Nadine until her death. Stella is baffled by his attention to her in introductions to the surrounding neighborhood, invitations to lunch or dinner, and offers to repair her lawnmower or help her with the gutters. We observe Richard's affection for her while she has always assumed he disliked her, basing her assumption on his steady profession as a civil servant and his role as a husband and father in contrast to her nomadic unmarried life. She is surprised when he tells her Nadine was often envious of her and that he has always admired her.

Stella's friendship with Judith, though more recent than with Nadine, has been sustained over thirty years as they have dropped in and out of each other's lives. Their friendship is elastic, including times of not seeing each other for long periods and then spontaneous holidays with shared rooms in spartan hotels. Now that Stella has moved not far from Bristol, where Judith lives with her lesbian partner, Mary, they are in frequent contact. On a visit to Stella, Judith asks why, after avoiding commitments for forty years, Stella has acquired a dog, Bracken, and she replies that in these parts he confers respectability. Judith notes that most people in cities also have dogs, primarily fangs on legs, and then remarks on the extent to which her and Stella's trades have put them out of touch with the real world, "the one we have to live in."

Judith and Stella share their nonconformity and recognize that "in other times or places they would either have been burned as witches or consulted as oracles." In their professional lives, they have tried to avoid the limits of gender, and now when it is too late, they finally have the protective camouflage they once sought. Stella muses on the discovery that she now poses no sexual threat or challenge and considers herself effectively invisible to young men. Even in this observation, Stella overlooks the fact that sexual invisibility is not necessarily protective. She is aware of a new persona "thrust upon her" by the ambush of time, and yet she imagines that her marginal position is merely similar to that of young people and that it increases her opportunity for observation of others.

Most poignant of her discoveries in retirement is her capacity for intimacy and connection with Bracken, the dog she introduced to Judith. He is the first pet she has ever had. She locates him through the Yellow Pages, bases her choice on the recommendation of Miss Clapp in the Animal Rescue Centre, and takes home a Springer spaniel mix that "comes from a broken home." Stella names her dog Bracken after her parents' dog that she barely tolerated when it was alive, and then learns from the postman that only hounds have that name. She takes Bracken on long walks along the old mineral

line that passes the Hiscox property, hoping to fit into the surroundings and chat with the neighbors. However, the Hiscox
boys kick Bracken when he rushes up to them, jolting Stella.
When they tell her they don't like dogs, she brushes off the
incident, saying, "Some don't."

Stella does find, over a relatively short period of time, that
she likes Bracken, but she resents his complete adoration. She
feels guilty that she does not reciprocate and wonders if all
dog owners are subjected to such "relentless emotional pressure." Yet when Bracken disappears after being left alone in
her cottage, Stella feels responsible and wonders if she had
forgotten to bolt the French doors. She searches for him for
days, and she is surprised when her eyes fill with tears in his
absence. She scarcely believes that she could feel so stricken
about an animal, and she finds that there is an entire dimension of human emotion of which she had been ignorant. She
feels a bleak space in her life "triggering this disproportionate,
lunatic response" in an otherwise "reasonable adult." When
she finally learns of the dog's murder, she recognizes she has
never personally experienced anything like this before.

Up to this point we've had hints that the boys are the per-
petrators of the various small fires reported in the *Herald*. We've
seen them kick at Stella's dog, call her names behind her back,
and assume she is mocking them when she is merely trying to
be friendly in the way she has always been with young people.
But it is not until Bracken disappears and his mutilated body is
eventually discovered that she begins to suspect the surly boys
as capable of having committed this crime. She tells Richard
that just as she is putting down roots for the first time ever, and
"supposedly a connoisseur of community life," she is "unable
to identify a community or even establish cordial relations

with my neighbors." She tells him she is unnerved by "this dog business," and she begins to notice that all along she has been expecting to move on and has not "taken root at all." The fate of the poor dog is what has thrown her, and she feels "entirely dispirited" and hemmed in by the house, taking Richard's offers of a trip to the Devon coast as an instance of unwanted therapy or charity, which she silently but viscerally rejects.

Stella has prided herself on not being tied to anyone, so perhaps we should not be surprised that she rejects Richard's attempts to comfort her and soon afterward rejects both his and Judith's offers to combine households for mutual support and friendship if not physical intimacy. Although Stella's tearful reaction to Bracken's murder hints that she may be on the verge of paying attention to her feelings after a lifetime of embarrassment at the expression of emotion, her rapid decision to flee Somerset and her friends suggests she may continue to avoid intimacy and to see her life as a series of snapshots rather than a continuing script in which she welcomes emotional development as much as she values independence.

By the end of the book, I found myself wondering where Stella will go and whether she would be better suited for life in a city than in a village. Perhaps her startled emotional experience after Bracken's disappearance may lead to a gradual awareness of her feelings, opening her not only to sadness but to joy. Despite her retirement from work that has been the central focus of her life, we sense that her intellectual profession and her commitment to independence will continue to define her.

The ending of the novel is abrupt and left me feeling wistful and curious. Judith had remarked about the disappointment and wastefulness of being sidelined from work, "when you've still got plenty of mileage left." Neither she nor Stella revealed much ability for introspection, seeing themselves solely in terms of their professional roles. Both have ignored their emotional development, caught up in the challenges and discoveries of their various projects. I wonder if they will be able to explore their underdeveloped emotional lives and figure out how to live in the "real world" even as they continue to live permanently "in a landscape of the mind," as the novel also suggests the boundary between these modes of being is neither clear nor fixed.

Lively's novel is stimulating, as it compels us to examine our assumptions about what matters to old women when they are forced to retire from work that has provided the primary meaning in their lives. Readers who hope to feel an emotional attachment to Stella are apt to be disappointed because she reveals so little emotion, and this is a novel of ideas about emotion rather than one designed to move us to experience emotion. Lively's cautionary tale ultimately exposes the limits of equating one's personal perspective with "truth." She calls into question how it is that we truly know anyone, the ways in which we relate in societal groups, and how we construct meaningful benchmarks to our lives.

Lively asks us to see beneath the surface of others and ourselves and to understand the "spiderweb" that connects us all, tasks not limited to the elderly. In terms of fiction, she makes it clear that the unconventional plot is no less fraught with tension and substance than the marriage plot. The protagonist makes equally momentous decisions and discoveries, and, in the case of Stella, we see a character remain open to new possibilities, an accurate depiction, Lively suggests, of how life actually unfolds.

# *VISITORS*

## by Anita Brookner

Unlike the elderly spinsters in nineteenth-century American regionalist novels or in the early twentieth-century novels of Barbara Pym, the protagonist of Anita Brookner's *Visitors* (1997), seventy-year-old Dorothea (Thea) May, has no romantic inclinations and is not caught up in the internal politics of church jumble sales or neighborhood garden clubs. She is not plagued by inheritance worries, troubled by ill health, or suffering from any loss. As I first read the novel, I wondered: *Where is the usual conflict we anticipate in works of fiction?* Like *Spiderweb*, *Visitors* explores a plot that is uncommon for an old woman character, but Thea's plot is even less familiar than Stella's. Death, divorce, and mandatory retirement are recognizable as major events for Olive, Candida, and Stella, whereas the plot event for Thea—hosting a wedding guest for a week—appears absurdly minor on the scale of disruption. The novel reminds us that sea changes in one's sense of self and one's circumstances are not only possible beyond a certain age, but that they may result from seemingly uneventful occurrences, even as simple as the breaking of a comfortable daily routine.

In part, the value of this novel is in its prose: the illuminating power and pleasure of the well-wrought sentence and the simple but lingering qualities of its development of character and plot. Critical praise for the novel includes the words *quiet, perfectionist, nuanced, subtle, elegant.* But Brookner's focus on Thea is not simply a beautiful rendering of the mundane. Rather *Visitors* insists on the intensity and importance of the ordinary to shift our sense of who we are.

Thea has become increasingly reclusive since her husband, Henry's, death fifteen years earlier. She reminds me of the ordinary old people in Doris Lessing's *Diaries of Jane Somers*, who are initially invisible to Jane as they go about their discreet routines, quietly shopping at corner stores, taking buses, seemingly beyond interest to the younger generations. The old in *Visitors* are drawn to the young while simultaneously envying and disliking them. In life, as in fiction, women like Thea often appear boring, at best merely bit players in life, secondary characters in fiction, yet Thea is the main focus in *Visitors*.

The novel is set in London in August, the month of holidays, the transition between summer and autumn, mirroring the cycle of human life as youth recedes and habits conceal increased frailty. Impending death is visible as older friends die, and symptoms of aging are palpable in breathlessness, heart arrhythmia, and increasing fatigue. What possible narrative interest are we likely to have in Thea, who has no outside interests, no employment, no children or grandchildren, no memberships in church or social organizations? She has no extended family of origin, and she maintains minimal connection through obligatory weekly telephone conversations initiated by her only "family connection," Henry's elderly cousins, Kitty and Molly, and their husbands, Austin and Harold.

The event around which the novel centers is the wedding of Ann Levinson, the granddaughter of Henry's cousin

Kitty. Ann was born in England but raised in America, and the young couple decides to get married in London. Brookner's focus, however, is not on the young lovers but on the older circle of family, who would traditionally be relegated to the edges of a romance plot. Kitty, accustomed to being in control, is thrilled to host the wedding celebration for a granddaughter she doesn't know very well, and whom she hasn't seen since Ann was a girl. The novel portrays both the external events of the week before the wedding and the internal psychological drama of the older generation. Brookner traces the multiple details of Kitty's elaborate social planning, complete with high drama on a small scale—focused on the chasm between the assumptions and behavior of the grandparents' generation and that of the young people. When Kitty asks Thea to house the best man, Steve, for the week before the wedding, Thea twice refuses before she reluctantly agrees out of a resentful sense of familial duty. Counterpoint to Kitty's public drama is Thea's tumultuous internal turmoil as she vacillates between her determination to keep her distance from Steve and to avoid entanglement with Kitty on the one hand, and the increasing pull toward connection and the surprising pleasure of intimacy on the other.

Although initially disinterested, Thea is invited to several pre-wedding events at the Levinsons'. At these events, she is helpful and makes connections that are unusual for her. She comes to the aid of Kitty and is confided in by Austin about the bank account he has secretly created to support their "hippie" son, Gerald, Ann's father. Thea starts to identify with Ann, as she, too, has felt distant from Kitty and the rest of Henry's family. She sees Ann being overwhelmed and ultimately convinces her of the benefits of accepting her grandparents' largesse. Perhaps because of her own sense of marginality, Thea develops a soft spot for her. As the events surrounding the wedding unfold, Thea begins to shift her perspective: she sees that she matters to Kitty, that Austin values her opinions, and that the young people rekindle her interest in the future.

Just as Olive Kitteridge takes for granted her own superiority prior to Henry's stroke, as Candida underestimates the importance of her friends before her divorce, and as Stella manages to avoid intimacy prior to retirement, so Thea considers her cautious and insular way of living admirable prior to Steve's arrival. For Thea, the prospect of hosting a strange young man in her flat is a frightening upset to her deeply entrenched routine, in which every day is carefully choreographed. Brookner's attention to the internal reverberations that belie the surface appearance of serenity reveals to us the gradual but significant change in Thea's self-perception.

Her marriage of fifteen placid and predictable years in her otherwise single life gave her quiet pleasure, and her habits are those of continuing self-sufficiency established as a young spinster in the years before she literally tripped and fell into Henry's arms when she was thirty-nine. Finally, she mattered to someone, and she provided for him a home life—a roof, food, and a haven away from his family home, where he had been living since his divorce with his sister, Rose. Before Henry's death, Thea took pleasure in their quiet days together, regular Sunday visits to see Rose, occasional walks in the park, and small dinner parties because they mattered to Henry. He provided for her a sense of meaning, took her on frequent holidays, and left her financially secure. During their marriage she considered herself his debtor, and it is only in the current timeline of the novel, years after his death, that she is able to think of herself apart from Henry, settled back into her pre-marriage routine. Thea now enjoys her solitude, welcomes her memories, loses herself in novels, is grateful for her garden, and realizes that her years with Henry have not changed her from the person she was before she met him.

Thea has chosen to be self-reliant and has been determined to appear satisfied. Yet in her old age, the mask of dullness she so carefully cultivated has "become the face, so that she was rigorously and genuinely dull." And she is no longer successful in controlling her awareness of "more troubled sensations" and metamorphosing them into detachment. Thea's careful routine as a single woman is an attempt to control potential emotional chaos by creating external order. She has repressed her sexuality since a traumatic and shameful affair in her youth that was driven by a desire to lose her virginity, having tired of waiting for "Mr. Right." He was an excellent lover and she an adept pupil, but their affair ended abruptly with the young man's suicide. Thea's mask of calm logic and routine was acquired the day she read of the suicide, and from that point forward she developed a reputation for being enigmatic and distant. After this experience, she resisted not only sex but also any affection, and focused on being an exemplary daughter and employee. After the death of both her parents, she sold the family house and purchased a flat, preparing for a solitary life as an old maid, a period that was interrupted by her marriage with Henry, and which she continues after his death. She never reveals her shameful secret to anyone. Not even Henry knew of her past, and he accepted her for what she had become: "a quiet, pleasant, rather dull, but infinitely reliable woman who never gave offence."

Thea considers her body solely in terms of function and

appearance, and her attitude toward it is troubling. Although the narrative describes her as trim and healthy except for a slight heart condition, she does not reveal any pleasure in her appearance or health. She has a bad moment every morning as she sees herself in the mirror as she applies cosmetics to keep up appearances while thinking of herself as packaged for the day once she gets dressed. She is convinced her body will betray her, and she is grateful Henry is not around to see her age. Thea is unknowingly shut off and shut down before the arrival of the visitors, and the wedding shakes her out of her cautious routine.

For the days surrounding the wedding, Thea is angry and resentful, not only at Kitty but also at her own disgruntled response to boarding a guest on her family's behalf. Thea is terrified by the idea of this man being in her flat, and it arouses in her an unidentified "archaic fear" that she has had to out-wit for her entire life. Kitty's insistence that he stay with her feels enormous, even as Thea recognizes how slight it must appear to others. She has plenty of room in her three-bedroom flat, but she has never hosted a guest and has avoided making any changes in the spare room where Henry took his naps and where he slept during his last illness. In fact, she has studi-ously avoided the spare room as if it were haunted despite her determined disbelief in all things nebulous or mysterious. She alternates between a determination to create boundaries and rules that will allow her to avoid interacting with Steve and a deeply ingrained sense of good manners that requires she at least make him comfortable.

Thea finally resolves to open the spare room and to brighten it up so that Steve will have no reason to criticize her hospitality. She ventures out to buy a new coverlet for the bed, is overwhelmed by the heat and the crowds, and, having forgotten to take her pills or to eat lunch, she nearly collapses getting out of the taxi in front of her flat. A neat, patient young man, who turns out to be Steve, rescues her, helps her inside, fetches her pills and a glass of water, and then silently waits for her to regain her equilibrium. She appreciates his help yet disapproves when he tells her he is not a close friend of the young couple and just tagged along on the promise of being put up by Ann's wealthy grandparents.

The unannounced early arrival of the young people and their lack of courtesy throw Thea and the other elders into a tizzy. The following day, when Thea and Steve meet Ann and David for tea at Kitty and Austin's apartment, the old experience the young as aliens. We see the politeness of the older generation in contrast to Ann's insouciance and David's false-seeming affability. Over tea, Ann casually mentions her pregnancy, and it occurs to Thea that what Ann really wants is to find her father. Thea begins to understand that Ann resents Kitty's elaborate wedding fuss because this is not her primary reason for being in London. Although Ann expected her grandparents to provide a wedding celebration, she wanted something very simple. Thea recognizes Kitty's attempt to bridge the chasm with expensive food and clothes as her customary response to fear. As Thea begins to feel empathy for Kitty and Austin, she also begins to enjoy the interruption of her placid life and to become interested in all the wedding preparations. She assumes the recent change in their relationship indicated by Kitty's plea for help and by Austin's unusual confidentiality is temporary, but she enjoys feeling included in the family.

Although Thea claims that Steve is no trouble, his pres- ence affects every moment of her day in that she is aware of him and constantly wonders what he is doing. Within just three days, she becomes increasingly attentive to providing hospitality, moving quickly from the initial disgruntlement to renting a car for his use during the remainder of his visit. She has no idea how he spends his days because he is as reclusive as she is. She admires him for qualities that mirror her own, and something about him makes her feel an unusual protectiveness, as if he needs nurturing. She sympathizes with him as the third party to David and Ann, a position with which she is familiar. At first, she is embarrassed that after so many years on her own, she is anxious and fearful of displeasing this stranger in her house. After never wanting children, she experiences an unexpected vulnerability at the sight of the young man's head moodily bent or the soles of his feet pressed together like a baby's under the breakfast table, and she recognizes how hard she has worked to create her stoic persona, and her disconnection not only from the erotic but also from the maternal. Although she has always been somewhat uncomfortable around men, her discomfort is eased when she discovers that Steve is gay when Ann tells Kitty that this is the reason no girlfriend has been invited to accompany him.

Although Thea is cautious with Steve, and even seems to disdain him at points, she notices that she feels alive in his presence. Before Steve leaves the house one day, she offers to make him dinner that evening, even loans him Henry's jacket because of the rain, and he good-naturedly offers to take her for a drive the next day. She gets caught up in anticipation, arranges an appointment at the hairdresser, shops for expensive dinner foods at the fancy delicatessen in Marylebone High Street. She prepares a lovely meal, accompanied by a good wine. As she looks at Steve across the dinner table, she feels a desire to appropriate a little more of her life while there is still time. She thinks of how provisional life is, and her spirits lift as she contemplates change. She is filled with a sense of living for the moment, she is flushed with the prospect of Sunday's drive to the countryside, and she drinks her wine gratefully, resolving to do so more often, and goes to bed feeling happy that she has more than a routine telephone call to break the silence of a dull Sunday. But the next morning Steve seems to have forgotten his invitation to Thea and leaves the house early to visit his parents in Cheltenham. She is devastated and mortified that she had mistaken friendliness for friendship. She gives no sign of her feelings, however, and rationalizes that nothing has actually been taken away from her.

After the wedding, when the three young people are in Paris on the honeymoon trip provided by Kitty and Austin, and Thea imagines she will never see them again, they send her a postcard with all three signatures. It sits prominently on Thea's table next to a kind letter from Austin, and she feels a new sense of connection to all of them. In response to this newly awakened sense of vitality, she surprises herself. In a single day she begins planning for a vacation, writes to an old friend, visits the new young doctor in the neighborhood rather than Henry's old doctor, and sees her solicitor. She changes her will, leaving her flat to Ann, sensing that this is the right thing to do and wondering whether it will eventually house all three of the visitors.

A dream near the end of the novel connects Thea with her childhood and puts her in touch with the repressed parts of herself. The dream takes place in a dull heaven that resembles her childhood neighborhood with its tedium and its air of obedience and allows Thea to "repossess her youth," while not being doomed to an eternity of such dullness. She realizes that her past exists only in her memory and cannot be shared by anyone else. Rather than insist on independence and solitude in her present life, she feels a new desire for closeness. She is newly aware of a certain collective fragility, and that it's important that she make connections with the family she has. After the dream, she begins to think of alternative deaths and heavens, and recalls the feisty elderly women she and Henry encountered on their travels in Italy, Spain, and Greece. She compares her daytime self of propriety to her waking fantasy of becoming like the loquacious old lady she and Henry encountered every day in Venice, drinking wine with strangers and not caring about public opinion. Thea realizes that the women in the sun are doppelgangers of sorts, signifying a part of her that is struggling for expression.

After her dreams, Thea feels refreshed and grateful for the family she has. The visitors have awakened her not only to the web of these connections but also to her long-repressed feelings and her physical senses: "She thought it marvelous that she could still stand at her window and watch the flight of a bird, could still (occasionally) eat with appetite, could still hear voices other than her own." Thea is also "aware of the need to make amends—for joylessness, for fatalism, for caution—in what time was left to her." More importantly, she has discovered that she matters, that she has a place in the lives of the young people and of Henry's cousins—not simply because of marriage but because of who she is.

Brookner's novel reminds me of the importance of taking risks, of accepting the initial discomfort of unfamiliar circumstances, and of the value of breaking out of imprisoning routines. The young, however ill-mannered, can be bracing to the old, and their inexperience can remind elders of their youthful selves. Whatever our age, we all want to matter to someone, and to sense that our lives have meaning. Thea begins to reprise her memories without repressing her feelings, and in allowing the resurgence of memories that she had surrounded with emotional scar tissue, she discovers an awakening to joy. Just as Olive and Candida begin to change after their losses and Stella reveals the possibility of opening to her feelings after Bracken's death, Thea begins to feel more alive after the visitors leave, and her awakening reminds me that it is never too late to face forward.

# BROKEN FOR YOU

## by Stephanie Kallos

Stephanie Kallos's *Broken for You* (2004) is a big, satisfying novel in which seventy-five-year-old Margaret Hughes, who is enormously wealthy and lives in a mansion in Seattle, learns that she has an inoperable brain tumor and may live only a year or so, even with treatment. Rather than sending her into depression, the brain tumor creates a sense of urgency, a carpe diem, and although we know the outcome from the beginning, the novel is not morbid because of the life she chooses before she dies. This novel's scope and large cast of characters with their multiple overlapping stories contrast with the narrow focus of Brookner's *Visitors*. *Broken for You* is a fairy tale for grown-ups, a cautionary tale about the costs of withdrawing from humanity, a reminder that broken lives can be pieced together, and a testimony to the resilience of the human spirit. Margaret's wealth allows her to be a fairy godmother, and her personal qualities allow her to be a surrogate mother, matchmaker, and financial guardian. She is finally able to express the love and compassion that have been frozen since the death of her eight-year-old son, Daniel, when she was in her mid-forties. This novel is gratifying to those who can temporarily suspend their disbelief and revel in its self-conscious and playful exploration of the tension between individual loss and historic loss. The novel, threaded with reminders of the Holocaust and the sins of the fathers being visited upon the children, nevertheless satisfies a reader's wishful fantasy that Margaret live out her remaining years.

Like the other books in this chapter, the novel's form is very consciously put together. In this case, mosaic, art made from repurposed broken objects, is the central metaphor of the novel, and Kallos intentionally creates an experience that's mosaic-like. The tripartite organization with its thirty-four chapters mimics a mosaic, as the narrative jumps from character to character, place to place, and moves both forward and backward in time. Kallos suffuses her novel with the importance of physical objects, which the novel suggests function as links to the past as well as to each other. In both obvious and subtle ways, the narrative portrays the breaking and mending, not only of objects but also of hearts, bodies, and lives.

Since the death of her little boy and subsequent divorce thirty years earlier, Margaret has lived alone, avoided most human contact, and tended the enormous and valuable porcelain collection she inherited from her father. Margaret married at age thirty-six, and her son Daniel's death was the result of a car accident. Her ex-husband, Stephen, was drunk behind the wheel. The marriage ended two years later, and Margaret was again alone, feeling cursed and doing penance for the sins of her blood (the ill-gotten wealth of her father during the Holocaust, when he smuggled out fine porcelain that had belonged to Jewish families and that now fills her inherited house). After decades of conversations with her porcelain objects, Margaret has nearly forgotten the sound of her own voice in public. Yet after learning of her brain tumor, she reaches out to strangers. Eventually, she not only fills her house with boarders who become her support system, but she literally breaks the porcelain, makes amends with the only original owner she can track down, and sponsors an art project that benefits the entire community.

The novel braids the lives of many emotionally wounded characters who each find some measure of healing and a sense of meaning in Margaret's home. However implausible its multiple coincidences, the novel gratifies our yearning for connection and happy endings, and creates a heroine who avoids many of the quagmires of the stereotypical limitations I outline in this book. I admire Margaret's spunk, her balanced approach to conventional medical advice, and her ability to listen and observe. Since her isolation after the death of her son, Margaret's talent for creativity and empathy has been restricted to her collection of objects; over the decades she has woven complex and individual background stories for them, and she draws on that finely honed imaginative power as a way to understand the emotionally damaged people who eventually become part of her supportive community.

Early in the novel, Margaret visits the doctor and discovers she has an inoperable brain tumor. We see the world through her eyes as the intimate third-person narrative portrays the physician's diagnostic explanation for her headaches, slips of the tongue, errors in cognition, apparitions. Although she has insisted he show her the images of her brain and tell her the names of things, Margaret is nearly nauseated by his references to "slices" of her brain, his tone-deaf questions about what interventions she wants, and his assumption that she will want to call her ex-husband with the news. I appreciate Margaret's irritation at his tone and his assumption that she needs a male shoulder on which to cry, and her internal response that having managed her own affairs nicely for most of her life, she would not be "railroaded, pitied, or bamboozled now." When she asks to be excused to use the restroom and then sneaks out of the building, the reader is on her side. We already know she will not recover; we sense she will want to change her life before her time runs out, and we trust that her defiance will continue.

Margaret's post-tumor transformation starts as the result of a seemingly random question she poses to a waitress shortly after her diagnosis. Although she usually avoids contact with other people, she feels hungry and nauseous and stops at a small, empty café, where she tries not to stare at the waitress's pierced nostril. She silently calls her "Nose Ring." Margaret orders four desserts, including whipped cream on the flan. While looking at her desserts, she reviews treatment options and recalls the prognosis is at best a 25 percent chance of prolonging her life by several years. She realizes her choice is between having invasive treatment and dying sooner or later, and having no treatment and dying sooner or later. When Nose Ring notices she has not tasted anything, she asks if something is wrong. Margaret poses what she assures Nose Ring is a trite question, asking her how she would spend her time if she found out she had only a short while to live. The girl replies that she would think about whatever it is that scares her most, "relationship-wise," and then do it. Do the opposite of what she's always done. Margaret is startled at the difference between the girl's answer and the cliché response she had anticipated. Nose Ring continues, "It would be a last chance, wouldn't it? To break all your old bad habits?"

As the café fills with customers, Margaret, for the first time in decades, does not mind that she is no longer alone.

Her appetite returns, and she drafts an advertisement on the back of the bill. "Room for rent in large Capitol Hill home. $250. All utilities included. Month-to-month. Private bath." She realizes she must first consult her housemates, the porcelain figurines with which she has lived for years and to which she is devoted. At first, I found her relationship with the soup tureens, the game pie dishes, the teapots and casseroles, the figures, the teacups, and the gold-encrusted inkstands amusing. But as she seriously considers which objects to consult first as she mentally travels through the many collections throughout the fifteen thousand square feet of the house, the reader sees the bizarre scope of her collection and the extent of her mental instability, showing the ramifications of her isolation over the years. Burdened by the terrible guilt of her father's financial gain during World War II, she devotes her life to caring for the objects and searching for their rightful owners. Fueled by the death of her son and her inability to locate surviving owners of the extensive collection, she had isolated herself and descended into a kind of madness. By renting out rooms in her house, she begins the frightening work of caring about people again.

Margaret and her first renter, Wanda, initially disappoint each other; they seem to have nothing in common and even appear a bit crazy to one another. When Wanda arrives at Margaret's house, we learn that she's a bit unbalanced, divulging her personal details to Margaret on the front porch before even entering the house. We later discover she is good at fixing things when she mends a broken teacup for Margaret. She is also a skilled stage manager with an unusual ability to manage sensitive people. We soon learn that Margaret and Wanda have more in common than they first thought. Both of them have experienced unusual childhoods, and both lost their mothers when they were children. When Wanda was only six, her father left her with her aunt and her family of eight children to go search for Wanda's mother. He never returned. A subplot of the novel follows Wanda's attempts to find a boyfriend who abandoned her and her chance encounters with a man who turns out to be her father.

Although the plot keeps us turning the pages to discover what happens next, and although Margaret's previously reclusive life becomes increasingly full and joyful, we never lose track of her death sentence and the symptoms of her tumor. As the headaches increase in frequency and severity, Margaret eventually returns to the doctor, who now offers noninvasive treatments that Margaret considers acceptable: prescription medications, biofeedback techniques, dietary and vitamin supplement advice, and regularly scheduled visits for CT scans, as well as encouragement to engage a live-in nurse.

After this second visit to the doctor, Margaret once again wanders the streets to regain her equilibrium. This time she finds herself in downtown Seattle for the first time since before her years of seclusion, and she tries to find any building that has not changed over the years. She finally locates the Hotel Orleans, where she and Stephen had spent their honeymoon. She stops to admire it and is approached by an elderly hotel valet, Mr. MacPherson, who initially offers her assistance and then reminisces about the beautiful old hotel. Their conversation continues, and he invites her inside for continental breakfast. As she reluctantly leaves after paying her bill, Mr. MacPherson runs halfway down the block after her, clasps her hands, and invites her to return and to call him Gus. Later Gus tells her "there's no point in goin' round the barn" at his age and that he would be honored if she would spend more time with him. She discovers that "spending time with him was the spiritual equivalent of building bone mineral density." With Gus and his infectious passion for the Hotel Orleans, for French language and culture, for books and ideas, for art, and for staying young, Margaret is "full of light, and laughing." She'd assumed she was "through with all this," but after their first kiss, she brews herself tea and reflects on Gus's remark that "We don't 'grow old' but rather 'when we stop growing, we *are* old.'" When Margaret asks Wanda to help break her wedding china the morning following, Wanda finds it "tremendously comforting" to be living with someone who is as "deeply aggrieved and crazy as she was."

Margaret's second boarder is Susan, a nurse seeking hospice work after being abandoned by the family for whom she had been a nanny for many years. As Margaret's tumor grows, she needs a live-in nurse, but she does not tell Wanda or Gus the real reason she rents a room to Susan. Margaret initially tells Wanda that Mr. MacPherson is not her boyfriend but her companion. But after she tells Gus about her health and confesses that she would like to spend whatever time she has left with him, he joins the household, "and the two of them began living in sin." The household thus grows to four.

After Wanda returns to the house after being hospitalized following a car accident, she moves into a first-floor room that's been fitted for a disabled person by Troy, her former assistant. She refuses to eat or to leave the room for weeks, chooses to remain mute, and seriously considers suicide. Margaret is unobtrusive and eventually tells Wanda the history of her family. It is at this moment that Margaret asks Wanda to help her break all the remaining porcelain, not only the objects filling the house but also those we learned are stored in warehouses. It does not occur to Margaret to try to sell the porcelain and donate the proceeds to Holocaust survivors. Wanda contemplates her choices: suicide or breaking things, or some combination of both, and two weeks later she finally emerges from her room and ends her silence by asking for a complete tour of the house. She asks Margaret for the stories she has imagined for each piece of porcelain and even has Margaret write down some of the stories. Margaret hires Troy to install an escalator for Wanda, knowing she will soon need it for herself, and invites him to move into the house. He chooses Daniel's room and handles all the building projects. Eventually the household includes a physical therapist and a sous chef, Bruce, who feeds them all and quotes his Jewish grandmother who taught him "cooking is a prayer, a gift of love, it's family. It's standing in the company of your ancestors and feeling their hands, helping you."

Wanda, who has always been skilled at mending broken objects, gradually postpones thoughts of suicide as she begins to create mosaics from the pieces of broken porcelain. "The more she worked, the more she became familiar with a kind of magic which only happened when she let go . . . Only when she was quiet inside, when her mind was a large empty room instead of many cluttered ones, only then did the magic happen." She enters the Land of No Words, where the physical rituals of her work—breaking, sorting, planning, adhering, and grouting, hold her together.

Just before Thanksgiving, when he is able to leave Seattle to continue his search for Wanda's mother, the man who turns out to be Wanda's absent father is summoned to Margaret's house in response to an urgent phone call from her attorney.

For years Margaret has hired experts to try to locate survivors from the camps so she could return their porcelain. Most had died, but a survivor whose daughter and husband died in the camps surfaces and is traced to Seattle. The woman has died, but because she named Wanda's father in her will, he is called by the attorney, interrupting his plans to leave town.

When he comes to Margaret's house on Thanksgiving Day, he is required to break a plate as part of the entrance ritual of the enormous house that now includes the Crazy Plate Academy, a volunteer organization that offers classes and fosters community through artistic collaboration. He eventually learns Margaret's story, is invited to stay for Thanksgiving dinner, and in response to his offer to help, he is told to visit Tink (Wanda's professional name) in her studio. He realizes who she is and does not tell her he is her missing father, but he does change his mind about leaving and decides to stay for dinner.

As preparations for Thanksgiving continue, Margaret's health is quickly deteriorating, and she must be lifted between her bed and a wheelchair. Her mind slips easily between her present reality and a dream state. Kallos devotes an entire chapter to Margaret's dream in which she is united with everyone of note in her life and is forgiven for her father's sins in World War II. Not until the following chapter do readers realize that Margaret, seated in her wheelchair, has been wafted away to her death as her surrogate family celebrates around the Thanksgiving table.

In her will, Margaret had distributed her enormous wealth with fairy-tale generosity. Unknown to her housemates, Margaret had wisely invested their rent money, and they each inherit a lucrative investment portfolio that will allow them to continue living in her house and will support the continuation and expansion of the art center. The novel ends with the remaining broken characters coming together and forging new connections. The narrator reminds us that "the broken are not always gathered together, of course, and not all mysteries of the flesh are solved. We speak of 'senseless tragedies,' but really: Is there any other kind?" We are told that we never stop looking in our dreams for the ones who have "become part of the unreachable horizon." And "although we can never stop carrying the heavy weight of love" in our lives, "we can transfigure what we carry." We also can "shatter it and send it whirling into the world so that it can take shape in some new way."

I include this novel of loss and redemption because of its refusal of the standard plots for old women. I appreciate the ways in which the plot is wryly self-aware in how it negotiates the familiar trope of deathbed epiphanies. Kallos embraces the possibilities of the classic plot but shifts it with her focus on the elderly woman as the protagonist who relishes a series of second chances. The doctor's report and Nose Ring's thoughtful speculation set things in motion. However implausible the accumulation of chance meetings, mended lives, and dreams fulfilled, the novel satisfies our desire for material and spiritual healing. I enjoyed the portrayal of Margaret's choice to come out of her self-imposed exile and learn to live and to create with the help of Wanda, Gus, Susan, Bruce, Wanda's father, and Troy. Filled with fairy-tale elements and the power of art to transform pain and loss into beauty, the novel is a joyful celebration of life right up to the end.

# ASTRID AND VERONIKA

## by Linda Olsson

Linda Olsson's 2003 novel, *Astrid and Veronika*, is a compact book with a simple plot—the development of a friendship between an older and a much younger woman. In the novel, the events that unfold reveal to each of the women much about themselves and about one another. Astrid, like Margaret in *Broken for You*, whose concern for Wanda allowed her to come out of her isolation, only discovers how to live in the final months of her life as she begins to care about Veronika. Both of these novels portray elderly women who have withdrawn into self-imposed solitude in large houses. Motherless, childless, and without friends, they avoid other people. Just as Wanda opens Margaret to paying loving attention to another person, so Veronika's illness soon after moving into the rental house stirs in Astrid tendrils of human caring. Also like *Broken for You*, *Astrid and Veronika* has fairy-tale elements that infuse its message that loss can create opportunities for acceptance and healing.

After an arranged marriage to a much older man and the tragic death of her only child, Astrid has avoided the outer world, secluding herself in the home built by her grandfather in a small Swedish village. Veronika has recently rented the nearby house as a refuge in which to write her second novel

following the drowning of her fiancé, James, in a surfing accident in Australia. The novel richly evokes the importance
of intergenerational connection for the old and the young, a
theme that threads through many of the novels included in
this book. Olsson uses the natural cycles of the Swedish countryside over one year, from March to March, to mirror the
thawing of Astrid's frozen spirit and the resurgence of Veronika's writing as the gradual outcome of voicing their pain to
one another. The narration alternates between a third-person
omniscient storyteller and first-person accounts by Astrid and
Veronika as they confide their stories to each other. Olsson's
spare and clear-eyed prose and her empathy for her characters
without either idealizing them or reducing their complexity
raise the book above cliché or easy sentiment.

Astrid's secrets are truly horrific; in many ways she resembles the witch of fairy tales. Later in the book it's revealed
to the reader, when Astrid shares it with Veronika, that she
smothered her newborn baby daughter, Sara, rather than allow
her to grow up in the world of pain that Astrid knew. Astrid's
account of the magical day she spent with her daughter in the
outdoors the day she killed her mirrors the account of another
perfect day with her mother, also named Sara, before she committed suicide, the details of which eluded Astrid for many
years. In both accounts, the love and the oneness with nature
make the unbearable acts even more inexplicable. What
internal pain or psychological disorder could ever explain the
devastation in both instances? As readers, we search for clues
in the story. We wonder if Astrid's father somehow caused the
pain in his wife, and in his daughter. I myself pondered other
tales in which mothers have killed their children to protect
them from abuse. Perhaps Astrid is like the grandmother in

Mary E. Wilkins Freeman's "Old Woman Magoun" (1909), or Sethe in Toni Morrison's *Beloved* (1987), trying to save an innocent young girl from inevitable suffering? Perhaps, yet Olsson's tale has more in common with fairy tales than with historical fiction. The tale does not provide sufficient attention to either the baby or Astrid's mother to create sorrow for them. Olsson, instead, provides the reader glimpses through Astrid's previously suppressed memories of the experiences that shaped her and that led to her belief that nothing good can possibly last.

Astrid has secluded herself for decades in the large family home outside the village where she has lived her entire life; local villagers call her a witch. Both Astrid and Veronika crave solitude, and each is trying to escape painful memories that interrupt their sleep and torment them by day. In order to cope, Astrid has established a strict routine: she tries never to leave home except to wander in the surrounding forest or to make rare visits to the village for necessities. She has reduced her living space to a downstairs bedroom and kitchen. Veronika has nightmares of the sea, the enemy that killed James on an otherwise perfect day together. Because she was abandoned by her mother as well, and raised by her father, whose work took them all over the world, she hopes that returning to Sweden, the place of her birth, will bring her some solace. Her plan is to pour her love for James into her novel.

Veronika arrives on a windy night in March with flurries of snow covering dangerous ice. She can barely distinguish the two isolated houses in the dark. She carries in her few belongings, following the path illuminated by the headlights of her rental car. Darkness, shadow, and absolute silence mark her arrival. For Veronika, feeling like an orphan tenant, "it was time to find new words." For weeks, however, she is unable to write and can only stare at the blank screen of her laptop. Each day on her solitary morning walk, she passes Astrid's house, waves to the empty window, and wonders whether the old woman described to her as a witch by the village storekeeper is aware of her existence. After three weeks of no contact between the two women, Veronika becomes ill on the last day of April, Valborgsmass Eve, the celebration of the end of winter and the beginning of spring. In her fevered state, she has nightmares about James. Curious after days of watching the house and seeing no sign of life, Astrid knocks on her door, sees that Veronika is ill, says nothing, but returns with a thermos of tea. The morning after Astrid's silent visit, Veronika vaguely recalls her neighbor bringing tea, and were it not for the evidence of the blue thermos on the kitchen table, she would have thought it was part of her delirium.

Their friendship begins in silence, and nearly a week later, when she begins to recover, Veronika walks to Astrid's house to return the thermos. She surprises herself by asking the old woman to join her on her first walk since getting out of bed. The old woman shakes her head, but after a shared silence, she says, "Wait," closes her door, and reappears wearing "a threadbare cardigan over a checked man's shirt, corduroy trousers, and a pair of black rubber boots with the tops cut off." On this first walk, Veronika finds herself falling into the rhythm of the other woman's steps as she follows her across the road through the strip of forest where there is then room to walk side by side. Wild anemones dot the bank on the southern side; the bright blue petals are surprising signs of new life among blackened leaves and flax-colored grass.

Suddenly Astrid stops and says, "My father used to grow flax here," and we sense the beginning of an inner thawing. She then remarks with scorn that her husband sold the land. She leads Veronika to a secluded spot beside the river where they rest for a while in silence. Eventually Astrid introduces herself, admitting she knows Veronika's name because there are no secrets in the village except those like her own, which have to be well guarded. She insists she has no interest in other people's lives and does not want to know Veronika's secrets. Uncharacteristically soon, however, she tells Veronika about her mother and her memories of coming to this very spot along the riverbank as a little girl. She blushes and wonders why she is saying all this, and Veronika responds by saying that she has no memories of the mother who abandoned her. Astrid tells Veronika about the day when she was six and her mother twenty-seven, the day her mother committed suicide; her mother was found three days later in a small hotel in Stockholm. She had slipped her little gold locket under Astrid's pillow, and though nobody told Astrid what had happened until years later, she knew instinctively that she had lost her mother that evening. From then on, she had accepted loneliness as inevitable and permanent. She abruptly breaks off her story to Veronika, and they return to their houses without speaking.

The following day, Astrid knocks on Veronika's door and invites her for afternoon coffee. She serves waffles on her mother's china that had been stored for many years. Veronika gives Astrid a copy of her first book, which she compares to a child that has to be left to live its own life. She tells Astrid about travelling with her father, a diplomat, and being looked after by nannies. Astrid tells Veronika about her only trip away from the village as a ten-year-old child sent to her cold and distant grandfather in Stockholm with no explanation. She offers to show Veronika her house and tells her about weaving rugs from her father's clothing after his death, and later doing the same with her husband's clothes when he was taken to the rest home. Without explanation, she asserts, "It gives me pleasure to walk on them."

Several weeks later, having had no further contact from the old woman, Veronika leaves in Astrid's mailbox an invitation to come for dinner. Olsson describes the meal in such detail that the reader feels present to the aromas and tastes, as well as the images of hot-smoked trout, wilting dill on steaming potatoes, sliced lemon, pungent cheese. Veronika plays a recording of Lars-Erik Larsson's "Förklädd Gud (God in Disguise)," and the music brings a sudden flash of memory in which she is preparing food with James. The memory hits her with an almost physical force; her hands stop moving, and she hears Astrid's footsteps on the porch.

It is over dinner that Astrid admits that lately she has felt it would be a relief to tell someone her version of at least some of the truth. After listening to a musical recording with lyrics by Erik Axel Karlfeldt, Astrid softly begins to sing and admits that she used to love singing with her mother. She provides liquor made and forgotten decades ago from wild strawberries and compares the recently rediscovered berry patch that she thought had completely died to the memories and secrets a person believes have been erased, but that are still there if they have a wish to uncover them. She shares with Veronika the story of her first love at age sixteen, meeting in the forest where the wild strawberries grew. He disappeared, and later she learned that he was killed in a fall from the loft in the hay barn during harvest. This experience only reinforced what she already knew since losing her mother—that nothing good could last. "It's more than sixty years ago, but my plants are still alive." She equates the strawberry patch with memories of that one summer—finally retrieved. Astrid confides, "Telling you about that summer has given it back to me . . . It was never lost, you see; I just refused to listen." Veronika compares her own memories to shards, fragments that still hurt to the touch. She tells Astrid about meeting James, about the growth of their relationship, and Astrid whispers, "Always remember your love."

Later that summer, as Astrid learns her husband is dying in his nursing home, and in the light of her new friendship with Veronika, Astrid realizes how much she has lost in her years of isolation. She tells Veronika about the marriage her father arranged against her wishes when she was eighteen: "I married death." We glimpse her lonely childhood, paternal abuse, and her loveless marriage to an older man for whom she was a possession that came with the property. After years of avoiding him, she insists, "I am not afraid of facing him, I am afraid of facing myself. Such a long wait. I allowed life to slip away while I nurtured my hatred inside this house. Now I realize I made it my prison . . . the only bonds were those I made myself." She has waited a lifetime for this release, starting with the day she married him. Now she tells Veronika, "it was never about him . . . The marriage was just the defining moment. It was the day I gave up my life." The following day, Veronika accompanies Astrid to the rest home, where Astrid tells her husband she has come to watch him die, although he is so near death she has no idea whether or not he can hear her. Veronika waits until Astrid tells her it is over, and they arrive home at the dawn of Midsummer's Eve. Veronika has stayed awake all night with Astrid, and that morning she tells her about Johan, her lover before James, whose grief at being abandoned by her after assuming they would marry was so great, "it was like watching someone die." Astrid tells Veronika it is important to remember the face of a loved one, and that she has lost her daughter's face.

Later, while preparing for dinner and listening to Veronika's recording of Brahms's Sonata for Violin and Piano, No. 3 in D Minor, Astrid bursts into tears. Unknown to Veronika, the second movement had been Astrid's mother's favorite. She has not heard this music in over seventy years. Astrid links the music with her mother and her daughter: "I killed the music, and I killed my child." Until hearing the music, she has never allowed herself to cry for her daughter, or for herself, "for the little girl who was me. Or for the young woman I grew up to become." She insists, "It was me. It was always about me. Because my love wasn't strong enough . . . perhaps it was that my hatred was too strong."

Over dinner that evening, Astrid tells Veronika the secret she has never told anyone, of how she smothered her baby, Sara, to death after spending an enchanted day together outdoors in the secret place in the forest where the wild strawberries grew. Afterward, she rocked Sara in her arms all night, screamed until her voice broke, and returned home the next morning. She bathed her, dressed her in her baptismal gown, brushed her hair, put her in her bed, and smoothed the blanket. Then she went downstairs and told her husband, "Your child is dead." Astrid ends her account, "and afterwards there was only silence." In response to this, Veronika gently pulls Astrid to her feet, holds her tightly, and whispers softly, "Oh,

Astrid, my dearest Astrid." Astrid lets out a cry of such enormous pain it seems unbearable to release. Their sobs mingle. Astrid tells Veronika that in listening to her own words, she realizes they tell a different story from the one she has carried all these years. "I think that if we can find the words, and if we can find someone to tell them to, then perhaps we can see things differently. But I had no words, and I had nobody."

Four months after Veronika's arrival in the village, Veronika and Astrid go into town to shop and celebrate Veronika's birthday. Veronika has not contacted anyone on the mobile phone James gave her on her previous birthday, nor has she listened to the recorded messages from her father. On her birthday, she is flooded with memories of her previous birthday with James, "on the other side of the earth. In another life." Astrid declares it will be her birthday celebration as well, and they spend the day together, going out for lunch, eating ice cream, and swimming in the lake. The day is filled with laughter, mutual support, and remembering to breathe. So simple and yet so essential. Astrid reads a poem by Karin Boye to Veronika, and repeats the line, "Let me sing you gentle songs." Astrid says she is taking in everything, and that this day is enough to satisfy her. Veronika wears her greenstone pendant from James for the first time since he died and says, "I think I can see the beauty again," to which Astrid responds, "Yes, there is beauty. You just have to have the heart and you can see it anywhere." That night Astrid prepares their birthday dinner using a recipe of her mother's, serves it on her mother's china, and dresses in beautiful clothes her mother had once worn. Since her husband's funeral, she has allowed herself to unpack more of her mother's belongings. Her birthday gift to Veronika is her mother's small leather-bound diary, with the admonition not to read it until she is ready. "I have read it so many times, each page is clear in my mind . . . I want to see it in the hands of someone who will protect it." Veronika tells Astrid she has given her the best birthday she ever had, and Astrid reassures her, " . . . it's mine, too."

Over the summer, they adopt a routine of daily walks and weekly dinners. In mid-August, Veronika invites Astrid for a traditional crayfish dinner. Veronika's father has called to tell her he misses her and is coming back to Sweden for early retirement. As Veronika wonders what to do next, Astrid assures her, "If we listen to ourselves we know what it is we have to do." She notes that Veronika has been there half a year and that when she is ready, she will know what to do next. In the following weeks, Astrid shows Veronika all her secret places. They pick lingonberries and forage for bright orange mushrooms. She takes her to her secret circle in the midst of the forest where the wild strawberries grow. Back home, she teaches her to make jam from the berries, and they eat an omelet made with the fresh mushrooms. She talks about why autumn is her favorite season, a time to set one's house in order and prepare for winter.

On All Saints' Day, the first Saturday in November, Veronika packs to leave the rental house to meet her father in Stockholm. She realizes this is the first time in her life she is facing a departure that would be tinged with sadness. She begins to read the diary from Astrid. That afternoon she and Astrid visit the graveyard, and Astrid points out the spot where she will be buried next to Sara, with the simple plaque bearing just their names and the words, "Now let me sing you gentle songs." They celebrate their final evening together with a meal of Astrid's pancakes, and they promise not to say good-bye, just to wave silently in the morning.

The narrative breaks after Veronika moves out and goes to visit her father. Suddenly it is March again, four months after the farewell dinner and exactly a year since Veronika's first arrival. She returns to Astrid's house after stopping in the neighboring village to pick up keys from the man who is managing Astrid's estate. This is where it's revealed to the reader that Astrid has died and that Veronika has inherited Astrid's house. In the envelope with the house keys and Astrid's mother's golden locket is a poignant letter in which she urges Veronika not to grieve. She indicates that she has chosen her death. She also thanks Veronika, and tells her always to remember her love and not to suppress her memories, reminding her that although you can make yourself believe that they have been erased, they are still there if you look closely and if you have a wish to uncover them.

In the letter, Astrid imagines Veronika entering the house she has readied for her and speculates that Veronika has been searching for a home and will find a refuge here. Astrid writes: "You have known me as no other person has . . . I am not sad that my insight came so late. I am grateful that it came at all . . . you have given me a new perspective. You pulled me out into the bright life again, opened my eyes. Made the ice thaw." She urges Veronika to live, to take risks, to see the beauty and the music in life. Throughout the novel, Olsson quotes poetry, and the gentle songs remain with the reader, softening the heartache that has been shared and allowing the light, the music, and the beauty to linger.

I am touched by this novel in which an old woman, for the first time in her life, is able to tell her painful story. In the telling, it is clear that she begins to understand herself. Astrid's gift of the large, sturdy home originally built with love is literally and figuratively a place of her own in which Veronika will have the space and the freedom to write. Astrid gives Veronika the legacy of home and story she was unable to provide her baby daughter, and she offers her the wisdom of a surrogate mother. Astrid's story becomes Veronika's second book. The novel closes in a single page where Veronika smiles and whispers that she has finished writing Astrid's story and given it the title "Let Me Sing You Gentle Songs."

Olsson's novel is a "gentle song" in which a very old woman who has lost everything and a young woman who feels as if she has lost everything find in one another the acceptance and love that allow them to remember the loving moments they had each nearly lost. They literally feed and nurture one another, and in telling one another their stories, they begin to heal. Veronika's terrifying nightmares end as she gradually learns from Astrid the cycles of nature and of grief that allow her to inherit not only the home but also the best of Astrid's hard-won wisdom. The witch and the young woman lost in the dark find each other, and in their connection and trust, light and hope, like the seasons, return.

# CONCLUSION

At first glance, the protagonists of the six novels chosen for this chapter appear to have little in common. They live in England, Sweden, and the United States, in cities and small towns and villages. Although five of the six have previously been married, two of them are estranged from adult children, two have mourned the early deaths of their children, and two of them have never had children. Only one of the six has always known that she never wanted a husband or children, preferring instead to focus on her career. Yet each of them values her independence and enjoys economic stability and generally good health, and each has not only a room of her own but also a home. I have grouped them into this chapter because of what they share: a late-in-life crisis that, like an earthquake, creates sudden fissures in the earth that propel them into unexplored territories of the self.

These narratives do not end "happily ever after." Rather, a crisis forces each woman to make unexpected choices, to examine her familiar sense of herself, to reprise her opinions of others, and to take risks she would otherwise not have considered. Changes in the self do not come automatically or easily. Because each protagonist is both believable and capable of discovery, compromise, forgiveness, and kindness, these stories help to deflect a common narrative that life after sixty is a downward spiral to death.

Olive Kitteridge has been relatively comfortable in her marriage and career for decades. Prior to her husband, Henry's, death, she has mourned the death of their shared dreams for their only son, Christopher. While Henry is alive, Olive holds him responsible for everything that disappoints rather than taking any blame herself. Yet even Olive is capable of psychological growth and of reaching out beyond her harsh judgments of others.

Candida Wilton, unlike Olive, has not worked for a living since her apparently perfect marriage to Andrew, her Prince Charming. Her coldness not only to him but also to her three daughters has estranged them all, and everyone takes Andrew's side against her when he abandons her for another woman. However, Candida is still capable of self-reflection, and it is satisfying to watch her start to temper her harsh judgments of others and begin to value friendship.

Of the six protagonists in this chapter, Stella, who prides herself on her anthropological skills in a career of examining kinship patterns, is the least capable of intimacy and self-knowledge. Her mandatory retirement leaves her disoriented, without the structure of her career to define her. As readers, we recognize the strength of narrative assumptions about marriage when we are surprised by Stella's rejection of offers from both Richard and Judith to combine households in retirement. At the novel's end, we wonder what her future will hold and whether or not the hints of intimacy Stella briefly experiences with her dog, Bracken, will develop in unexpected ways in her future.

Thea's crisis—hosting a wedding guest—would seem trivial if we did not recognize her fear of change in the routine and ritual that provide scaffolding for her life since her husband, Henry's, death. Their congeniality and friendship, while not apparently sexual, created for her an identity that allowed her to be part of something beyond herself. She remains in their house, which had been hers since before their marriage, and she carefully maintains a distance from others up until the time of the wedding. Her transformation is perhaps the most nuanced and subtle, and yet her development from quiet despair, bordering on depression, to a sense of hope and expectation is powerful and gratifying.

The stories of Margaret and Astrid move into the landscape of fairy tale or elder tale, and their tragedies are nearly impossible to comprehend. Yet their movement beyond isolation into new friendship after so many years of pain is deeply satisfying. Each of them leaves a legacy, as does Thea, to the next generation. Each faces her own death with a quiet assurance that she has been unconditionally loved and with the knowledge that her life and her death will make a difference to someone else who has been deeply wounded and has blossomed in the shared community of truth-telling and acceptance.

I set aside these novels with appreciation for their authors' imaginative exploration of life beyond happily ever after into unfamiliar territory where what comes next includes forgiveness, growth, and love. In this chapter I celebrate the importance of opening up rather than shutting down in the face of unbearable loss. I celebrate the possibility of change— subtle or profound—when one has assumed its impossibility. Each of these stories includes the risk of a step out of solitude, a giving of space, sometimes literally. Thea allows a guest into her very private house, Margaret takes in boarders, and Astrid reaches out to her visiting neighbor.

Each of these women of a certain age suffers unwelcome change that she experiences as earth shaking—the death of a husband, divorce, retirement, housing a stranger, an untreatable brain tumor, the loss of a mother. And in each situation, instead of shutting down and feeling helpless, she eventually takes unexpected risks, gains insight into herself, and deepens her life. Such narratives encourage us to share our stories of loss and grief, to face our own fears and biases, to reassemble the broken pieces of our lives after profound loss, and to seek the hidden strawberries and the lost music, realizing it is never too late to find wholeness and joy.

Chapter 5

# Defying Expectations

*They May Not Mean To, But They Do* (2016)
by Cathleen Schine

*All Passion Spent* (1931) by Vita Sackville-West

*The Fountain of St. James Court; or, Portrait of the
Artist as an Old Woman* (2013)
by Sena Jeter Naslund

*The Love Ceiling* (2009) by Jean Davies Okimoto

*The Little Old Lady Who Broke All the Rules*
(2014) by Catharina Ingelman-Sundberg

*Etta and Otto and Russell and James* (2014)
by Emma Hooper

M any of the stories gathered in this book end in death—as do all lives. However, in the final years of life, an old woman can still make choices and resist the norms, not only of the larger society but also of her immediate family. In the previous chapter, I discussed books in which a woman who has walled herself off from new connections and experiences is challenged by a late-in-life crisis to open herself to new possibilities for growth, friendship, and healing. The women in this chapter make even more drastic changes, stretching the common plots about domesticity and creativity and breaking the mold for fictional old ladies. Each of these six novels portrays a woman who defies expectations, which makes them particularly delightful for the reader who may not have anticipated such surprises.

In each of the first two novels, Cathleen Schine's *They May Not Mean To, But They Do* and Vita Sackville-West's *All Passion Spent*, an elderly woman who has always put her husband and children first defies the wishes and interference of her adult children after her husband's death and determines how she wants to live the rest of her life, choosing her own friends and deciding where she wants to live. Both novels use humor in their depiction of the strongly held opinions of the children and their surprise at the determination of their strong-willed octogenarian mothers. Schine's Joy Bergman refuses to move in with either of her children, preferring to remain in her rent-controlled Manhattan apartment with her small dog. Sackville-West's Lady Slane shocks her six children by refusing their greedy offers to manage her finances and living conditions, and she announces her purchase of a small house in Hampshire, where she moves accompanied only by her beloved servant, Genoux. She forbids her family to visit, saying she welcomes no visitors younger than seventy.

The protagonists of the second pair of novels share a passion for artistic expression and a love of their children, but they are otherwise very different women. In Sena Jeter Naslund's *The Fountain of St. James Court; or, Portrait of the Artist as an Old Woman*, Kathryn Callaghan completes her third novel—the fictional account of the real-life eighteenth-century painter Elisabeth Vigée-Le Brun, which provides the backstory of the novel—and manages to brandish a gun and save the life of her adult son at the end of the novel, which takes place over the course of a single day. Jean Davies Okimoto's *The Love Ceiling* portrays Anne Kuroda Duppstadt, who begins to pursue her art late in life, honoring her dying mother's request to reject the internalized put-down by her father, a narcissistic and famous artist. Okimoto's novel depicts Annie's struggles to pursue her painting and firmly but gently bring her husband and adult children on board. Ultimately, Annie, unlike Kathryn, manages to have all three—husband, motherhood, and art—in this unusual but realistic account of the ways in which the people we love can be the ceiling we must break through to realize our talents.

The final two novels are the most surprising. Catharina Ingelman-Sundberg's novel *The Little Old Lady Who Broke All the Rules* is set in Sweden, but its portrayal of stereotypes of old people translates easily into American society. Martha Andersson, age seventy-nine, and her four best friends break out of their dismal retirement home, call themselves "The League of Pensioners," and pull off a museum robbery that lands them in prison, which they imagine will be an improvement over their retirement home. This rollicking tale is plot driven, amusing the reader while subtly exposing the ageism in a society that underestimates the intellects and appetites of the elderly. Emma Hooper's *Etta and Otto and Russell and James* is an enchanting, strange, quirky tale in which eighty-three-year-old Etta leaves her husband, Otto, a handwritten note and a stack of his favorite recipes before setting off on foot to see the Atlantic Ocean. She is joined by a talking coyote she names James. This delicate portrayal of love among Etta, Otto, and their childhood friend Russell is as mysterious and magical as it is precise in rendering memories and current events, dreams and magic.

For readers who feel limited by the habitual roles of their lives, each of these novels reminds us that regardless of expectations and habits, even in advanced age, it is possible to be true to one's inner desires.

# THEY MAY NOT MEAN TO, BUT THEY DO

## by Cathleen Schine

Cathleen Schine's 2016 novel, *They May Not Mean To, But They Do*, opens with the Philip Larkin epigraph "They fuck you up, your mum and dad. They may not mean to, but they do." Yet by the novel's end we agree with the protagonist, Joy Bergman's, clever rephrasing of Larkin, "They fuck you up, your son and daughter. They may not mean to, but they do." Eighty-six-year-old Joy flouts the well-meaning expectations of her adult children by insisting on caring for her beloved husband single-handedly at home as he slips into dementia and then, after his funeral, pursuing her relationship with one of his friends, against their objections. She loves her family deeply yet rejects their good intentions, instead following her own fiercely held sense of herself and living on her own terms. She shows how even in the face of loss and conflict, it is possible to flourish in old age.

Feisty, opinionated, and set in her ways, Joy is admirable. She has been the breadwinner of the family for decades since her charming but impractical husband, Aaron, lost the company he inherited. She loves her New York neighborhood with its cacophony of voices, its take-out places, the familiar doorman, and the nearby park. Her children and grandchildren adore her, and she has lifelong friendships. She strives to avoid being viewed as eccentric yet freely carries three shopping bags filled with food, drink, and whatever else she imagines she may need whenever she leaves the apartment. Although the novel includes scenes without Joy—focusing on her adult children too, Molly and her wife, Freddie, in California and Daniel and his wife and two daughters in New Jersey—the matriarch is the heart of the narrative. Flashbacks provide an account of Aaron and Joy's life together, and the novel moves beyond Aaron's death into Joy's renewed friendship with her widowed college sweetheart, Karl.

We learn that Joy is both loved and unloved for the same reasons, and that she has shared an enviable closeness with her husband. She is disconcerting, intimate and remote, talkative and "yet she heard everything you said or thought you might say." Although she is wise, deep, and intuitive, and a person to whom people confide their darkest secrets, she is also scatter-brained and easily distractible. Her husband was sentimental, unreliable, brimming with love and charm, and a man who made people feel they did not have to work too hard because good things were coming from somewhere. Their two children had always been able to recognize the differences between their parents, although "they were as one." They're described as holding hands when they walked down the street and feeding each other tidbits, like lovebirds, which embarrassed their children and yet reassured them. But such descriptions are of a distant past, and much of the novel portrays a present time in which Aaron is rapidly sinking into dementia and Joy is laboriously caring for him.

The novel provides an intimate portrayal of Joy tending to Aaron as he deteriorates. Though she pushes herself beyond her mental and physical capacity, she refuses to put Aaron in "a place" because he would be miserable and even more disoriented. Schine's detailed account of their interactions—Joy's deep love for Aaron, the excruciating pain of slowly losing him, the delight when he sings to her or holds her hand—are juxtaposed with his irritable responses to her frequent practical reminders, such as to tilt the wheels of his walker to negotiate a curb. She has always been the practical one in their marriage, and she continues to be a source of both comfort and annoyance.

Joy's adult children are acutely aware of how much their father has declined and see the overwhelming evidence of the toll his caregiving is taking on their mother. She no longer sorts or even opens her mail, fails to pay bills, exists on takeout food, and neglects to clean the apartment. Every ounce of her energy goes into caring for Aaron around the edges of her job as a curator at a museum. The children mean well as they nag her to hire help and urge her to sell her vacation home to pay the bills. But that small home is her only inheritance from childhood, and she sees owning it as all that keeps her from dying penniless and leaving no inheritance to her family. Schine's humor infuses the novel even as Aaron's illness and Joy's exhaustion become increasingly difficult for their adult children to bear and for us to witness. After Joy calls Molly and begs her to fly home immediately from California because Aaron has fallen out of his chair, she chides Molly as disrespectful for saying he has dementia. We empathize with her frayed unreasonableness even as we sympathize with her daughter's frustration and worry. During these weeks of decline, Joy's adult children assume they know what is best for their mother, wanting to protect her. Yet Joy makes her own efforts at protecting them from the horrors of Aaron's condition, particularly when he can no longer communicate in recognizable language. She does not want them to scold her in tones similar to those they use with the grandchildren, even though it is obvious that she is overwhelmed and that she holds on to her part-time job at the museum to avoid going into debt and having to sell the vacation home.

Accounts of Aaron's decline and Joy's emotional and physical strain are interspersed with lighter sections in which Joy is at work in the museum or lunching with girlfriends. She enjoys their monthly luncheons, when she can escape caregiving and also disobey all of her own doctor's dietary rules. Joy laughs with her friends, and cries as she confides that Aaron is dying. And yet she staunchly insists she is fine and needs no help. When asked about how she and Aaron spend their days, she tells them he watches TV and eats frequently, while much of her life—when she is not at work—is spent giving him showers, applying creams, dressing him, and other things she won't discuss. She checks on him during her lunch breaks and never knows what she will find. She keeps secret her own dizzy spells and prays she won't fall.

Everything takes on a new urgency after Aaron suddenly starts to howl in pain partway through the family Thanksgiving dinner. Both Daniel and Molly fret over what to do when Aaron is released from the hospital. They commiserate that their parents are "killing each other," and that they don't "want them to be old." When Molly tries to convince Joy to hire help, Joy insists, "I can cope. I have always coped," and then declares, "Next thing I know you'll be sending both of us off to assisted living." The novel comes to a crisis as the indignities pile up and Joy finally becomes overwhelmed. Her work and her own health are threatened, and her sense of herself begins to fray. Schine portrays how even a strong and determined person can simply break under the pressures of what can be seen as the routine indignities of life, but in fact are the cracks in the parts of ourselves and our resilience that holds us intact. When Joy returns to work after Thanksgiving, the museum has been moved into a new building, she has a young new director, and her office is a tiny windowless storage room the size of a closet. She accurately assumes they are trying to get rid of her, especially when she learns that after months of her work on a comprehensive guide to protect the museum's photographs in the new museum display cases, her project has been assigned to somebody else.

Joy reaches her breaking point when Aaron lashes out at her for trying to help him. He yells at her in a stream of demented abuse, "You can't do anything right!" over and over. "You did this! *You* did this to me! It's your fault!! You do everything wrong! . . . You can't take care of anything." After Molly steers her mother out of the room, Joy suddenly becomes fierce: "I've had it. Am I not flesh? If you prick me, do I not bleed? After everything I've done. Everything I've lived with all these years. Everything I've had to do. I am a human being." And then she slumps to the floor wordless. His outburst, so unlike his previous sweetness and delight in her, literally knocks her off her feet, and for the first time she reveals the emotional and physical cost of her devotion. Joy is hospitalized for a minor stroke and then put in isolation for C. diff, a highly contagious antibiotic-resistant infection she probably acquired from nursing Aaron. By the time she recovers enough to realize she is a patient, she learns that Aaron is doing fine at home, attended by others. When she finally is released from the hospital, she slowly recuperates at home with the loving assistance of Aaron's aides hired by Molly and Daniel. Too weak to resist, Joy appreciates everyone's kindness, and she does not care what anyone says or does "as long as she did not have to move, as long as she could lie on the couch and rest. Never had fatigue been this heavy, never had it been this welcome." When the weather finally warms up, she and one of the aides manage to push Aaron's wheelchair out the door, and Joy uses his walker to steady herself on their outing to the small park, where she silently recognizes her college sweetheart, Karl.

When Aaron goes from palliative to hospice care at home, Molly and Freddie fly in from California. Schine adds humor to what might easily be a traumatic bedside scene as Joy continues to address Aaron even after he dies. When Molly enters her parents' bedroom, she immediately realizes from her father's off-color skin and ice-cold hands that he has died. But when she tells Joy Aaron is dead, Joy quickly leads her out of the bedroom after telling Aaron they will be back in a minute and asks Molly not "to have any discussion in front of Daddy." Schine lightens the scene as Joy returns to have a private conversation with Aaron, and Molly tells Freddie and Daniel, "I think Daddy died . . . but Mommy doesn't want him to know." Even after the hospice nurse says rigor mortis has set in, Joy is not sure he is dead.

After Aaron's funeral, Joy experiences herself as if she has become a completely different person, a boring, fearful, sickly person for whom she must take responsibility, but then she runs into Karl in the nearby coffee shop. When she tells him she has been fired from her museum job, Karl understands because he has been eased out of his law firm. They commiserate and acknowledge that it was good they ran into each other when they did. The remaining plot traces their renewed friendship, their shared loneliness, and their mutual irritation with adult children who mean well but suspect their parents may be susceptible to being taken in by the needs of another old person. As Joy and Karl begin to see more of each other, she finally tells Daniel she is too tired for their weekly dinner, and he becomes worried about "that Karl guy."

Soon after Aaron's funeral, the extended family tries to go through the familiar rituals. Molly and Daniel plan a family Passover in their parents' apartment and are outraged when Joy invites Karl to join them. Afterward, Molly and Daniel determine they must protect Joy from taking care of another old man by getting her out of her apartment. They each suggest she move in with one of them, which Joy refuses. However, she reluctantly agrees to an extended visit with Molly and Freddie in California. The visit is a disaster, and she is so miserable outside her familiar neighborhood that she returns home early, accompanied by the small dog they had given her to try to make her feel needed during her visit. Molly and Daniel feel great relief when they can again get Joy away from Karl for the family's annual summer trip to the upstate cottage, but the much-anticipated trip is a complete failure. Everything Joy had hoped for—the scent of the honeysuckle, the spring in which she always waded barefoot, the comfortable familiarity of a place she has loved her entire life—is changed and unfamiliar. The trip ends abruptly when Joy's insistence on inviting Karl to her granddaughter's bat mitzvah leads to a huge fight with Daniel and Molly. Joy hires a taxi and storms back to the city, feeling she no longer belongs anywhere since Aaron's death.

Her grandson Ben accompanies her, and the novel concludes with several amusing episodes. When Ben is asked by his new employer to provide a urine sample for drug testing, he tells Joy that his future is ruined. Learning he's concerned about marijuana use at a party the previous night, she says, "Oh, for heaven's sake," grabs the empty specimen jar, fills it for him, and indignantly concludes, "As if it's any business of theirs." In the final chapter, Joy shows up in court on Ben's behalf with his citation for public urination when he is out of town earning money for law school after acing his LSATs. Somehow, the clerk misreads the name, calling out "Bea Harkavy" rather than Ben. Joy is not embarrassed. She feels completely at home among the motley crowd in the court as she acknowledges the charge. The novel ends with her words to the judge: "This is exactly where I belong."

The novel is funny, sad, realistic, and surprising. Prior to the upstate vacation, Joy rejected Karl's proposal to marry and move into his luxurious apartment, just around the corner. Although she loves him and appreciates their renewed intimacy, she tells him she can't leave her apartment because it is rent-controlled. They burst into shared laughter before he kisses her hand and comments good-naturedly, "We are star-crossed lovers." After she returns from the disappointing vacation and after the bat mitzvah she and Karl attend together, he tells her he has told his adult sons of his intention to marry her, and she asks if he also told them of her refusal. They laugh together at the reactions of their two families and thoroughly enjoy their own satisfaction of "putting the fear of God in them." She tells Karl, "no wedding" and "no oldies shacking up" but is still irritated at their adult children's interference. She suggests they "get engaged . . . Nothing decided, nothing certain, no plans, but always that possibility. It's very existential. And it'll keep those kids all on their toes." Karl laughs, lifts her hand and kisses it, and tells her she takes his breath away.

Joy defies expectations throughout her life. As a young mother of two children, she earned a PhD when she realized her dapper young husband had no business sense and that she needed a profession. As an old woman, she defied expectations by caring for her beloved husband at home even when his body and his mind deteriorated. She stood up to her adult children when their good intentions went against her will—whether to hire in-home care or to follow her own heart and include Karl in her family's life after Aaron's death. Perhaps most delightful is her insistence on staying in her own rent-controlled apartment instead of moving into Karl's more luxurious apartment, maintaining a home of her own while also enjoying her late-life love and not allowing well-meaning but muddling children to "fuck up" her life! The novel reminds us that old people are still complicated humans, and they can be capable of thriving even after very difficult losses. We put it down in satisfaction, grateful that Joy has the resilience and determination to defy her well-meaning children, to choose happiness with Karl, and even to thrill to the adventure of being mistaken for Ben in the city "where [she] belong[s]."

# ALL PASSION SPENT

## by Vita Sackville-West

Vita Sackville-West's *All Passion Spent* (1931) opens with a dedication to her sons that reads "For Benedict and Nigel who are young. This story of people who are old," followed by a four-line epigraph from John Milton's *Samson Agonistes* that ends, "And calm of mind, all passion spent." This utterly English novel is so feminist infused and such a delicious fairy tale for the contemporary woman of a certain age, who may be inspired to consult her own heart in her final years rather than try to please anyone else—including extended family. Like *They May Not Mean To*'s Joy Bergman, Lady Slane has been a devoted wife, but after her husband's death she's determined to decide her own future, not worried about the opinions of others. Sackville-West's novel combines the insights of Virginia Woolf's *A Room of One's Own* with the magic of a fairy tale. The beautiful young girl who follows external expectations and marries the prince discovers she does not live happily ever after, having killed her dream of being an artist, although she appears to live a magical life of riches, travel, and acclaim. Her adult life has been one of luxury, of servants, and of good health. Yet it has required the stifling of her most valuable self. Only in her late eighties does she live according to her own wishes.

Narrated in third person, the novel is divided into three parts, and moves forward chronologically from the day Lady Deborah Holland Slane is widowed at age eighty-six until her death. Part I opens with the public response to the newspaper announcement of Sir Henry's death at age ninety-four and continues for seven pages before Lady Slane is introduced and the narrator suggests that her opinion is at odds with his public image. After patiently listening to the opinions of her six adult children, she announces her plans, not only to move from London to a house in Hampstead that she fell in love with thirty years ago but also to forbid any visitors who are not over seventy. In contrast to the conventional opinions of her children and their spouses, who assume she will rely on them as she has on their father, she is delighted finally to manage her own affairs and to escape the public life she has endured for seventy years. In the brief part II, Lady Slane is in Hampstead, where she has the leisure to "survey her life as a tract of country traversed . . . so that it became a unity and she could see the whole view." In the closing section of the novel, Lady Slane deepens her friendship with chosen friends, has the opportunity to make significant defiant choices that align with her personal values rather than the expectations of her grown children, and connects briefly with her great-granddaughter shortly before death.

Most memorable after first reading this novel is Lady Slane's quiet determination to live the final years of her life as she wishes, with no attention to the opinions of anyone else. She is gracious to her children, listens to their assumptions about how she should live as a widow, and then quietly but firmly tells them she has her own plans. Such self-knowledge—even after decades of hiding her opinions and being a perfectly agreeable wife to Henry—is unusual in life and in fiction. She has perfected the art of listening to others, of keeping her thoughts to herself, and of hiding her wild spirit from everyone around her.

Much of the pleasure of reading part I comes from observing the contrast between Lady Slane's persona and the resulting assumptions made by her offspring and her strong inner will that allows her to defy those assumptions. Her six adult children go from calling her "Dear Mother," and assuming she is a simpleton with no will of her own before the funeral, to assuming she has lost her mind when she refuses their plans for her life. She shocks them, saying, "I have considered the eyes of the world for so long that I think it is time I had a little holiday from them. If one is not to please oneself in old age, when is one to please oneself? There is so little time left!" And when she further insists she wants "no one about me except those who are nearer to their death than to their birth," they decide she has gone mad.

Perhaps such distance from her children is a result of their being raised by nannies and servants. Perhaps no intimate bonds ever existed between Lord and Lady Slane and their six children. No evidence exists in the novel one way or another. Surely Lady Slane in her silences, outward behavior, and persona has prevented not only Henry but also her children and grandchildren from ever knowing her most private self. Yet the novel never critiques her or Henry individually; rather, it critiques the patriarchal and imperialist values of their social world.

Having never known poverty, Lady Slane has little appreciation for wealth. She benefits from the selfless caretaking of Genoux, her French maid, throughout her marriage, and continuing through her retreat to Hampstead. She takes Genoux for granted, not even curious about her life until they are both quite elderly. She never has to concern herself with planning meals or maintaining a house, or even with setting out her own clothes. She ignores politics and commerce, and as much as she resents the pontifications and intrusions of her adult children, she has relied on them for all sorts of practical assistance prior to Henry's death.

A reader who has grown up in less wealthy conditions may not be able to identify with Deborah Holland, Lady Slane. Yet even a middle-class wife and mother with none of Lady Slane's endowments can appreciate the still-prevalent assumptions that romance and marriage is the ideal prize of a woman's existence and that a vocational desire to become a painter or musician is somehow less important for a "true" woman. Similarly, the assumption that an old woman desires nothing so much as to cradle a newborn grandchild or great-grandchild is not necessarily accurate (as we saw earlier in Tillie Olsen's "Tell Me a Riddle"). It makes complete sense that a woman who has nurtured others for decades may welcome an opportunity for solitude, for companionship with her own generation, for a release from needing to care how others see her.

The calm, serene tone of Lady Slane in part II allows the reader vicariously to consider the cost of marriage for a woman with the potential of becoming an artist and the satisfaction from reprising life without feeling disloyal. Lady Slane luxuriates in the leisure to examine her vivid memories of the girl she had once been. The novel's most beautiful passages are set in nature—particularly in recounted memories as they are brought to Lady Slane's consciousness in Hampstead. We see her sensibility to flowers, to color, to light, to a swarm of butterflies, her sense of values in stark contrast to the values of others. With her we enter the colorful, emotionally drenched scenes in which she assumed she could both marry and become an artist. Sackville-West insists upon the love Deborah felt for Henry even as she hated his refusal to encourage her art. He insisted her life as wife and mother would more than make up for abandoning her dream, and she did not protest. Marriage exists primarily for men, not for women, and after his death Lady Slane's muted anger is against the institution. She briefly wonders if she had been "happy," and quickly dismisses the word itself as incapable of bearing any relation to "the shifting, elusive, iridescent play of life" and "too simple" to sum up her life with Henry.

Lady Slane reflects on the ways her marriage has shaped her existence. "Her love for him had been a straight black line drawn right through her life," the novel reads. "It had hurt her, it had damaged her, it had diminished her, but she had been unable to curve away from it." She recalls that she could never be the same self with him as when she was alone, and without bitterness she knows she substituted a life with him for a life of her own. Yet she reveals no regret. It is as if once caught up in the pressures to marry Henry, she accepted that role as pre-determined. She became Henry's wife, a mother, the Vicerine, the public figure on whom others projected their own fantasies of her perfect life. At age seventeen there had been no possibility for her of running away from home and pursuing an artist's vocation.

Part III portrays Lady Slane at peace with herself, having taken the time to revisit her girlhood and her long marriage. I commend her acceptance of herself and her lack of regret or guilt. She finds it "difficult to summon up the sensations of her youth," and she begins to feel an affection for her aged body, including its "hint of lumbago . . . the small intimacies of her stomach . . . the pain of neuritis in her left hand." Even her physical ailments do not destroy her essential and time- less beauty, not only from her inner spiritual qualities but also from her still-slender form, her posture, her lovely face, and her hair—all of which radiate fairy-tale loveliness, tempered but not ruined by age. She feels younger than she has in years and enjoys immensely the atmosphere at Hampstead: "modest, warm, affectionate, respectful, vigilant, and generous," where nobody is in a hurry and nothing is artificial.

After her move to Hampstead, she makes new friends with eccentric old men, who each love her in their own profound ways. I am enchanted by portrayals of love and friendship among these few characters in their eighties who choose not to worry about the opinions of others. None of the men who become Lady Slane's friends has chosen marriage and family, and yet each is convinced of his own worth and content to let others live as they please. As men, unlike women, they were not constrained by their families to choose marriage as their only vocation. In quite differing ways, they all love Lady Slane and enjoy her company. Each is unconventional, and each one respects integrity and a lack of posturing. Her land- lord, Mr. Bucktrout's, theories entertain the others, and he does not try to convince them to accept or reject his opin- ions. Mr. Gosheron, the builder who remodels the Hampstead house, respects the materials with which he works, and he's as perceptive in sizing up a person as he is in recognizing the beauties and flaws in a piece of wood. Each is an original, complete in himself, enjoying the company of a kindred spirit but not needing emotional bolstering from Lady Slane, as Henry did. With each of these new friends in her old age, she can be herself as a whole person and enjoy the company of men, unlike Henry, who do not rely on her to make them feel complete.

I enjoy the defiance she shows in choosing where and how to live, as well as her responses to the unexpected new adventures and challenges she encounters. One wonderful new adventure is her friendship with Mr. FitzGeorge, a connoisseur and long-time friend of her son, who waits until after Henry's death to appear in her life. He has loved her since he met her in India when she was a young mother, and now as an old man he scolds her for allowing marriage to kill her spirit. He becomes her soul mate. He visits often, and they share memories and quiet times together, taking walks up the Heath. His love—not wanting to possess her—survives after death, when his final will reveals how well he understands her need to make an informed choice before she dies. He leaves his huge fortune to her, knowing of her disdain for wealth. She is initially horrified by this turn of events, but eventually she realizes that in leaving his fortune to her, he has actually allowed her to make a defiant decision against the social conventions she disdains.

In spite of her family's greed and their assumptions of a huge inheritance, she gives it all away. That action, removing the possibility of wealth from her great-grandchildren, leads to the final adventure of her life, the unexpected visit of her great-granddaughter and namesake. Although they had never met, Lady Slane has followed the newspaper clippings about this youngest generation of relatives. The younger Deborah, learning of Lady Slane's refusal of riches, has felt supported in her own resolution to break her engagement to a man who, it turns out, had based his proposal on the widespread news of Lady Slane's inheritance and his assumptions the young girl would therefore be wealthy. Deborah is relieved by her escape from her fiancé and her freedom to pursue an artistic career in music, a dream that was never realized by Lady Slane, but which she enters imaginatively in their conversation just before her quiet slip into death. Lady Slane and we have no way of measuring her musical talent, any more than she can measure the potential talent of her great-granddaughter. What matters is that young Deborah, bolstered by Lady Slane's belief in her, will have the opportunity to choose her vocation rather than being entrapped by her parents' limited expectations. In reading this book, I am delighted by the ways in which the adolescent Deborah and the old woman mirror each other's spirit.

When I contemplate Sackville-West's dedication to the novel, I wonder what she wanted her sons to take away from this story. Was she warning them to question traditional assumptions about marriage and money? Was she providing them a glimpse into her own desire to seek adventures outside social expectations of a good wife? Perhaps she is urging them to appreciate her love of beauty, flowers, spirit—to combine idealism and realism. Or maybe she has portrayed for them, as for us, a glimpse of the intimacy and friendship that—in spite of contracts and bloodlines—are possible at any age.

Lady Slane's defiance comes only in old age, after she has fulfilled the role she innocently accepted in marrying Henry. She not only defies her children's expectation regarding how and where to live in the final years of her life, but because of FitzGeorge's fortune, she is also able to avoid any compliance with conventional expectations of inheritance and to turn down the inheritance that would—however unknown to her—imprison her great-granddaughter. What a satisfying tale!

# THE FOUNTAIN OF ST. JAMES COURT; OR, PORTRAIT OF THE ARTIST AS AN OLD WOMAN

## by Sena Jeter Naslund

Sena Jeter Naslund's 2013 *Fountain of St. James Court; or, Portrait of the Artist as an Old Woman* is a novel filled with literary references: its title echoes James Joyce's *Portrait of the Artist as a Young Man* and its structure Virginia Woolf's *Mrs. Dalloway*. Naslund's prose is often lovely, and the novel is charming, and ambitious in its scope, recalling Joyce in its attention to the making of an artist and Woolf in its use of metaphor. The contemporary front story takes place in one day in the life of the protagonist, Kathryn Callaghan, like *Mrs. Dalloway*, and the backstory is the chronological life story, as told in novel form by Kathryn, of an eighteenth-century painter, like *Portrait of the Artist as a Young Man*. While Joyce's *Portrait* is about a man who is on the verge of becoming an artist, Naslund's portrait of Kathryn Callaghan is the story of an accomplished writer as an older woman who has created for herself a fulfilling life of artistic achievement against enormous odds.

Kathryn is a successful, self-supporting, and thrice-divorced writer nearing seventy. She is on good terms with her son, Humphrey, a sculptor who lives with his husband in Sweden. She has close friends, loves her upscale neighborhood, and enjoys the ordinary daily details of her self-chosen home and its furnishings. Kathryn, or Ryn to her friends, is an unusual protagonist in that she is content with her life. Unlike the women in the previous pair of books in this chapter, Ryn remains close with her child even as she pursues her own happiness. In most novels, including those of Woolf, creative intellectual achievement and successful motherhood are portrayed as mutually exclusive. Elderly mothers in fiction tend to be concerned about their grown children—whether mourning about geographic or emotional distance, or trying to escape the interference of adult children who mean well. Ryn, however, in addition to being respected as a writer by Humphrey, is also a gun-toting thriller heroine who literally saves his life, not by providing emotional or financial support but by being an aging and elegant action hero. Naslund's novel insists on the possibility of mutual artistic and maternal success and portrays an older woman who is vital and courageous.

Structured as a novel within a novel, the book's interleaved segments alternate. *Portrait of the Artist as an Old Woman* is Kathryn's novel about Elisabeth Vigée-Le Brun, who in real life was famous for her portraits of Marie Antoinette. *The Fountain of St. James Court* is the main story, which takes place in a single day in 2000s Louisville, Kentucky, in a neighborhood surrounding a public square with a beautiful fountain of Venus rising from the water. The story begins with the completion of Kathryn's novel shortly after midnight and ends after a full day of activities that provide an opportunity for Naslund to showcase her protagonist's sensitivities, artistic sensibilities, bravery, and connections with other talented women.

The novel emphasizes the importance of bonds between

female artists. The opening scene of *The Fountain of St. James Court* shows Kathryn walking across the square just after midnight to deliver her newly finished manuscript, *Portrait of the Artist as an Old Woman*, to her best friend, Leslie, an African American musician and writer. Their friendship began in college and has continued for decades. Both are divorced from husbands who did not understand or appreciate them as artists, and their friendship is rich and supportive. In fact, Leslie moved to Louisville to be near Ryn. The novel's theme of female attachment is amplified through the two protagonists of the parallel storylines, Elisabeth and Ryn. Though they live in separate centuries and countries, Naslund focuses on the qualities that they share and implies that Ryn's choice of her subject reflects a desire to recuperate and also connect with this earlier, brilliant woman, a long-ignored artist who was once famous and is recognized as one of the premier painters of eighteenth-century France.

In her historical novel, Ryn writes in Vigée-Le Brun's voice. Even as a little girl of six, Vigée-Le Brun responds to color and light. She experiences the "colored patches of sunlight, hovering high" as if they were angels in the Church of Saint Eustache. Similarly, Ryn observes the fountain of St. James Court as "a ceremony of light," and her cells sing "with the joy, the thrill, the fulfillment that Beauty offered. Light, invisible and elusive but here given form, stood for the miracle of art. How water made light visible; that was how the art of writing must capture and irradiate life." Naslund makes clear a connective spirit and perspective between the two female artists whose lives structure this narrative.

Elisabeth and Ryn both marry men who are unfaithful to them, and both take comfort in their art. Elisabeth parenthetically comments on the "loose behavior" of her husband but asserts that although she is forever yoked to him, given the structure of eighteenth-century marriage, she is capable of independent thought and feeling, which drive her artistic practice and success: "This is the art of living: to feel what I feel; to be in no way repressed, mentally or emotionally, and to find the means both artistically and personally to let out the light that is within me." Ryn has the modern ability to divorce more easily and maintain social independence, and feels "curious and happy doing what she wanted to do when she wanted to do it." While missing her third husband, the brain surgeon who left her after fifteen years for a younger woman, she reminds herself of her relief "not to be in the presence of a spouse who discounted her value in dozens of ways." We get the sense that the contemporary woman who is true to herself and her art may not easily find a worthy male partner.

For both women, the most important outcome of their marriages is motherhood. Each gave birth to one dearly loved child she raised alone after the dissolution of the marriage. And each tries to protect her grown child from an unhappy romantic partnership. Vigée-Le Brun is unable to prevent her daughter, Julie, at age nineteen from marrying a man who eventually destroys her spirit and leads to her early death, a tragedy that haunts *Portrait of the Artist as an Old Woman*. Where Vigée-Le Brun fails to save her daughter, Ryn successfully intervenes in her son's romantic liaison. Ryn had hated Humphrey's "subservience" to his boyfriend three years earlier and even then had wanted "to lead a cavalry charge, riding a silver-white horse against the evil smirk of Jerry," who was abusive and repeatedly beat their dog in fits of rage. When his ex-boyfriend returns after Humphrey's marriage and move to

Sweden, she is both terrified and angry.

While motherhood is central to each woman's life and sense of herself, each woman's art is equally essential. It is foundational to who they are, and it brings them economic and social connections and choices. Shortly after realizing her mistake in marrying her husband, Elisabeth reassures her mother, "There is no need to worry. I have my painting. As long as I can paint, I will always be happy." She later reflects that her "happiest hours have always been those when I stood or sat in my chair before my easel." Ryn, similarly, after her third divorce, realizes she wants most to dwell in her own skin, "scavenging for myself, happy and complete in myself, my friends, my work, my home, my claimed territory: Old Louisville." After asking Leslie to read the draft of her novel, she recognizes, "*Portrait* was not finished: revision, revision, revision. And she would love the revising, her hands falling in love with the grain of the words as surely as a woodcarver loved to touch again what he had carved." For each woman it is the doing that matters, the seeing and the creation of a new aesthetic object rooted in that seeing.

Elisabeth's experiences as a very old woman, as imagined by Ryn in *Portrait*, provide sustenance for the sixty-nine-year-old Ryn as she writes them. In her old age, Elisabeth looks back on the fact that the French Revolution forced her husband to divorce her after she fled to Italy. She recalls her relief as a young woman "to become legally what she already was spiritually: an independent woman who defined herself as an artist and a mother." She eventually is allowed to return to France, but as a once Royal favorite, she no longer has access to power or to wealth. Her comments, as imagined by Ryn, offer the comfort of a life lived true to one's self; she states: "I have enough . . . while my stepfather and my husband spent my money, I learned how to paint better and better, and how to converse in society, and how to find pleasures in nature in small glittering moments. I knew I could rely on myself to provide. Sheerly because of my delight in my painting, I have had a rich life."

Near the end of *Portrait*, as Elisabeth drifts off to sleep, she wonders if she is lovable as an old woman, but she knows she is a "loving old woman—my nieces, many friends—and happy in my love of art. Painting was innate in me, and my love for it has increased rather than diminished over time." And as Ryn drifts off to sleep, in the closing chapter of *Fountain*, she, too, affirms the importance of her art and looks forward to the next morning, when she will begin revising *Portrait*, reminding herself that practicing the art of revision was the best part of writing: "Then you had something, instead of nothing." This theme of enjoyable self-directed revision, of art, of life, offers a delightful view of aging creatively.

Older readers who see their own lives in terms of literary resonances and metaphors are likely to enjoy this novel. Ryn frequently alludes to writers and artists, including Woolf and Joyce, but also G. M. Hopkins, Sara Teasdale, Keats, Hemingway, Whitman, Paul Tillich, and others. Familiarity is not necessary to understand the points she makes through her allusions. For example, Ryn contrasts her life to that of Virginia Woolf's Clarissa Dalloway and compares her third husband, the brain surgeon, to the egoistic Mr. Ramsay of *To the Lighthouse*. In her luxurious life, surrounded by material comfort in her lovely home, Ryn is remote from readers who struggle daily with financial challenges, abusive partners, physical or mental disability, or who have not achieved artistic or professional success. However, she does suffer loss, fear, and disappointment.

Even within Ryn's protected environment, her son's abusive former lover haunts her. Hints of his reappearance in the neighborhood are threaded through her day. Neighbors see his beat-up car tearing recklessly through the square, Ryn's housekeeper reports that he stopped by the house looking for Ryn while she was out, and she has a general sense of foreboding as even the weather turns from sunny skies to a torrential downpour. Ryn thinks frequently during the day how strange it is that when she first started living alone, a friend had given her the small .38-caliber Colt revolver she keeps hidden in her bedside drawer. Ryn assumes she will never need to use it. Nevertheless, she remembers the sense of satisfaction she had as a young girl with perfect marksmanship in the shooting galleries to which her father took her, and we get the sense she knows how to handle a gun.

After dusk, when Ryn arrives home during the storm, she settles in with a glass of wine to savor the entire day following completion of her novel draft and to anticipate seeing Humphrey the following morning. However, her short-lived peace is interrupted when Jerry belligerently shows up at her front door and demands Humphrey's address. Their verbal confrontation is intense as she refuses to give it to him. He then bursts into her living room, breaks the delicate coffee table, and threatens not to leave without it. In that confrontation, Ryn does the unexpected. She claims to go upstairs for the address, but instead she grabs her gun from the drawer of the bedside table. When Jerry realizes she does not have the address for him, he lunges toward her, and she manages to graze him in the foot with a bullet. He flees, bleeding, and we sense she and

Humphrey are rid of him.

Ryn protects Humphrey from ever again being harassed by Jerry, and we applaud her heroic behavior. Never underestimate the fury of a mother protecting her child. We hear echoes of Angela Carter's retelling of the "Bluebeard" fairy tale, in which a heroic mother charges in on a stallion at the critical moment and saves her daughter's life.

Ryn defies expectations overtly in her brandishing of the gun. More importantly, the novel challenges literary notions of whose lives are worthy of telling in its close attention to the formation of the artist as an old woman, both in the eighteenth century and in the present.

# THE LOVE CEILING

## by Jean Davies Okimoto

Women in the stories I collect seldom have more than two of the three following ingredients in their lives: a satisfying relationship with husband or partner, children, and creative expression or career. Most female protagonists in fiction are either divorced or widowed by the time they are in their sixties. They have made choices between artistic and maternal fulfillment, rarely having both. In Tillie Olsen's "Tell Me a Riddle," the demands of motherhood and the pressures of financial need prevent Eva from writing. Sackville-West's Lady Slane in *All Passion Spent* has benefited from wealth, but she gave up any pursuit of art to fulfill the expected role of wife and mother and asserts her own will only after the death of her husband. Kathryn Callaghan in *The Fountain of Saint James Court* is able to combine her maternal and artistic lives but does not sustain a satisfying marriage. However, in *The Love Ceiling* (2009), Jean Davies Okimoto's sixty-four-year-old protagonist, Anne Kuroda Duppstadt, maintains a long marriage, raises two children who continue as adults to enjoy her company, has a beloved three-year-old grandson, and flourishes as an artist late in her life. Okimoto is not the first woman writer to examine the difficult tension for women between family life and creative potential, but her novel is unusual in allowing

Annie to achieve satisfaction in her marriage and as a mother and artist.

In *The Love Ceiling*, set in Seattle in the 2000s, the death of Akiko, Annie's adored Japanese American mother, leads Annie to pursue a lifelong dream of painting. Her artistic ambition had been stifled by years of being put down by her cruel father, a famous artist who always disparaged her talent, was never challenged by his wife to do otherwise, and continues to make demands of his housekeeper and Annie after Akiko's death. The novel takes its title from Annie's discovery that when she finally begins to pursue her dream and not settle for her job as craft lady in a senior center, the complications she faces come from the very people she cares about most—her husband, her daughter, and her grandson—leading her to remark, "There is a glass ceiling for women . . . and it's made out of the people we love." Okimoto is best known for her many books for children and young adults, and *The Love Ceiling* reveals her familiar, gentle sense of humor and compassionate insight into the workings of family relationships. She is sympathetic to her characters, and we like Annie. Although she is challenged by family dynamics, the tone of the novel is hopeful, and we anticipate a happy ending. Part of our delight comes from watching Annie increasingly stand up to her family members and define a clear role for herself, particularly when she frees herself from her oppressive relationship with her father.

When she was fifteen, Annie's art teacher at school had written on the back of her pastel: "You have a gift. An unusual sense of color. An intuitive feeling for light." But when Annie tentatively approached her father with the pastel after school, he cruelly destroyed it, smearing it with brown paint and gouging it with his palette knife. He claimed he was saving her a lot of pain by letting her know that the art world was filled with rejection. He announced, "You'll never be a serious painter." Annie suppresses her talent and puts her family first until after her mother, shortly before death, apologizes to her for her complicity in indulging Annie's father, "the great Alexander Gunther," and allowing him to be the only artist in the house. Her mother elicits a promise from her to move beyond her father's prohibition and start painting. "You must do it . . . promise me, Annie," she says. In barely audible words, Akiko whispers, "I'm sorry. I'm sorry about him." Okimoto writes that this apology in "those few hard-fought, rasping, tortured words meant she understood. And she was deeply sorry she'd been helpless to do anything about it." Annie wryly thinks that knowing this forty years sooner "might have saved me a lot of shrink bills," while also knowing that rather than "too little, too late," her mother's remorse was an "unexpected gift."

It is easy to understand Akiko's fear of opposing Gunther, who had been cruel to her as well, making the story all the more surprising when he discovers from his lawyer that several months before her death, Akiko had revised her will and named Annie the executor of her half of the joint property. He contests the will but is overruled. That action and his fury, following Annie's promise to Akiko, allow Annie finally to confront him and become emotionally free to study painting with Fred Weiss, a retired art professor who knew her mother. He gives her his card and invites her to visit his studio on his daughter's Vashon Island property, where he mentors a few students.

At home, her husband, Jack, struggles with his own diminishing career and the contemplation of retirement, initially assuming Annie will continue to meet his emotional needs and their established routines that include her preparation of all meals except for their weekly night out. Soon after she tells Jack of her plans to study with Fred, he makes a ridiculous comment about him probably being an old lech, wanting to get her into his garret. He has trouble adjusting to the changes in Annie, and although she feels sorry for him, she finds his comments about Fred to be completely off base. She wants to "start a career, begin taking [herself] seriously—before it was too late." She wants to age with grace.

Any wife who has prepared decades of nightly meals will appreciate the difficulty with which Annie tries to shift some of the household responsibilities to Jack. In one amusing scene where she is painting at home, he interrupts her to ask if she is hungry. When she says no, he asks if she could "just take a break," and she suggests he fix something for himself, to which he responds that he doesn't want another sandwich. At Annie's suggestion that he find something else, they spar briefly until finally in exasperation she suggests he eat peanut butter or tuna fish. "But just figure it out," she says. She realizes that although she has always been a traditional wife, she is sure he will eventually adapt, which he does. He begins by trying to make a big pot of soup, in the process "covering the kitchen counter with almost every pan, skillet, and pot" they own. She muses: "He was trying. He really was trying; I had to give him credit." He had never seen a father cook except on Mother's Day.

Okimoto manages to portray not only Annie's frustration but also Jack's attempts to be supportive when he finally realizes how serious she is. For example, he urges her not to move her studio out of their daughter, Cass's, old bedroom when after three years of living with her boyfriend Cass returns, heartbroken, after their breakup. Jack suggests Cass sleep on the couch rather than have Annie paint in the basement. While Annie does let Cass take the bedroom, Cass does not easily settle into being under her parents' roof as an adult; her presence and the visits from Annie and Jack's grandchild, Sam, their son's three-year-old, make it more difficult for Annie to paint.

During this time Annie finally completes her first painting and knows that Fred requires all of his students submit a painting to be included in the upcoming exhibition. One morning, when she and Jack are babysitting Sam, Annie leaves Jack in charge while she runs a brief errand to buy groceries, But Jack fails to keep an eye on Sam, setting him up instead with a video. When Annie returns home, she finds Jack in his office and Sam in her studio. "Clutching a tube of paint like it was toothpaste, Sam was squishing it over the canvas . . . Dark blue paint was spread over the lower third of the canvas as high as he could reach. The foreground, the lower part of the meadow I had struggled with day after day, week after week, had been destroyed, obliterated with ugly smears of thick paint." After cleaning up, she tells her grandson, "Those aren't your paints. They belong to Gran. You are never, ever to do that again. Do you understand?"

She hugs Sam and postpones confronting Jack so she doesn't scar Sam for life. But she is furious with him. She takes her painting to Vashon that very afternoon. After bursting into tears on the ferry on the way there, she is reassured by Fred that the painting can be saved. He shows her how to carefully scrape off Sam's paint and then how to begin over again. He reassures her that her instincts will take over and that she will recapture the basic feeling of her painting. After hours of work, she gets a phone call from Jack that her father has had a heart attack or a stroke and medics are taking him to the hospital. She feels as if once again Gunther is trying to take her away from her art, but nevertheless she rushes to the ferry and accompanies Jack to the hospital, where they learn that her father is likely to recover many of his abilities but will need extensive rehabilitation.

When she visits the hospital the next day, her father immediately starts making demands. Because his speech is mumbled, he grabs a pad of paper and scribbles "Leslie M" in large childlike letters. Annie understands that he wants her to contact his girlfriend, a woman she saw him with only three weeks after Akiko's death, the latest in a series of women with whom he cheated on his wife. Annie tells him, "Not this time." Finally she finds the strength to talk back to him. "You've treated me with contempt my whole life. In fact, you wished I'd never been born. But you were even worse to Mom—you were hostile and cruel to her." She tells him he has a mean, sadistic streak, but that she appreciates his genes and that she is starting to believe she has a gift that came from him. She promises she will not abandon him, but she also won't "tolerate his abuse."

When she goes home after a return visit to the hospital several days later, she discovers Cass and Jack loading her unfinished painting into the car. Fred's other student, Martha Jane, had phoned to say they were hanging the show and that Fred had insisted that her piece be in the Vashon Island art show even though it was a work in progress. Ninety-year-old Martha Jane, Annie's new friend and mentor, titled the piece "Three Steps Forward, Two Steps Back." Annie, vowing never to use her official maiden name, lovingly substitutes

her mother's, and she knows she will always sign her paintings Anne Kuroda Duppstadt. We learn of her later success
from the epilogue, which lists Annie's many art shows and
announces that she is still painting in her eighties, that her
work is known for its "unique use of color, and the juxtaposi-
tion of contrasting colors found in ukiyo-e prints," that it "has
found a wide audience in Japan."

Often authors do not allow their protagonists to have
everything they desire so late in life, perhaps because their
own life experience has not allowed for that. But Okimoto
allows Annie a full family life, and then after her mother's
death, Annie finds the strength to defy her father and become
an artist. Okimoto's narrative is believable in its portrayal of
family life, the power of relationships between children and
parents both to harm and to help, and the ways in which
even long-married adults can change their established routines and assumptions, take risks, and grow. Annie eventually
has it all—a husband who learns to accept her new life as an
artist, children who love her, and new friends and mentors
who help her develop her potential as an artist. Even more
uncommonly, she becomes well-known as a painter in her old
age. Her achievement is not the stuff of fairy tales. Rather, it
reinforces our awareness that it's never too late to confront
external impediments and to move beyond internal barriers.
Life after sixty can be wonderful and surprising, and coming to
age can be profoundly satisfying.

## THE LITTLE OLD LADY
## WHO BROKE ALL THE RULES

by Catharina Ingelman-Sundberg

Translated into English in 2014, Catharina Ingelman-Sundberg's *The Little Old Lady Who Broke All the Rules* follows the escapades of a group of five elderly choir singers, The Vocal Chord, who have known each other for twenty years and all live in the same Stockholm retirement home. At the age of seventy-nine, Martha Andersson convinces her four closest friends—Brains, Christina, Anna-Greta, and Rake—to turn to white-collar crime rather than put up with the new management of their retirement home. Naming themselves "The League of Pensioners," they see themselves as a band of Robin Hoods, on a quest not only to improve their own lives but also to benefit the lives of pensioners throughout Sweden.

In contrast to other novels I introduce in this collection, this novel is primarily plot driven and entertaining. Rather than exploring individual character, examining psychologically acute responses to the many losses that accompany aging, or relying on exquisite prose or experimental structure, the novel is witty and episodic. It is also one of the most surprising in this chapter, and part of the reading pleasure comes from following The League's antics as they plan and carry out their outrageous crimes and then grapple with their unexpected success. But the humor is undergirded by a heartbreaking reality: Ingelman-Sundberg's novel relies on our recognition of the social stereotypes that render elderly people invisible, disempowered, and too often warehoused. *The Little Old Lady Who Broke All the Rules* is enjoyable because its characters take advantage of the way older people are treated as helpless and insignificant in order to engage in a fantastical revenge caper.

*The Little Old Lady* makes readers gently aware of unexamined ageist beliefs, our shared underestimation of the mental and emotional capacities of people who appear physically frail. The novel uses humor to call attention to the devaluation of the elderly, and it entices us into colluding with these elderly characters' lawlessness and rooting for their success. We relish the "everyman" takedown of a satisfying villain; in this case, the specific individuals and corporations against whose draconian policies The League plots. But just as Robin Hood's story was not just about a particular sheriff or king but a corrupt system, Ingelman-Sundberg's novel offers a critique of the cultural and social stereotypes that put profit over people and result in the elderly being shunted into care homes, which we recognize as often unworkable, often dire, options for the end of life.

The Lily of the Valley Retirement Home was initially a welcoming, if dull, residence; it promised delicious meals in elegant surroundings, and for people who could no longer keep up a home and lived alone, it seemed a reasonable alternative. Each of the characters who ends up there presumes relief from household tasks in the company of friends, and the common spaces are comfortably furnished. In their individual rooms they have freedom to pursue their interests. Brains is able to use his tools to continue inventing, Anna-Greta enjoys listening to her favorite recordings, Christina paints her watercolors, and Martha reads her crime and detective novels and keeps a secret stash of cloudberry liqueur for entertaining her friends. Residents play card games, celebrate holidays, and enjoy guest lectures and group outings.

However, things soon turn for the worse when, under new corporate management and with a new name, Diamond House, the focus shifts to profit rather than care. New administrators enact numerous cost-cutting measures that deprive the residents of pleasure and freedom, and their role becomes similar to that of inmates. The administration replaces home-cooked meals with plastic-wrapped, tasteless food. Coffee is restricted to three times daily and served without any biscuits or buns. There are no holiday celebrations. Outings are curtailed, and the residents are secretly being drugged with small pills slipped among their usual medications that cause them to be placid and decrease their hunger. These dehumanizing measures are the stuff of nightmares and exemplify the horrors of profit-based care (for any vulnerable population), though Ingelman-Sundberg narrates her story within the parameters of a novel whose warmth and good humor promise that all will work out for the pensioners in the end.

In the face of these abuses, the novel's characters are saved, emotionally and literally, by their affectionate connections to one another. In their fifties, over twenty years before the novel takes place, the group had determined to live together in retirement. They had hoped to pool resources to buy a mansion surrounded by a moat, but all they could afford was to move into the same retirement home. Still close friends in later life, they rely on each other to continue to feel human in a society that no longer sees them as real people. Their well-meaning children seldom visit, believing their parents are happy. It is not family but familiar friends, the chosen community of the choir, who can "see" one another and whose understanding and acceptance of one another allow them to organize and revolt. They, not their families or the state, save themselves, and they do so not by working within the law but by circumventing it—by illegal conspiracy, in fact!

As an older reader myself, I am delighted that the ringleader of the aging gang of five is a demure-seeming retired teacher. Martha Andersson, who grew up in Osterlen, "where people didn't just sit and wait for somebody else to take action," determines that the friends need to do something to improve their lives: "It's about time we made a stand . . . a little mutiny." She insists to her friends that they must demand improvements and that in the meantime they are due some pleasure. She instigates their first foray into "crime" by convincing the group to sneak into the staff kitchen to help themselves after hours. Although she looks deceptively unassuming, with her knitting in her lap, she is a keen and radical thinker, a woman whose desire—for food, intimacy, money, and independence— is strong, and who infuses the others with hope. She becomes the mastermind for their eventual robberies.

The members of The League follow Martha's lead and create an effective criminal gang, as well as a likable cast of characters whose intensity, erotic desire, humor, greed, and complexity refuse stereotypes of the elderly. Oscar "Brains" Krupp is a retired engineer and the inventor ("solution finder") of the group. He knows how to pick locks and outfit their walkers with special features, such as enlarged side tubes to hold wire cutters. He is also Martha's romantic interest, in spite of his pudgy build, because of his ingenuity, sensitivity, and respect for her ideas. Erotic desire is keen in this group of pensioners, and the novel suggests it is key to their liveliness, in contrast to the ways they are misread by younger people, including their adult children.

Christina Akerblom, the youngest member of the group at only seventy-seven, was once a milliner who dreamed of becoming a librarian but married young and endured an unhappy marriage until her divorce after her two children were grown. She is an amateur landscape painter with a strict religious upbringing who worries about what her adult son and daughter will think if they hear of her criminal activity. Ironically, when they learn about the group's museum heist, they realize they have underestimated their mother and are proud of her. Christina often comments on situations by voicing literary quotations, such as "It is better to dare to cast the dice, than to fade away with a withering flame," and "It is more beautiful to hear a string that snaps, than never to draw a bow," which Martha suggests they adopt as their motto.

The fourth member of the group, Anna-Greta Bielke, tall and thin, worked in a bank all her life and is the only one of the group with a hefty savings account. She is the member who understands finance and is comfortable using the Internet. She is preoccupied with her appearance, hoping to attract a rich gentleman, but her loud laugh tends to scare off would-be suitors.

Bertil "Rake" Engstrom, the fifth member of The League, is a retired seaman with vast travel experience and a love of gardening. Since his divorce from a short-lived youthful marriage that left him with one son, he has fancied himself a ladies' man. His humor often embarrasses the three women, who nevertheless enjoy his company. He suggests their motto should be "It's better to be in the bed that broke than always to sleep alone."

The friends' initial foray into illicit activity begins promisingly but ends badly. Their trip to the staff kitchen results in a marvelous dinner of real food, and they drink expensive wine and champagne and dance late into the night. Unfortunately, they drink too much and fall asleep without cleaning up the mess. Nurse Barbara, manager of the home, clearly smitten with the parsimonious new director and trying to impress him with her money-saving changes, retaliates by locking the five friends in their rooms and allowing them to leave the residents' floor only if accompanied by one of two remaining staff members. She also adds small red pills to their daily regimen for the sake of "calming them down." When she realizes they take turns sneaking outside during the day, she locks the front door as well. This is the point when they essentially become prisoners in the space they thought would be their shared home. They grow increasingly dull and drowsy, no longer breaking into spontaneous song, or inventing, or even playing Solitaire in the common spaces. When Martha spills her red pills, she is too listless to pick them up. Over time, Martha begins to cut back on the extra pills management has added to her usual medications and sees how her normal energy returns. She shares her discovery that they are being drugged and convinces her friends that actual prisoners have more freedom than they do, and that they must plan their revenge and regain their freedom.

After viewing a television documentary on life in Swedish prisons, Martha convinces her friends that if they are arrested for nonviolent crimes, they will be sent to a prison where they will have good meals and daily exercise rather than waste away at Diamond House. They come up with a plan to quit taking their pills and secretly begin daily exercise in the staff gym they discovered in the cellar while searching for an escape route. For months, they plan as they improve their strength and stamina. When Martha decides they are ready, Brains picks the cellar door lock and they escape unnoticed. Nurse Barbara, caught up in preparations for an upcoming vacation, leaves a substitute, Katia, who does not notice the residents' absence for several days. When she finally does, she assumes they are on a choir outing.

The friends revel in their freedom, happily taking taxis to Stockholm's luxurious Grand Hotel, walking distance from the magnificent National Museum. They rent the penthouse suites, usually reserved for dignitaries or rock stars, where they are as giddy as children over the expensive furnishings, multiple gleaming bathrooms, and spaciousness. They immediately order the best champagne on the menu and charge all their room service meals to Anna-Greta's credit card. They love living beyond their means and promise to repay her from their robberies, which they assume they'll be able to carry out. They bask in this unaccustomed luxury, although they know it can't last. They are in no hurry to go to prison but still prefer their notion of prison over Diamond House. Their escapades are hilarious, and they could easily become the ingredients for a light-hearted comedy film.

Their initial "practice robbery" is of the hotel guests in the sauna. The account is humorous. Brains trips the electricity, which makes access to private lockers impossible, so that guests store their belongings in an unlocked cabinet near reception before entering the sauna. Martha hides Rake's small bags of henbane and cannabis in her cleavage before dumping them in the heating system of the sauna. Guests in the sauna become lightheaded, and when the lights go out, nobody notices Brains emptying the contents of the cabinet into his gym bag. After their initial glee, back in their suite, they discover that the loot is mostly room keys, glasses, and just a few pieces of jewelry—not enough to land them in prison.

Martha cheers them up by suggesting they rob the nearby museum rather than individuals, assuming the museum will be able to pay a ransom, after which they can return the precious paintings and be remanded to prison for white-collar crime. Once again, they carry out the crime without calling notice to themselves. Their antics are amusing as they disconnect the alarm system. Anna-Greta pokes at a painting with her gnarled walking stick and then fakes a fainting spell to attract the attention of the guards, while Brains posts an "out of order" sign on the elevator. The rest of the group spray-paints on the security cameras, and eventually they wheel out two small paintings in Martha's walker, covered by her coat.

Their crime makes headlines in all the newspapers as the heist of the century. The League removed two small paintings from the National Museum—a Renoir and a Monet—and left no traces, surpassing all former such attempts by organized criminals. However, back in their hotel room, the friends have no idea what to do with the paintings while they plan the best way to get ransom money. Christina finally comes up with the idea of hiding the paintings in plain sight by hanging them on the walls of their suite in the place of former paintings. Using her watercolors, which can easily be removed, she adds a few extra features—a mustache, a hat, long hair, and spectacles—to Renoir's *Conversation: An Impression from Paris* and a modern yacht to Monet's *From the Mouth of the Scheldt* and alters his signature.

In the hotel library the next morning, they savor newspaper accounts of the robbery and begin to focus on how to obtain ransom money before they turn themselves over to the police and are sent to prison. They finally draft a letter to the museum director promising to return the paintings "in exchange for a ransom of 10 million kroners in two black Urbanista shopping trolleys and placed on the Silja Serenade cruise ship bound for Finland and leaving Stockholm on 27 March, before 16:00 hours," which is the following day. They promise to return the paintings as soon as they have received the ransom money and threaten to destroy the paintings "if you contact the police." Martha mails the letter and is exuberant, suddenly feeling years younger. She looks forward to the cruise with her friends and the excitement of sneaking the money home and wonders, "How many people her age got to take part in such adventures?"

Once they're back from the cruise, the friends confess to the robbery at the local police station, but nobody believes them at first. Even the police chief thinks the group is a bit wacky and could not possibly have accomplished such a theft. He offers to call a taxi to return them to Diamond House. It's only when Martha produces one of the ransom notes and insists the police chief check its number that he begins to believe her account. The comedy relies on a combination of elderly outrage, defiance, and lack of fear—surely prison would be an improvement over Diamond House—and the stereotype and underestimation of old folks. Readers of the novel begin to cheer these Robin Hoods of the Rich as the indignities and invisibility of The League of Pensioners are repeatedly portrayed.

It is strange to be in the position of colluding in crime, yet as a reader I want the gang of five to succeed. The whole tenor of the book is comedic, and there is something delightful because the real social crime is the dehumanizing treatment of the elderly. Even when the friends are finally believed and are sent to prison as white-collar criminals, they assume they won't be there very long. They intend to resume their crimes because of the excitement and decide they want to donate most of the money to improve eldercare. Nothing in the novel suggests a dreadful outcome or even normal illness, let alone dementia or death. And because we know they're well-intentioned and don't mean to harm anyone, we don't blame them for the fallout of their crimes.

In prison they experience a huge gap between the documentary and actual conditions, but their surprise and disappointment are quickly replaced by ingenuity and secret plans for future escapades. Exercise in the prison yard with its high walls, daily life in tiny cells with only a cot, a table, and an open toilet, no privacy or personal items, is even worse than life in Diamond House. The pensioners are completely surprised that they won't be kept together in prison and instead are kept in individual cells in the men's and women's prisons. However, Martha develops a way of communicating through an exchange of romantic poems to Brains, delivered by the prison chaplain, who thinks their courtship is sweet and who's oblivious to the coded messages that plot their next crime. In prison, the elderly friends all meet experienced criminals who become fascinated by their widely published escapades and determine to locate the paintings and steal the pensioners' ransom money. But the exchange of information goes both ways, and the group learns much from their fellow prisoners, including a mafia plan for a major robbery of Loomis security vans that inspires their next crime.

After an unspecified amount of time, the five friends are moved to Asptuna, an open prison, to allow them to "acclimatize" to their new freedom before being released home. Of course, none of them have a home to go to, so they return to Diamond House, where they discover Nurse Barbara has been replaced by Katia, who is kinder and who's reinstated many of the former luxuries. Perhaps inevitably, the pensioners grow increasingly irritated and bored. In the end, The League pulls off the robbery of the Loomis van that they learned about from the mafia while in prison. With all the money they get from the robbery of the Loomis van, they escape to Las Vegas, where they plot future robberies, but only after making sure the original paintings they stole have been safely restored to the museum and the ransom money hidden in the hotel drainpipe has been reported to the police and donated back to the museum. They establish a special fund for charities that benefit eldercare. No real harm is done, and the old folks have discovered renewed energy from relying on their ingenuity, taking risks, and enjoying themselves in new adventures.

This is an enjoyable and fun novel that hinges on the age and good nature of its protagonists. The League's escapades would not be so funny if they were young people, and we would not feel so kindly disposed if they were less generous. We look forward to following their escapades in the sequel, *The Little Old Lady Strikes Again*. We want them to escape prisons of all varieties, to enjoy good food and champagne, to experience affection and sensuality, and to continue fighting against the idea that old people can't relish being fully alive.

# ETTA AND OTTO
# AND RUSSELL AND JAMES

## by Emma Hooper

My favorite story of defiance in this chapter is *Etta and Otto and Russell and James* (2014), Emma Hooper's unusual novel in which eighty-three-year-old Etta leaves a note for her husband, Otto, telling him she plans to walk from the middle of Canada to see the ocean. She leaves Otto instructions and handwritten recipes to help him manage during her absence. The tale of her journey vacillates between realism and magical realism, between waking and dreaming, and between the fluctuating tenacity and fragility of memory. Her steady companion is James, a coyote with whom she carries on conversations even as she sometimes wonders if he is real. I am enchanted by this book, by its delicate portrayal of love, its simplicity and intense focus. It is not plot driven, though I was captivated by the accounts of Etta's journey. I read it slowly, to savor the beautiful, evocative prose and the narrative's empathy and grace. The author loves her characters and presents them simply, without any critique or sense of pulling narrative strings. She somehow reveals their essence, portraying the elderly with both compassion and clear-eyed precision, and in the telling fills us with wonder.

The book moves the reader through time and into different characters' points of view, assembling a story that contains lists, poems, recipes, snippets of letters, and newspaper clippings. Time shifts between past and present, with blurred boundaries between memory and dream, even between life and death. We get an intimate sense of Etta's journey across Canada and of Otto's past journey to fight in World War II. We glimpse Otto's tangled friendship with Russell and their respect and love for one another since age six, and we learn that they've known Etta since she arrived as their teacher at age sixteen, barely older than they were—just before rumors of war began seeping in over the radio. We get to know Etta, Otto, and Russell intimately as we accumulate specific details, facts, and anecdotes, including the fact Etta and Otto exchanged letters while he was in the war and that later Russell and Etta had an intimate relationship when it seemed that Otto might not be coming back. Emma Hooper's prose is spare, and each precise detail matters. The language conveys the arid land, the lack of excess, the simplicity of living close to the earth and within the close-knit boundaries of family and home.

With no introduction or context, the novel opens with these strange remarks, verbatim:

> Otto,

The letter began, in blue ink,

> *I've gone. I've never seen the water, so I've gone there. Don't worry. I've left you the truck. I can walk. I will try to remember to come back.*
>     *Yours (always),*
>     Etta.

What follows is equally compelling, as the reader learns that under the letter Etta has left a pile of recipe cards for all of Otto's favorite foods. His reaction is as unusual as her letter. He sits at the table and arranges the recipe cards in columns and rows. He considers going to look for her, but instead he remains at the table with the letter and the cards, his hands trembling. He notices his gun is missing, then goes to get their globe and traces the 232 kilometers she must walk from Saskatchewan to reach Halifax on Canada's eastern coast.

The novel's details are concrete, giving the reader a sense of accuracy, even when narrating the seemingly impossible. A talking coyote, rather than seeming absurd or sending a clear indication of Etta's dementia, is believable. Because James is real to Etta, he is real to the reader. Early in her journey when her feet are bleeding through her boots, she wakes to find him licking her feet and asks: "Are you helping me or eating me?" The coyote does not answer, but he follows her into town to buy shoes, and the salesman insists, "No dogs in the shop." The coyote remains, following Etta, and she names him James. While noting that he is visible to the salesman, the narrator places James's comments in italics. Later in their journey, the narrator tells us "James liked singing; he was always singing," and Etta hums along with his hymns and cowboy songs.

Similarly, the novel seamlessly interweaves past and present. In parallel chronologies, the narrative itself moves forward in two strands: one from Etta's opening letter, following her journey on foot from Saskatchewan to Halifax, and the other from the childhoods of Otto and his friend Russell, a boy who practically lives with Otto's family after being orphaned at age six. This second narrative, like the past histories of their lives, both precedes and informs the present experiences of Otto, Etta, and Russell, and it unfolds simultaneously, the ways memories fold and unfold. The two boys alternate days spent farming with attending their one-room prairie school, where Etta is their young teacher. Each scene provides a glimpse, like a series of photographs in an album, where we make sense of the specific details caught in a frame, forever set in time and yet always alive in the memories of those who lived it, both separate from and part of the "current" story. We know why and how Etta has needed to strike out on her own and also that her leaving does not reflect a lack of care for Otto but rather her awareness that she is forgetting who she is.

The novel is hung on Etta's journey across Canada, which gains a cult following. An article in the newspaper goes viral, and people flock to catch a glimpse of the magical old lady. We understand the excitement of the cashiers in the grocery store who want to give her free groceries and have their picture taken with her. We understand how Etta's journey—on foot, accompanied only by a coyote—creates a following of people who entrust her with tiny talismans—a button, a green ribbon, a photograph. We know why strangers want to send bits of themselves with her to the sea just as we entrust bits of ourselves as readers.

Each outsider's encounter with Etta—from the clerk in the small store where she buys crackers, to the journalist, Briony, who wrote the original article for the local newspaper, to the ordinary people who follow her story—validates our sense that the journey exists in the outer world and not simply in Etta's muddled head, although her thoughts are confused and she often has to remind herself who she is by consulting the folded piece of paper she carries in her pocket. The paper reads:

*You:*

*Etta Gloria Kinnick of Deerdale farm. 83 years old in August.*

Family:
  Marta Gloria Kinnick. Mother. Housewife. (Deceased)
  Raymond Peter Kinnick. Father. Editor. (Deceased)
  Alma Gabrielle Kinnick. Sister. Nun. (Deceased)
  James Peter Kinnick. Nephew. Child. (Never lived)
  Otto Vogel. Husband. Soldier/Farmer. (Living)

In that short list, she compresses her skimpy family line with its many losses.

During her absence, Otto adopts a baby guinea pig for company and creates a collection of life-size papier-mâché animals as he awaits her return, accepting Etta's need to see the ocean. It is as if they trade places. She who had never left Saskatchewan travels to the ocean Otto had crossed as a young man, and Otto develops the nurturing skills Etta has perfected since girlhood. Otto accepts her note, her recipes, and her need to leave. As Otto grows increasingly fragile and outside the rhythms of ordinary time, his assembly of papier-mâché animals attracts the attention of the public and of a local art museum. As readers we somehow believe that Otto teaches himself to fashion realistic life-size creatures out of flour and water and all of the newspaper he's accumulated after purchasing 326 copies of the *Canadian National* from the surrounding towns and clipping out the articles with Etta's picture. Their nephew William had telephoned from Manitoba to tell him about the article that describes Etta as having "moments of fumbling confusion contrasted with moments of startling clarity" and "a striking presence." Otto is pleased to know she is alive and well and discourages William from trying to locate her, insisting, "She's okay. There's a plan. She'll be okay." However, we are never given a plan.

Russell's determination to track Etta and bring her back is a much more normal response than Otto's quiet acceptance.

He confronts Otto with questions about her unreliable memory: "And if she forgets? Her name, her home, her husband? To eat or drink or where she's going? . . . She could die out there! She could be dead already!" But Otto refuses to search for her, and Russell stomps out, kicks the door, and insists he will go alone. Otto knows that being returned home is not what Etta wants, and when Russell finally tracks her down and says he has come to take her home, Etta of course refuses and tells him that is "silly" and "a lie." She tells him "it's your turn," and insists that he does not need her permission "to do whatever, wherever. Go do it alone, and now, because you want to and you're allowed to and you can. You always could have if you wanted to enough." They kiss deeply. The narrator describes their connection with intense compression and poetic repetition:

> And they held like that
> and held
> and held
> and then,
> You and Otto both, said Russell, as he pulled away.
> Yes I know, said Etta.
> So much and so different. So so much.
> Yes, said Etta.

On Etta's insistence, Russell says he will trade his truck for a horse and ride north to track the caribou that have lingered in his yearning since he first saw them in an illustrated book given to him on his sixth birthday by his father just before his death.

The novel's ending refuses a clear conclusion—instead, it formally enacts what Etta defines as the structure of life:

"It's a loop," she tells Otto. "It's just a long loop." At the end of her journey, Etta somehow merges with Otto, dreams his watery dreams and embraces a unity that she had intentionally avoided in recent years. In a surreal textual moment, in this dream at the end of her loop, "they sat together underwater on the rocky sandy floor"; Otto tells her he's missed her, and Etta tells him she will miss him but assures him she will be okay. Etta kisses Otto and then surfaces, but she was "facing out, away from the land. Everything was gray and green and moving as far as she could see." Whether, finally, Otto dies in bed at home or Etta dies in the Grand Falls Hospital and Care Home is unclear. Briony, the journalist responsible for the newspaper article, later returns to tell Etta her own story of loss and to complete her own journey. She tells the Care Home receptionist that Etta has "lost herself." On the novel's final page, the narrator concludes with a line from the past when Otto was returning on furlough: "Otto's train was due in seven minutes. Etta stood on the platform and waited for the wind it would bring." This conclusion connects present with past, where long-term memories linger even when short-term memory is unreliable. We know that Etta is dreaming Otto's dreams, dreams of war, but perhaps what matters most is that the three old people of this novel are intertwined by invisible strands of love and dependence across distance and time.

This ending's defiance of narrative closure enacts the wonderful and strange defiance of the novel as a whole. A very old woman is not too old to fulfill her dream; her very old husband accepts her unconventional way of making the best of her dementia, and their lifelong friend tracks her down but lovingly accepts her refusal to return home and also is empowered by her insistence that he follow his own dream. Etta and

Otto and Russell reveal their quiet dignity in remaining gentle and caring through incredible hardship, knowing themselves and one another with love and acceptance. They live simply, without material grasping or bitterness. Otto never questions Etta's love, understanding without jealousy her affection for Russell and Russell's need to follow her. Without any trace of sentimentality, the novel represents the simple truth that ultimately we each die alone, and rather than leaving the reader sad or disappointed, it provides a refreshing sense of completeness and mystery.

# CONCLUSION

Although these novels include many of the losses that accompany age—death of husbands, divorce, lessening of physical and mental health—they are not depressing. Youthful choices to marry and become mothers result in considerable happiness but do not destroy artistic yearnings for Lady Slane, Ryn, or Annie. Lady Slane, Ryn, and Joy all make important choices about where they want to live in their final years and who they want as friends—from Joy's insistence on remaining in her rent-controlled Manhattan apartment and pursuing her romantic relationship with Karl to Lady Slane's move to a less opulent home of her own choosing and friendship with three eccentric old men to Annie's development of her artistic gift while remaining married and connected to her children and grandchildren.

Martha and Etta differ from the other women in this chapter, not only in their location—Sweden and Canada—but in the strangeness of their journeys. Martha and Etta share a fierce sense of survival, and both determine to break out of their ordinary lives. Both have been schoolteachers in harsh environments, and both have a strong sense of connection to others. Romance is muted in these two final novels, though we see glimpses of desire in both. Martha is a leader, with a sense of external adventure, whereas Etta makes her journey alone, knowing Otto and Russell will survive her departure.

I love each of these stories for their shared sense of determination and hope, their celebration of women whose kindness and loyalty does not extinguish their creativity, self-reliance, or desire. I love their authors' attention to the beauty of life and to the spiritual qualities beyond formal definition. They make me notice easy-to-overlook details of the natural and material world, and they celebrate the importance of listening to the music of one's own heart.

# *Conclusion*

## Margaret Drabble's

## *THE DARK FLOOD RISES*

n her 2017 novel, *The Dark Flood Rises*, British writer Margaret Drabble gives us a two-month window into the lives of a small group of elderly characters who are all connected directly or indirectly with Francesca "Fran" Stubbs in two settings, England and an expat community in the Canary Islands. In both places, natural disaster threatens, and the crises of the Middle East create an ominous instability. I include Drabble's novel in a short separate section because it, like this book, deals with the way attitudes about aging and dying inflect our daily lives. In the novel, death is ordinary, not only because of the advanced age of its central characters, who are "already too old to die young," but also in the fabric of the human and natural world. Only its timing is unknown, whether in the rising of the flood tides in England, the tsunamis and earthquakes of the Canary Islands, or the wars between nations. Everything is in flux, yet nations and individuals live as though life were endless and change resides in the past recorded in books, art, and human memory. In the midst of these serious subjects, Drabble finds humor and offers hope.

Set in the precarious present, the novel moves steadily forward while also looping backward in characters' thoughts and conversations. Without formal chapters, the short sections are separated by a repeating colophon to indicate a shift between scenes or characters, and Fran's point of view is the glue loosely connecting all the parts. The title *The Dark Flood Rises* comes from a poem by D. H. Lawrence, which rather ominously calls us to consider our preparation for death: "Have you built your ship of death, O have you? / O build your ship of death, for you will need it." This serious tone both fits the novel and also misses its terrific humor.

Drabble's elegance, restraint, and wit mean the novel never falls into sentiment or reductive cliché as it tackles the truths of aging, in a particular body in a particular place. She writes that Fran has "a great tearfulness rising up in her, a grief for all things"—and we cry with her, for her, for ourselves—individually and collectively. Or as Fran herself puts it, "Old age, it's a fucking disaster." There are no excruciating bedside or battlefield scenes to evoke our feelings. Rather, death just happens. Fran thinks about the recent deaths of two friends—one smoking in bed and the other undergoing chemotherapy—and decides she much prefers the first. She recalls her childhood fascination with the heroic deaths of literature, for which she has since substituted a conviction that ordinary old age requires courage and that "old age itself is a theme for heroism."

This novel is notable because of its acceptance of change, aging, and death as normal occurrences. Fran and her friends Josephine and Teresa are realistic and fully alive in their old age. Although they have all downsized from the homes in which they raised their families, they are determined not to burden their adult children, and they retain their independence. Apart from these similarities, each has a distinct attitude toward aging. Fran thrives on constant activity, and although she is well past retirement age, she thoroughly enjoys her current job as an expert on housing for the elderly. She visits retirement homes and writes up reports on each of her visits. She enjoys driving to occasional conferences on the motorway, regardless of weather conditions, loves the familiarity of the chain hotels where she meets with colleagues, and relishes writing up her reports. In fact, she is proud of her perceptions, and she knows that "when she ceases to enjoy perceiving, she'll know she is about to be dead." Her ideal death would be on the motorway on one of her visits. Until then, she hopes to see all of her beloved England. She is constantly seeking new adventures, dyes her short, thinning hair in multicolors, and dresses flamboyantly to please herself. Rather than live in a home for the elderly, she rents a third-floor walk-up apartment in an area of London that her family and friends consider sketchy. She enjoys a sense of living on the edge, prides herself on her physical stamina, and gains some sort of inexplicable satisfaction from preparing packaged dinners for her first husband, who always complained about her cooking during their marriage.

Josephine Drummond, Fran's friend since they were young wives and mothers, is determined to make friends with Old Age, which she sometimes calls "La Vieillesse" after the title of a "terrifying book on the subject by Simone de Beauvoir." Josephine has formally retired from her academic job but continues to teach a weekly poetry course for adults, "On Old Age and the Concept of Late Style." She still rides her bicycle to the library, where she is working on a research project she considers a "harmless indulgence." Unlike Fran, Jo dresses conservatively in neutral shades, determined to avoid looking like "mutton dressed as lamb." She is slightly uneasy about appearing to be a stereotypical old woman who is hopeless about money and technology but decides that she is already the worst stereotype just by being elderly. She lives in Athene Grange, a lovely retirement home with ample amenities, and meets weekly for literary conversations over drinks with a distinguished retired male professor. She is proud of her scholarship and her taste, which she contrasts to the interests of her friend Fran. Libraries mean as much to Jo as exploring England means to Fran, confirming status and identity. Jo faces death philosophically, recalling and questioning phrases from her vast literary background.

Though both Fran and Josephine think often of death because of their age, only Teresa is dying of cancer and receives hospice care in her home. Raised Catholic, Teresa Quinn is familiar with the rituals of the church, and although she is not quite sure about the truth of life after death, she keeps up the motions for the sake of her children and her priest. She accepts her dying with composure and speculates about possible causes of her mesothelioma. Teresa "has learned not to blame. She has learned the hardest lesson, which is not to blame herself," which Fran attributes to Teresa's faith. Fran and Teresa were childhood friends just after World War II who recently regained contact. Fran visits Teresa in her home, and as they reminisce and recall long-forgotten incidents, they piece together a shared story about their childhood that enlarges their sense of themselves as they reflect on girlhood from the vantage point of old age. Their opportunity to see their past from that vantage point is one of the satisfying gifts of this novel.

Despite its ominous title, *The Dark Flood Rises* is no more threatening than our own everyday reality. The novel captures our daily lives in the present moment, in which we sense our own aging and deal with personal health concerns while also being surrounded by and ever aware of conflicts among individuals and nations, of mass weapons, dysfunctional social contracts, state violence, and the effects of climate change. But, in privileged spaces, many of us continue to carry on our daily lives as if we would all die in our sleep in our own beds, having settled our grievances and left behind a sense of kindness and grace. We look for and find humor, and we try to work toward bettering the conditions not only for ourselves but for others of our kin and beyond it. The Dark Flood approaches as death approaches, but it does not drown our need for stories that celebrate love, erotic desire, imagination, human connection, defiance, discovery, and hope for all of us who have lived too long to die young.

# Postscript

I n the early days of this project, I looked forward to completing the book within two years, hoping to benefit from my discoveries about how to age gracefully and well, but a car accident changed not only my plans but my entire life. While our Volvo was totaled, I had no visible signs of injury. I was preoccupied with the recent death of my younger sister and the always competing pulls of work and home life, grateful the accident was not worse.

But over the weeks, I was not entirely myself. I could not recall if I'd already taken a shower or where my keys were. I was assured these were normal signs of being overwhelmed by the grief of loss and being busy and run-of-the-mill aging. But then I started forgetting why I was in rooms. I lost words, lost my quick response time, and most terrifyingly for me, I could no longer read easily. Words jumped, plots were lost, even menus proved challenging, let alone novels or student papers. The neurologists assured me I was fine, my comprehension solid, nothing amiss, just "normal" slowing down with age.

But I knew it was not "normal," and that I was not "okay," and I lived for six months with what I feared was the onset of dementia. Finally, after continuing to insist that something was wrong while hiding my deepest fears, I spent a day taking neurological tests. I underwent a PET scan and learned I had sustained a traumatic brain injury. That's why my reading tested at a second-grade level, why my processing speed was abysmal, and why I could not recall the names of my students or call to memory my telephone number or where I lived.

Rather than experiencing a gradual decline into old age, I had been hurtled into that strange terrain in an instant. Loss of mind as I had known it, and a sense that I had forever lost myself, thrust me inside, rather than outside, the geography of loss that was a familiar landscape in the stories I read and studied. Happy not to be in the early stages of a progressive dementia, I was still in unfamiliar territory, in which learning to read again and developing new ways to write were accompanied with losses I would not regain and a new understanding of invisible disabilities and strategies of compensation. I adjusted to being overwhelmed by visual and aural stimuli by avoiding crowded spaces, listening to novels on tape, and limiting my driving to neighborhood streets. In my classroom, without my former nearly perfect memory, I took copious notes on student presentations and discussions. I talked less and listened more. Instead of directing discussions, I recorded them and then provided write-ups for my students. As I became increasingly a more serene older woman, my students and colleagues blossomed, and my course evaluations rose rather than dropped. While impersonating my former self, I was becoming a changed self, still acutely aware of loss but not defined by it.

As I made my own journey to a new self through multiple rehabilitation paths, I viewed my book project through a changed perspective from the one I'd held pre-injury. When I regained my ability to read—a painfully slow process—I returned to the texts I'd originally chosen for this project and saw them differently. My readings here are, simultaneously, more sympathetic and more critical than when I began the project, and they are written with more urgency. Fiction sets a cultural tone for what we believe to be true about ourselves. *The Book of Old Ladies* encourages readers, young and old, to think critically about the ramifications of fiction in all of our lives, inspiring dialogue and ultimately more profound and plentiful storylines from future novelists that will feature older women as the fascinating, dynamic, and complicated subjects they truly are.

Now it's been fifteen years since my accident, and I've been on a journey to discover all the ways in which aging women not only imagine a different future for themselves than that of their mothers, but also redefine aging and choose to rein-vent themselves and explore what it means to be themselves in later life. *The Book of Old Ladies* offers a selection of works that I hope you will want to explore yourself, and I hope my discussion of these stories uncovers a broad picture of older women's range of lived experience over the course of their lives, including the surprises, illuminations, and intensities of old age. I have now lived longer than many of the female protagonists whose stories I had hoped would inform me and offer alternative visions to inhabit as an older woman, just as a young girl tries on costumes and inhabits multiple roles as she matures. I have discovered through my own experience that loss does not need to define us, and that old women have at our disposal many ways we can adapt and learn and continue to see the world with wonder and joy.

# ACKNOWLEDGMENTS

Thank you to all of the students who have kept reading lively and urgent for me, and whose insights and community have been crucial for me for the past forty-six years, with particular thanks to my "Coming to Age" seminar students of 2015 and 2020.

Thanks also to the staff and faculty of Mills College, who have for decades nurtured my teaching and professional life and provided an intellectual community. And to the Huntington Library, whose reading room, gardens, and staff offered space and quiet support for much of the thinking and writing of this book.

Thank you to the friends who read drafts—Sandy Ponce, Margaret Simon, and Paula Skene—and to all those who offered insights: the neighborhood women who have met every Super Bowl Sunday for over forty years, the mothers from my daughter's high school, and the folks at the Downtown Oakland Senior Center.

Thanks to the talented research and editorial assistants whose help was critical after my traumatic brain injury: Elizabeth Mathews, Emily Travis, Monique Iles, and Linda Gray. Thanks to the team at She Writes Press, with special thanks to Brooke Warner and Samantha Strom, and thanks to Caitlin Hamilton Summie for publicizing the book. I am grateful to the writers and readers who have supported the book through early reviews, including Eileen Barrett, Sky Bergman, Julie

Chappell, Jennifer King, Yiyun Li, Viji Nakka, Patricia Powell, Roberta Rubenstein, Julie Shigekuni, and Kortny Stern.

I appreciate everyone whose professional skills helped me recover after my brain injury, including Laurie Chaiken, Beth Harris, William Johnson, Neil Kostick, Jen Tellier, Lisa Yang, Robert B. Zeiger, and the doctors and staff of Kaiser Permanente Oakland and the head injury clinic in Vallejo.

Thanks to my beloved family—my husband, Paul, my children, David, Katherine, and Kirsten, and their partners and families. And to my loyal dogs, past and present, who provide love and support. And finally, thank you to my mother, Edith Halsey Olsen, and to my grandmothers, Mabel Halsey and Amalia Olsen, none of whom completed high school but who all loved words and lived rich, full lives as old ladies. And to the women, such as Libby Pope, Roussel Sargent, and Genie Walker, who pushed me to take myself seriously as an academic and whose legacy continues to inspire me.

# ABOUT THE AUTHOR

Over the course of her forty-two-year career, she has studied, taught, and published works on fiction by women for decades, focusing on how narratives limit or expand what we imagine to be possible. Dr. Saxton served as Mills College's first Dean of Letters, cofounded the Women's Studies program, and founded the Rhetoric and Composition program. Her scholarly works include *The Girl: Constructions of the Girl in Contemporary Fiction by Women*; *Approaches to Teaching Woolf's Mrs. Dalloway* (with Eileen Barrett); and *Woolf and Lessing: Breaking the Mold* (with Jean Tobin).

# SELECTED TITLES FROM SHE WRITES PRESS

She Writes Press is an independent publishing company founded to serve women writers everywhere. Visit us at www.shewritespress.com.

*Anchor Out* by Barbara Sapienza. $16.95, 978-1631521652. Quirky Frances Pia was a feminist Catholic nun, artist, and beloved sister and mother until she fell from grace—but now, done nursing her aching mood swings offshore in a thirty-foot sailboat, she is ready to paint her way toward forgiveness.

*What is Found, What is Lost* by Anne Leigh Parrish. $16.95, 978-1-938314-95-7. After her husband passes away, a series of family crises forces Freddie, a woman raised on religion, to confront long-held questions about her faith.

*Tzippy the Thief* by Pat Rohner. $16.95, 978-1-63152-153-9. Tzippy has lived her life as a selfish, materialistic woman and mother. Now that she is turning eighty, there is not an infinite amount of time left—and she wonders if she'll be able to repair the damage she's done to her family before it's too late.

*Duck Pond Epiphany* by Tracey Barnes Priestley. $16.95, 978-1-938314-24-7. When a mother of four delivers her last child to college, she has to decide what to do next—and her life takes a surprising turn.

*Eden* by Jeanne Blasberg. $16.95, 978-1-63152-188-1. As her children and grandchildren assemble for Fourth of July weekend at Eden, the Meister family's grand summer cottage on the Rhode Island shore, Becca decides it's time to introduce the daughter she gave up for adoption fifty years ago.

*A Cup of Redemption* by Carole Bumpus. $16.95, 978-1-938314-90-2. Three women, each with their own secrets and shames, seek to make peace with their pasts and carve out new identities for themselves.